Sept 7, 1988

ZAPATA

For all the legends surrounding his name and all the romance attached to his deeds, Zapata has never been the subject of a full-length biography in English. Roger Parkinson, noted military historian and author of the widely acclaimed biography *Clausewitz,* has filled the void with this welcome book.

Emiliano Zapata, one of ten children in an affluent Mexican home, was a rebellious boy. Orphaned at 14, he developed into a skilled horseman and became a well-known horse trainer. Then in 1910 he organized his village's defenses against the oppressive forces of President Diaz and, at the age of 31, was thrust into the role of revolutionary leader.

Zapata's efficiency, honesty, and popular appeal brought him swarms of followers, as others flocked around the equally colorful Pancho Villa. Under Zapata's strong and inspiring leadership his ragtag army embarked on a heroic and desperate campaign.

The assaults of the two revolutionary forces and a general civil war at last toppled Diaz in 1911. But Madero, the new revolutionary president, was unable to unify the country, and the victorious revolutionaries were soon at war with one another. Zapata became embroiled in the subsequent bloodshed, cruelty, and organized massacres which constitute some of the darkest pages of twentieth-century history.

In creating the now classic film *Viva Zapata,* John Steinbeck and Elia Kazan caught segments of the sweeping life story. In this satisfying, carefully researched biography, Roger Parkinson has developed for the reader all the rich background detail, to burnish every facet of his subject's complex life and personality.

Roger Parkinson was a war-correspondent and a renowned military historian. Among his other books are *Clausewitz: A Biography, The Encyclopedia of Modern War,* and *Tormented Warrior: Ludendorff and the Supreme Command,* all available from Stein and Day.

Emiliano Zapata

ZAPATA

A Biography by
ROGER PARKINSON

🜲B

A SCARBOROUGH BOOK

STEIN AND DAY / *Publishers* / New York

FIRST SCARBOROUGH BOOKS EDITION 1980
Zapata: A Biography was originally published
in hardcover by Stein and Day/*Publishers*
Copyright © 1975 by Roger Parkinson
All rights reserved
Designed by Ed Kaplin
Printed in the United States of America
Stein and Day/*Publishers*/Scarborough House,
Briarcliff Manor, N.Y. 10510

Library of Congress Cataloging in Publication Data

Parkinson, Roger.
        Zapata.

        1.   Zapata, Emiliano, 1879-1919
F1234.Z327   972.08 '1 '0924[B]   74-28202
ISBN 0-8128-6072-1

Contents

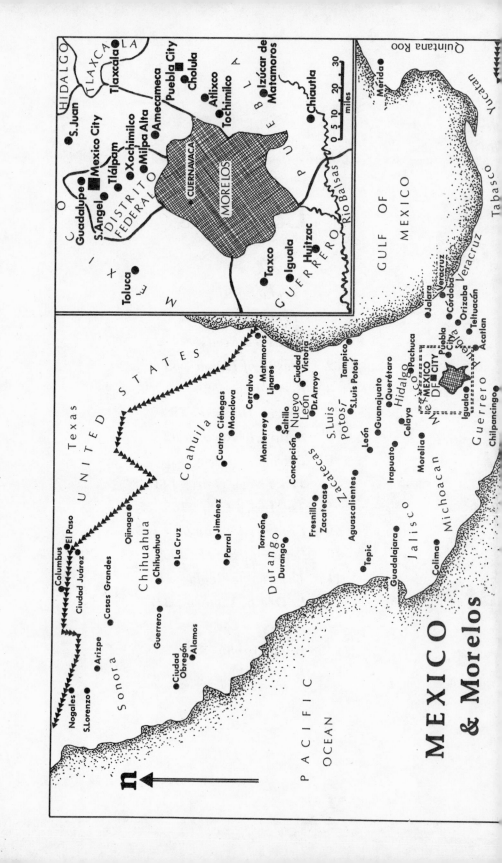

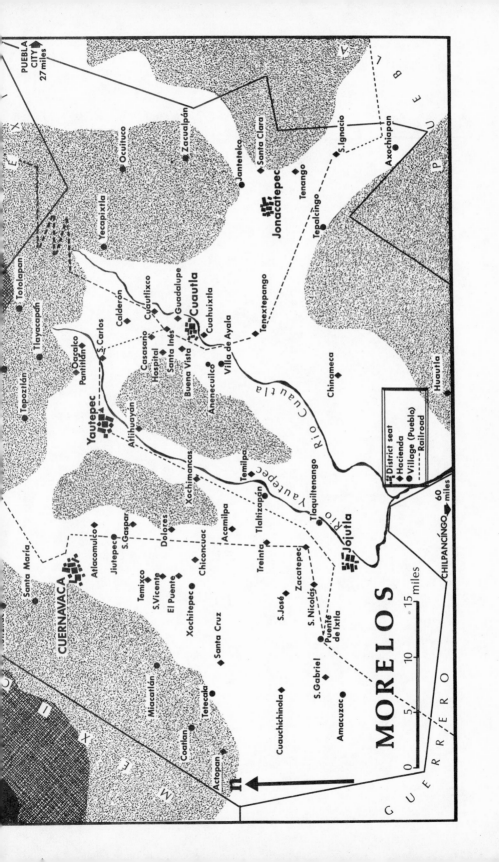

Preface

A peculiar fascination surrounds the story of Emiliano Zapata, the peasant leader who directed the farmers of south Mexico in their 1910–19 revolution. History treats him with either romance or horror: a man who battled for the good of the people, or one who fought with gross cruelty and wanton destruction. This biography attempts to describe the real Zapata, and while not claiming to have uncovered new source material, I found that discovering the truth proved just as fascinating as reading the legends. Moreover, such a study seemed to have a contemporary relevance. Zapata's struggle formed a classic example of revolutionary and guerrilla war, a type of conflict thrown into painful prominence during recent years. His campaigns provide much information, and the revolutionary leader himself offers an appeal equal to that of other folk heros, including the famed Guevara. If recent would-be revolutionaries, or those who tried to oppose them, had paid closer attention to Zapata's experience, then many tragic mistakes might have been avoided. Outside Mexico, Zapata has been too much neglected, despite the excitement, the terrors, the endurance, triumphs and failures which emerge in his story and in the whole drama of the Mexican Revolution.

Any biographer owes a great deal to those who went before. With Zapata, the path was hardly trodden by English language authors: works have been largely fictional and unreliable, with one very notable exception. I am indebted to John Womack, whose analytical and scholarly study so admirably cleared the way for others to follow. Mexican biographies are numerous, but of especial value were the works, unfortunately unfinished, by Gildardo Magaña and the more recent book by Porfirio Palacios. Details of these and all other books and papers consulted are in the bibliography. In addition to these authors, I also express gratitude to friends in Mexico City and Washington, the Mexican Embassy and Public Records Office, London, and to the staff of the London Library. As ever, my humblest thanks go to Betty, for her partnership, patience and understanding far beyond a wife's normal care.

ZAPATA

Prologue

Men slept in their sarape capes huddled between the rocks. Nearby stood their horses and mules, tethered together and to stakes driven into the ground the night before. Embers still glowed from the fire. Other men nestled in the boulders, silent shadows ringing the camp, awake and alert with their Mauser rifles in their hands. To the east, the dark outline of the Morelos mountains began to show against the sky. Dawn began to break over the south Mexican countryside on this Thursday, April 10, 1919.

The guerrillas roused and began the routine familiar to countless nights on campaign, checking weapons, harnesses, ammunition, kicking the fire into flame to cook the food. At 7 P.M. the men mounted. Moments later the camp was abandoned, and the riders filed through the rocks toward the northern slopes of the hills. Among the leading guerrillas rode their commander: Emiliano Zapata.

By 8 P.M. the guerrillas were slithering down the slope into the valley, following boulder-strewn gullies which split the volcanic hillside. The ground leveled, the grass spread thicker; the *Zapatistas* ceased to ride in file formation and moved out into a rough line. Most wore the white peasant tunics, their cotton trousers tucked into the socks to prevent them from catching in the stirrups, wide sombreros on their heads to protect them from the April dry-season sun already rising over the mountains.

Zapata wore different clothing: white collarless shirt, black waistcoat and frayed black jacket. Silver-colored buttons were stitched down the outside seams of his black trousers. Across his saddle was slung his favorite weapon, a .44-caliber Winchester rifle, lacking the range of the Mauser but more lethal with its larger bullet. Zapata's horse felt unfamiliar: he had ridden this sorrel for the first time only the day before, but the reddish-brown stallion, high-necked and thick-haunched, promised well. Zapata rode his new horse easily, his slight, 120-pound body controlling the mount with usual skill. Few in Morelos could match him as a horseman.

Zapata spoke few words during the ride this Thursday morning, but his guerrillas were accustomed to his silences. He seemed cheerful, "like someone who knows he is going to finish a good job," remembered one of his aides, in contrast to his manner over the previous weeks when he had been described as "crabby, irritable, somewhat raw-nerved." Yet his men saw no reason for their leader's sudden high spirits. This day promised to be one of the most dangerous of their revolution. The task to be undertaken appeared to them foolhardy, one which Zapata's aides urged him to abandon. Zapata refused to listen.

Ahead lay the hacienda of San Juan Chinameca, now less than half a dozen miles away. The countryside was familiar to most of the 150 guerrillas, and especially to Zapata. Only forty miles to the north was his native village; in his youth he had ridden many times along these trails, taking horses to market or leading a string of trading mules. Then came the revolution. For almost ten years Zapata had fought. He had led his peasant army in triumph to Mexico City. But after each victory the struggle began again, the endless guerrilla ambushes, the deadly hunts in the mountains, the battles swirling around the towns, the starvation and slaughter. So many friends lay dead: his brother Eufemio, shot down in the street, his old colleague Otilio Montaño, one of the first to join and recently shot by Zapata's own troops for treachery, so many friends executed by the enemy . . . Zapata survived the batterings well, until recently. He had even found time to get married and have children. His eldest boy, the illegitimate Nicolás, was now thirteen, and other illegitimate children—perhaps as many as five—were scattered throughout the state of Morelos. But lately the strain of revolution had started to tell. Zapata, four months from his fortieth birthday, had still to win the final victory.

His men rode on, increasingly anxious. At Chinameca waited the enemy. A meeting had been arranged: the federal officer at Chinameca insisted he wished to defect to the revolutionaries. Many guerrillas disbelieved this colonel, who so recently boasted he sought to kill the *"Zapatista* trash." The guerrillas swore it must be a trap. They found it impossible to understand why Zapata, normally so cautious, should expose himself to such danger. Perhaps Zapata really believed the colonel to be sincere, but some *Zapatistas* said their leader must be crazy and no longer cared.

None spoke of another, almost unthinkable, reason: perhaps Zapata wished to die. His murder would be his last sacrifice for the revolution and for the peasants. At 8:30 A.M. Zapata and his guerrillas approached Chinameca, near to the place it had all begun so many battles ago.

1

• • • • • • • • • • •

Scattered Seeds

His battlefield stretched south through the wild mountains of Morelos. On the northern boundary lay Mexico City, the ultimate target, beyond which spread the desert domain of Pancho Villa. Emiliano Zapata fought in the land of the Aztecs, of Cortés, of rich valleys and mist-covered snow peaks. Here lies the city of Cuernavaca, white-walled and glistening in the deep heart of the Morelos valley, now an easy weekend holiday center for tourists from Mexico City. Four centuries ago Cortés marched up the tortuous valley to attack Cuernavaca, and clashed with Aztec warriors under Cuauhtémoc, "the Eagle That Falls," son-in-law of the famed Moctezuma. Cortés seized the city despite its natural protection from the twin ravines gashing the earth on either side; his troops and their Indian allies sacked the houses and swept on. Sixty years ago the city again lay devastated, all communications with the country's capital severed by *Zapatistas:* so too did Yautepec, Cuautla, Jonacatepec, and towns and villages spreading from the dark volcanic mountains southward into the rolling, lush landscape of the state of Guerrero, on to the Pacific and Acapulco.

Zapata, at the height of his power, controlled an area three hundred miles long and two hundred wide, the richest in Mexico and almost one third of the total. Behind him rode an army of up to 20,000. In 1914, when his peasant troops swarmed into Mexico City to saunter in the boulevards and breakfast at sophisticated Sanborn's restaurant, Zapata had only just celebrated his thirty-fifth birthday. His fame would mushroom through the years, tinged with romanticism, tainted black by exaggerated tales of ghastly cruelty. When facts are sifted from fiction Zapata emerges as a highly skilled guerrilla leader, a born leader of men—and a man who could, if he had wished, have seized even greater power. Zapata is one of the few participants in the Mexican revolution who emerge with credit from the turmoil; his story is one of tragedy rather than triumph. His evil reputation, resulting from propaganda put out by his enemies and boosted by later journalistic sensationalism, plays him totally false; as a man Zapata was far from a monster; shy, reserved and almost self-effacing, he avoided personal glory and, directly contrary to the tales of terror, he rejected battles fought purely for the sake of military conquest. He remained a peasant, but one with unique qualities of military leadership—skills which were all the more remarkable since they were entirely instinctive.

Only four years before Zapata's victorious entry into Mexico City in 1914, where his soldiers found the new world of tramcars, limousines, luxury, and Paris-dressed women, Emiliano had been no more than a villager in a remote Indian community, seeking merely to train his horses in the nearby stony fields. Each day he rode his slender string of horses from his village of Anenecuilco. The seven-hundred-year-old hamlet nestled on the slopes above the terraced fields. Around lay the southern folds of the Mountain That Smokes—the 17,887-foot Popocatepetl—with its spurred cap and black volcanic flanks scarred by deep ravines. Anenecuilco formed a typical peasant settlement in this state of Morelos, comprising about ninety straggling houses. The poorest homes were built in *jacal* style, from cane, roofed with thatch; others were tiled, fashioned from the *caliche* mixture of adobe and lime which reflected the sun, and with one or two earth-floored rooms. Houses were separated from each other by yards or small gardens, some with a few fruit trees or a corn patch. Alleyways smelled of bougainvillea blossom, cooking, and an underlying stench of urine. Trees overhung the streets to provide shade in the dry season and shelter from the rains sweeping down the dark sides of Popocatepetl. The central street had been stone-paved to prevent erosion. Always the village seemed subdued and quiet, save for occasional yapping of scrawny, scratching dogs and a constant slap-slap as women in their open doorways shaped moist corn paste into thin tortilla cakes.

Zapata spent solitary days working his horses beyond the *milpas*—the plots of corn surrounding the village. Some men labored on these plots; most were employed as dayworkers on the local hacienda estates. Haciendas, and the serf system on which they relied, dominated village life. These vast plantations were situated in the richer lands lower down the valley, at places like Hospital, Buenavista, Cuahuixtla, and Tenextepango along the fertile banks of the Cuautla River; each had long drives leading from massive iron gates through overflowing sugar-cane fields to the central buildings—long, one-storyed houses with lines of graceful arches, glass windows, and sometimes large enough to include sixty or seventy rooms. Most villagers had traveled no farther than to these haciendas or to the nearest town, Villa de Ayala, two miles to the south. There the houses were sturdier, some even with windows and built in Spanish style with high, concealing garden walls; shops were better stocked, and the streets smoother paved. Just beyond the town, higher on the hillside, loomed a strong building constructed from huge hand-squared blocks which had been ripped from some ancient Aztec ruin; no windows were let into the walls of this building, merely yard-high firing slits. Here, in this old fortress, Zapata would establish his headquarters, from which he would lead his peasant army to fight.

Zapata's family history and upbringing perfectly suited him for this leadership and provided him with perhaps his greatest strength. He always remained one with the peasants, despite the power he rapidly obtained. His peasant face revealed Indian ancestry: swarthy, high cheekbones, dark eyes, thick black hair. One recruit described his first glimpse of him: "He was a tall man, thin and with a big moustache. And he had a growth on his right eyelid, but it was later cut off. He had a thin, high voice, like a lady's. He was a *charro* and mounted bulls and lassoed them, but when he spoke his voice was very delicate."[1] In his undemonstrative fashion he shared peasant values: he loved the land, respected nature; believed in the intrinsic good of agricultural labor; he held a typical peasant's restraint on individual self-seeking. Like a peasant he also proved authoritarian, fatalistic, suspicious, obstinate, and cunning.

Mrs. Rosa King, an Englishwoman who ran a tea shop and later the Bella Vista hotel in Cuernavaca during the revolution, questioned peasants on their reasons for following Zapata; she wrote: "Their shrewdness told them that no man could walk wisely among matters he did not understand, and it was for this they despised the federal generals sent out to them. It was, I sensed, the essence of their trust in Zapata that he stayed close to the soil of his *tierra*, whose needs were part of him, eschewing honours and wealth, and sleeping always away from the towns. . . ."[2]

Yet in the early months of the revolution Zapata's close identification with the ordinary people sometimes even counted against him: Zapata was so much one of them that they sought something more. Villagers heard about his exploits, shrugged, and turned away; how could a mere peasant hope for success? "It was in 1910 when his name was talked about," a villager from a remote corner of the Morelos mountains remembered, "but we just criticised. Then you began to hear about Emiliano Zapata everywhere. It was Zapata this and Zapata that. But we said that he was only a peasant, not an intellectual man."[3] Although Zapata could read and write, his schooling was virtually nonexistent—occasional days at the Villa de Ayala school. He would always rely on others for the "intellectual" ideology of the revolution.

And yet Zapata was more than a mere peasant. He was born on August 8, probably 1879, and his parents were slightly more prosperous than their neighbors in the village: they lived in an adobe and stone house, not a drafty, leaky cane-screen hut. Emiliano's father, Gabriel, was hard-working, quiet, and had a slight stutter. His mother, Cleofus, was unpretentious and popular. Both came from highly respectable and even renowned families, whose histories passed on to Emiliano, to his brother Eufemio, and their two sisters. José-Salazar, the mother's father, fought as a young man against the Spanish in the War of Independence: when Spanish troops besieged the rebels in Cuautla, almost seventy years before Emiliano's birth, his maternal grandfather smuggled food and ammunition to the trapped insurgents.[4]

The surname Zapata was even more respected. Two of Emiliano's father's brothers, Cristino and José, fought against the French intervention in the 1860's, and another José, probably Emiliano's great-uncle, led local forces during the same war: when fighting finished in 1867 this José became chief elder in Anenecuilco and held elected posts in the Villa de Ayala municipal government. He died in 1876 and fellow villagers lamented in a letter to the Mexican President, Porfirio Díaz, on "the death of our beloved president, whom we considered almost as a father."[5]

Emiliano Zapata therefore inherited a family willingness to fight for a just cause and a readiness—and ability—to lead. Moreover, Emiliano's upbringing set him slightly apart from ordinary peasant life, although this was insufficient to create a gap. His parents owned some land and livestock and gained income through trading, all of which was inherited by the two sons. Eufemio, easygoing and often indolent, sold his share and used the money to start an obscure business near Vera Cruz as a nefarious pedlar. Emiliano, six years younger, and about fifteen when his parents died, worked his land, and in addition farmed a few acres of hacienda land on a fifty-fifty basis. This status as a sharecropper, or *mediero*, marked him as above the ordinary laboring peon. He grew melons and sold them at a slight profit. Added financial independence derived from running a string of mules through the scattered settlements south along the Cuautla River, and above all from his horse dealings. He bought promising ponies, trained and schooled them well, and sold them to hacienda owners. His reputation as a skilled trainer gradually spread through central and eastern Morelos into the neighboring state of Puebla to the west, and even north to Mexico City. Zapata spent his money on better mounts, finer harnesses, and an occasional gaudy saddle. He seemed to shun belonging to a group and had few close friends; he courted a local girl, Josefa Espejo, about his own age, dark like Zapata, with snub nose and expressive eyes; he also had a child by another woman.

But despite his relative comfort and contentment Zapata remained surrounded by the poverty and frequent misery of Mexican village life. He knew well the hardship of struggling to obtain subsistence food and the drudgery of daily existence which so many peasants endured. One Morelos villager wrote of his fellow men: "At dawn, when God awakes, off they go to the fields, and from the fields back home to supper, and from supper to bed—and that is all. These men are like dead ideas . . . . In my judgement these men are absolutely dead. Here we call a man like that 'a chunk of meat with eyes.' "[6] Above all, despite his semi-independence, Zapata knew the overwhelming hold enjoyed by the haciendas. This power was increasing dramatically and fatally; already, in his teens, Zapata showed opposition, and soon he would do so again in far greater and more devastating form.

Sugar production in Mexico centered on the fertile valleys of Morelos. The industry received a boost in the 1870's when new milling machines were developed which extracted high proportions of sugar from the stalk. By the 1880's this boost had become a boom. Production soared with increasing international demand. But the need for complex and expensive machinery entailed large-scale production: this in turn meant increased yield from existing land, and beyond this the acquisition of new acres by the hacienda owners. Plantations grew in size and importance until they became company towns, organized on an agricultural factory basis. Small haciendas were either swallowed or merged with others into larger, more economical units. Always the pressure for more territory remained, spurred by the fear that present production might exhaust the dark volcanic soil.

This movement had a fundamental effect upon the peasants in Zapata's region. Rich planters seized communal village land, using legal means where possible and dubious, domineering methods if necessary. Acre by acre the plantations spread. In the 1880's, when Emiliano was still a child, a local hacienda seized the village orchard at Anenecuilco; according to a local story the young Zapata witnessed his father's tears and vowed to win back the precious orchard when he grew older. Lack of land had obliged his father to turn to another means of livelihood, raising and selling animal stock. Others were less able to switch their way of life and suffered disastrously as a result. Whole villages disappeared, their ruins covered by waving sugar-cane. Other villages and towns dwindled drastically in size and population: Anenecuilco itself dropped from 411 inhabitants in 1900 to 371 in 1910, and the population of the municipal seat at Villa de Ayala fell from 2,041 to 1,745 over the same decade.[7] The trend stretched throughout the state. Plantation owners denounced village rights over areas of land and paid lawyers and judges while court cases dragged on, bankrupting those villages that attempted to fight them. Individual protestors were often arrested and deported to the penal settlements of Yucatán and Quintana Roo, or were impressed into the federal army.

Thousands of villagers lost the fields upon which they relied for food. They either attempted to find other means of livelihood, as did the Zapata family, or became fully dependent on the haciendas. The only other avenue lay down the dangerous path of banditry. Groups of bandits became more numerous in the mountains, and these local thugs, with their desperate followers, would later complicate Zapata's revolutionary operations. Meanwhile, in 1896 the seventeen-year-old Emiliano almost joined them: he quarreled with the district authorities, presumably over a land dispute, and found himself forced to flee the state. He hid at a family friend's ranch in south Puebla for several months before considering it safe enough to return.[8] Reports that Zapata was impressed into the army as early as 1908 have yet to be backed by solid evidence; nevertheless, he clearly intended to fight, and this determination would inevitably precipitate trouble. Despite his natural reticence, which remained one of Zapata's most prevailing features, he always displayed another prime characteristic—his dogged stubbornness.

Yearly the misery grew for the villagers. Inadequate income led to mounting debts. Increasingly they had to turn to the plantations for work, first as day laborers, and finally, as they were forced to quit their crumbling villages, moving into the plantation as *gente de casa,* permanent resident laborers. Serfdom became complete. Those who spoke against the system were beaten, starved, and sometimes murdered into silence.

But some continued to fight, legally if possible. The inhabitants of Anenecuilco provided one example. The four village elders were respected and revered: Carmen Quintero, Eugenio Pérez, Andrés Montes and, above all, José Merino, the village president—and Zapata's uncle. This group struggled to protect the village land titles and water rights. They repeatedly journeyed to the municipal seat at Villa de Ayala, over the mountains to the state capital at Cuernavaca, even to Mexico City, to plead, to see lawyers, to deal with hacienda managers and estate foremen. Still the haciendas pressed for more land, and especially domineering was the vast Hospital estate four miles to the north of Anenecuilco. Then, in late 1908, came another upheaval, and from this the peasants would gradually be prodded to revolution.

Manuel Alarcón, governor of Morelos, died on December 15 at the age of fifty-seven, a victim of gastroenteritis. Only four months earlier he had been reelected for the fourth successive time as governor. Alarcón had proven himself a clever manipulator. Himself a plantation owner, he nevertheless managed to convince some villagers that he would do all possible for them. He listened carefully and politely to their petitions; sometimes, although rarely, he even found it possible to grant their requests. Opposition to the planters had thereby been kept within reasonable grounds, through Alarcón's dexterity, through the dulled, fatalistic inertia of the peasants themselves, and through the power of the planters.

But now a successor as governor of Morelos had to be found. The task should have proved easy: almost inevitably, the candidate favored by Porfirio Díaz, the seventy-eight-year-old dictator of Mexico, would in normal circumstances have been elected. But Díaz himself had already injected dangerous uncertainty. He had occupied the luxurious National Palace in Mexico City since 1876, three years before Zapata's birth. Then, in February 1908, he declared to James Creelman, writing for the American monthly journal *Pearson's Magazine,* that he intended to retire in 1910. He said he would dismiss all pleas for him to remain; Díaz, previously ruthless in his actions against rivals, now declared that if an opposition party emerged capable of ruling, "I will stand by it, support it, advise it, and forget myself in the successful inauguration of complete democratic government." Whether or not Díaz meant these words, they encouraged potential opposition candidates. In Morelos, on the death of Alarcón, the opposition movement now began to grow, with the post of state governor selected as the initial target.

Díaz considered the question of Alarcón's successor at conferences in Mexico City during December. Three days before Christmas the official candidate had been chosen. The choice could not have been less fortunate. The Morelos planters sought someone they could use; someone from their own class, respectable, malleable, ineffectual. They believed they had found the perfect man in Díaz's aristocratic chief of staff, Pablo Escandón. He owned the fifteen-thousand-acre Atlihuayán hacienda near Yautepec, and would surely respect the demands of the landowners. Moreover, unlike Alarcón, he would not be sufficiently skilled in pretending to consider the wishes of the villagers. Escandón was too mild, too well mannered to stand up against the planters, even if he had wished to do so. His name graced the society columns of Mexico City newspapers; one journal, the *México Nuevo*, provided a fitting description on January 2, 1909: "Colonel Escandón's prestige among the military is only the prestige accorded a perfect sportsman." Like many youths of his social standing, he had been educated abroad, at the Jesuit College at Stonyhurst, situated in the clean, green countryside of peaceful Lancashire in England, and his mind constantly returned to those pleasant days. In Cuernavaca he soon befriended Mrs. King and complained to her of being thrown into "these beastly local politics." She wrote in her memoirs: "He often dropped in in the afternoon for a cup of tea. We would talk together of our school days in England and towns we both knew, and the homeliness of the English countryside. Like so many of his class, Don Pablo was more at home in Europe than in Mexico; while he loved his own country he found it a little barbarous and the broad new boulevards, frequent parks, and the magnificent public buildings that were being erected in Mexico City were a source of great satisfaction to him. 'It is almost Paris!' he said. He was pleased when I repeated to him the admiring comments of the cultured foreign travellers who visited my tearoom."[9]

Díaz, although his personal friend, had reservations over Escandón's suitability as candidate for the governorship. But pressure from the planters became more insistent, especially from Manuel Araoz, who owned three Morelos haciendas totaling 31,000 acres. Araoz's main plantation, Cuahuixtla, was the closest to Zapata's village. A crucial meeting took place at Cuernavaca on December 30, 1908. Principal Morelos planters and professional men crowded into the elegant Hotel Moctezuma. They filled the big, arched, mahogany-floored dining room; others stood outside the open window on a patio brilliant with crimson blossoms. And as the vivid red, green, and blue macaws squawked their nonsensical chatter, these leading Morelos citizens heard that Díaz finally approved their request for Escandón's candidacy. They began to plan their campaign. A convention was arranged for the following day, and this took place with no signs of opposition to the official choice.

But already a rival party had begun to form among local elected municipal officers, teachers, respected village elders, and other spokesmen for the peasants. During December meetings were held in villages, schools, and bars to discuss a plan of campaign. An opposition candidate had emerged. First, an approach was made to General Francisco Leyva, hero of the fighting against the French in the 1860's, when he had been military commander in the Morelos area, and the state's first govenor—after defeating Díaz in a free election for the post. In the last week of December the seventy-three-year-old Leyva was asked if he would stand, but he refused because of his age; instead Leyva proposed one of his two sons, and the Morelos opposition faction settled on Patricio, a civil servant. On December 28, forty-eight hours before the planters' meeting in the Moctezuma Hotel, Cuernavaca, General Leyva obtained an interview with Díaz and warned him of the developing situation. Díaz, apparently outwardly supporting his sentiments expressed in the Creelman interview, told *México Nuevo* on January 7, 1909, that "anyone whom the citizens of Morelos freely elect would be welcome."

Throughout Morelos the opposition movement stirred, slowly at first and always apprehensive of vicious governmental retaliation. Political clubs formed in the towns and even among the normally unpolitical villages. To the more intellectual citizens, the Creelman interview had shown that the existing rule over the country might end, and the apparently inexorable grip over the land by the planters might therefore be altered. With the ordinary peasants, decades of accelerating oppression by the landowners finally started a movement for change. Almost inevitably the inexperienced opposition showed signs of disorganization during the first week of 1909, but a semblance of cohesion gradually emerged, and on Friday, January 22, the *Leyvistas* began to display their strength. Despite the occasion's falling on a work day, hundreds of peasants left their fields and their plantation employment to travel to Cuautla, eight miles up the valley from Anenecuilco. Emiliano Zapata probably joined the 1,500 people who crowded through the city's narrow streets and into the main square. There, resplendent with his old campaign medals, stood General Leyva. Beside him stood his son Patricio, earnest, erect, and seeming almost surprised by the boisterous reception he received. The mob cheered and shouted; the police did nothing—and throughout the state the opposition groups crept further into the open.

Forty-eight hours later three men met in a tree-shaded house at Villa de Ayala. This trio sitting round the table was influential: Refugio Yáñez, a former president of the town, Pablo Torres Burgos, the town's schoolmaster and an amateur lawyer, and a small-time professional lawyer, Luciano Cabrera. All three were well known for the help already given by them to local villagers over land questions. Now they formed a *Leyvista* group and invited anyone else to join. Almost eighty people put their names to the list of supporters, and among them was Emiliano Zapata, the thirty-year-old horse trainer from Anenecuilco.

Similar scenes were enacted throughout the state: on the same day as the Villa de Ayala meeting, January 24, over a thousand people gathered at Jojutla, down the Yautepec valley, close to the state border with Guerrero; one by one the *Leyvista* groups summoned dissidents to the opposition banner. For villagers these weeks were always the busiest of the year, the days when the corn harvests were cut and carried down from the hills, when women rose two hours before dawn to prepare tortillas for the long hours in the fields, and when families suffered severest financial hardships— all money gone until the corn could be sold in the February markets. Yet despite the activity and domestic preoccupations, the peasants responded to the opposition call, and the yeast of rebellion began to rise.

Reaction resulted, as vigorous, ruthless and unjust as had been feared. The primary instruments for the planters in their attempt to stamp out opposition were the district political officials, the *jefe político*, many of whom were local tyrants for the Díaz regime. First the local *Leyvista* leaders were warned that the struggle was useless—Escandón would win since Díaz "has disposed of it." Then the opposition spokesmen were threatened with transportation to labor camps if they refused to disband their groups. Then the beatings and arrests began. At noon on February 1, the chief Escandón agent arrived in Cuautla on a whistle-stop visit: the huge, high-chimneyed engine clanked into the station and the el-

egant Mexico City politician Hipolito Olea stepped onto the platform. He began praising Escandón—to be answered by shouts of
"*Viva Leyva.*" Olea lost his temper. "Imbeciles!" he roared. "Un-
grateful bums!" A barrage of stones thudded against the wooden
railway station; policemen raised their rifles; the mob scattered.

The incident at Cuautla—it failed even to achieve the scale of
a riot—provided the *Escandonistas* with their pretext for counter-
action. Scores of *Leyvistas* were dragged to jail, many of whom had
not even attended the rally, and persecution spread rapidly. Pablo
Torres Burgos, the schoolmaster at Villa de Ayala and Zapata's future revolutionary colleague, was imprisoned without even the for-
mality of a trumped-up charge. Octaviano Gutiérrez, from Anenecuilco, soon joined him. Police swooped on Genovevo de la O,
soon to be a revolutionary general, but found he had fled from his
Santa Maria home: they carried away his family instead. The government retaliation reached the opposition candidate himself: on
the day following the Cuautla disturbance Patricio Leyva was
sacked from the Ministry of Public Works.

Zapata remained physically untouched by the dictatorial crushing of the Morelos opposition. So far he had not been sufficiently
involved. Nor had he time to become committed before polling,
for the election took place on February 7. The result was now inevitable. Police and troops continued to imprison prominent opposition agents, even on election day; they stood by with loaded rifles and swinging batons while the peasants made their marks;
ballot distribution was often rigged and vote counting seemed
highly suspect. Details of the votes cast remained secret: officially
it was merely made known that Escandón enjoyed an "absolute
majority." Probably the proportion of votes for Escandón over
Leyva reached about two to one. And on March 15, 1909, the new
governor was officially sworn into office, still complaining over his
unwilling involvement.

Escandón tried his best as governor. He even altered the Morelos tax system in a way that helped the humblest peasants, and
many supported him as a result. One Morelos villager explained:
"Before, every citizen paid a personal tax of 20 *centavos* a month.
When Escandón came in he abolished the personal tax. Now we
didn't pay it. Then he taxed capital instead; he charged capital a

certain percentage. And so, all of us peaceful men who were against him before changed."[10] But, typically, Escandón's revised taxation alienated one group while pleasing another: his General Revaluation Law for Real Estate, enacted on June 21, 1909, increased the levy on capital, but mainly with regard to smaller farmers and middle-level property owners. Large plantations received favorable terms, even better than before. The main effect of the law was to turn town merchants and shopkeepers against the new governor.[11]

Meanwhile, the power of the large planters continued unabated. Two months after the election *Leyvista* spokesmen such as Pablo Torres Burgos and Octaviano Gutiérrez remained imprisoned; others suffered hellish conditions in the labor camps; still more, like Genovevo de la O, remained in hiding, their families still kept as hostages. Escandón, mainly through mismanagement and ignorance, placed corrupt or ineffectual officials in charge of the bureaucratic process and in the *jefes políticos* structure. Above all, the steady takeover of land by the largest haciendas seeped onward; already the seventeen owners of the thirty-six major haciendas owned over 25 per cent of the entire state area, and almost 100 per cent of the most fertile land. The largest property owner, Luis García Pimentel, owned 168,420 acres, with his main hacienda at Santa Clara in the state's eastern corner.[12] Land disputes brought before the governor were almost inevitably settled in favor of the planters, and in late summer 1909 the city council of Jojutla failed to find satisfaction when a nearby rice plantation began to tap substantial proportions of the city's water supply.

Small villages found themselves in an even more helpless situation. And on Sunday evening, September 12, 1909, the four village elders at Anenecuilco called a meeting to admit they could do no more: others in this small community must take up the struggle —younger and perhaps more ruthless. José-Merino hinted that guns might have to be used, rather than mere words, and then this highly respected figure, Zapata's uncle, stood down from his position as village council president and asked for nominations for the office. Three names were put forward, all young men, all potential fighters for the village rights. From them the shy, stubborn Emiliano emerged as clear victor. Zapata took his most important step forward so far in his progress toward revolution, and, in the words of the Mexican historian Gastón García Cantu, "like a wound, the country's history opens in Anenecuilco."

Yet Zapata began his career as village president by showing restraint. This was typical; he continued the attempted village policy of protecting village rights through peaceful and legal methods, as pursued in vain by previous elders. On October 16 the village council paid one hundred pesos to the lawyer Luis Ramírez de Alba to plead their case in the courts. The lawyer proved either incapable or unwilling to obtain results. Zapata and his council colleagues sought additional help, and in doing so moved onto dangerous ground: village representatives made the four-day journey to Mexico City, where they contacted notable opponents of the Díaz regime, possibly including Paulino Martínez and Jesús Flores Magón. These two intellectuals had spoken at the *Leyvista* rally in Cuautla on January 31, which gave impetus to the whole *Leyvista* movement; since then they had been closely watched, as had all who talked to them. The authorities in Mexico City relayed news of the Anenecuilco villagers' visit to the *jefe político* in Cuernavaca, where the information caused especial apprehension: reports were accumulating of the possibility of armed resistance in the Villa de Ayala municipality, and this region had a history of militancy. Some of the most stubborn fighting in the War of Independence against Spain had taken place here: the municipality and seat were named after the local hero in the conflict, Francisco Ayala; since then the proud locals had proved capable in self-defense against bandits, and the region remained heavily armed. Now an attempt at linking with dissidents in Mexico City seemed imminent. The Cuernavaca authorities reacted immediately. No direct evidence exists that Zapata himself journeyed to meet the controversial *Leyvistas* in the Mexican capital, yet it made no difference. Zapata, as village president, young, outspoken, with a family tradition of willingness to take up arms, had to be removed. In February 1910, Emiliano received notice that he would be drafted into the army. No time was allowed for escape: on the 10th he was taken under escort to Cuernavaca and enrolled as an ordinary trooper in the 9th Cavalry Regiment, commanded by Colonel Ángel Bouquet.[13]

To the state authorities, forced drafting of dissidents into the army acted as effectively as imprisonment. Deserters would be hunted and shot; day-and-night custody could be imposed in the barracks and victims would learn not to quarrel with the regime. Pay was minimal or nonexistent; the common soldiers — *"juanes"* (johns) — were ill fed and badly clothed. Zapata suffered the indignities and deprivations, yet doubtless he also benefited. No better way existed of knowing the methods and attitudes of his future enemy. Especial advantage could be obtained from discovering the potential of the modern artillery pieces held by the regular army: such weapons would provide government forces with their strongest form of arms against the revolutionaries.

From the moment of his induction Zapata sought all possible means of escape short of desertion. His efforts brought rapid success. He enlisted the help of influential customers from his horse-dealing activities, among them Ignacio de la Torte y Mier, son-in-law of Díaz himself and a federal deputy for Morelos. De la Torre y Mier's representations could hardly be refused; nor could Zapata decline his benefactor's part of the bargain: in return for his release Zapata was obliged to act as chief groom at de la Torre y Mier's stables in Mexico City. For most humble villagers such an opportunity would have seemed a godsend. To Zapata the experience made him almost literally vomit. Immediately after his arrival in Mexico City on March 29—after one and a half months in the army and no increase in rank from lowest *soldado*—he felt intense revulsion at the obsequious behavior of his fellow servants, and above all at the luxury of the stables, with their marble floors and heavy brass fittings, which made an even greater mockery of the hovels in his village.[14]

In Cuernavaca, the amiable Escandón continued to bungle his way toward disaster. His inclination to govern, never strong, dwindled even further. Increasingly he sought release, however temporary. He bombarded the state legislature for permission to make visits to Mexico City, claiming he wished to attend to "affairs of public interest" but really seeking a rest from the constant haggling and anxiety surrounding his unpleasant office. He presented his first request for leave only two weeks after being sworn in as governor; thereafter one, two, or even three pleas were put forward each month for up to ten days of absence.[15] The trend accelerated in 1910, as Zapata sought equally fervently for a return home from Mexico City.

Affairs in Zapata's village rapidly deteriorated in late winter and spring 1910 and pressure from the planters now threatened complete ruin. Anenecuilco's main danger arose from the actions of Hospital hacienda, with its flourishing sugar mill, its own bustling shops, stores, and maintenance plants and covering 2,614 acres of prime agricultural land—and greedily reaching for more. Hospital sought to obtain land around Anenecuilco where the villagers farmed their corn patches: without this area the inhabitants would be unable to support themselves. Each year for centuries the villagers had planted and harvested their vital crops upon these few acres; now, in late March and April 1910, the time for planting arrived again. But officials from Hospital moved in to stop them: the Hospital managers, acting on behalf of Vicente Alonso's widow, owner of the hacienda, warned villagers they would be driven off if they attempted cultivation. The hacienda field guards, thugs armed with rifles, staves, and broad-bladed machetes, squatted in the shade of nearby trees as villagers clustered around the gates.

Zapata remained helpless in Mexico City. In his absence the other members of the village council wrote a pleading and almost servile letter to Escandón, dated April 25, "As the rainy season is about to begin, we poor working men must begin getting the land ready for planting. For this reason . . . we turn to the Superior Government of the state, imploring its protection so that, if it please, it might concede to us its backing so we can plant the fields without fear of being plundered and run off by the proprietors of Hospital hacienda." The village council even agreed in the letter that they would forfeit their ownership rights of the land, provided they could farm the area on a rental basis. "We are disposed to recognize whoever turns out to be the owner of these fields, be it the village of San Miguel Anenecuilco or someone else. But we want to plant the fields so as not to be ruined, because farming is what gives us life. From it we get our sustenance and that of our families."[16]

Each day became vital. Soon, in mid-May, the rains would come. Planting must be completed well before the clouds massed, allowing the corn to make roots strong enough to prevent the shoots' being washed away. Normally, planting would already have begun, with the young shoots carefully nurtured by daily watering.[17] But not until May 3 did a reply reach Anenecuilco from Cuernavaca and this, signed by a minor secretary at the state executive office, merely prevaricated. "Informed of your note of the 25 April last, in which you ask that you be permitted to prepare and sow the fields which you have claimed . . . the governor ruled that ·you be told that you ought to identify the fields to which you refer."[18] Clouds were beginning to gather over the mountains; each morning the weather seemed more humid. The village council sent an urgent note to Cuernavaca on May 8 requesting attention.

On May 15 the villagers received a bureaucratic and completely useless reply. "The proprietor of Hospital hacienda has already been informed of your note of the 25th April last and of the 8th of the current month, so that he might say what he considers proper on the request you make in the said notes." The manager at Hospital, speaking for the owner, who, like so many estate proprietors, rarely visited her property, snapped his answer: "If that rabble from Anenecuilco wants to farm, let them farm in a flower-pot, because they're not getting any land, even up the side of the hills."[19]

Rain spattered the parched fields around Anenecuilco. In the third week of May council members traveled over the clouded hills to Cuernavaca and lobbied the state executive. On the 24th they managed to obtain an interview with Escandón's deputy, Lieutenant Governor Antonio Hurtado de Mendoza, who asked for a list of villagers who had previously cultivated the disputed land. Within forty-eight hours the names were supplied. But then followed more delay. The lieutenant governor, a judge from outside the district who knew little of local agriculture affairs, believed the matter could be left awhile. Perhaps his tardiness stemmed from a deliberate pro-planter policy: the Hospital officials now swooped on Anenecuilco, seizing the land and renting it to farmers from Villa de Ayala. The rains had begun. The farmers from Villa de Ayala planted the trenches long since hoed by the Anenecuilcans, who could do nothing.

Escandón spared no time for these problems. As the villagers at Anenecuilco stood desperately by and pleaded for help from the governor, his preoccupations lay elsewhere: during June he spent many hours helping Mrs. King prepare for the grand opening of her Bella Vista hotel in Cuernavaca. She wrote afterward: "In my great dining-room upstairs, Don Pablo Escandón, the governor of the state, cocked his head to one side and sighted down his aristocratic nose at one of the potted palms. 'Move it three inches to the left, Carlos,' he said finally, to the Indian boy at his elbow. . . . He turned his attention once more to the room. 'Yes, it is all very fine,' he said to himself, with a sort of personal pride, for it was he who had urged me on to this enterprise."[20]

Yet even Mrs. King, in her luxury hotel and belonging to a class inevitably linked with the aristocracy and the planters, recognized the hardships endured by peasants. "I would see the poor wretches as I drove about, their feet always bare and hardened like stones, their backs bent under burdens too heavy for a horse or mule, treated as people with hearts would not treat animals." And she realized the failings of the hacienda owners on the one hand and the link between the Indian peasants and the land they tilled on the other. "If they [the planters] had lived more at home on their haciendas they would have seen that the golden stream was tainted with the sweat and the blood of their labourers. . . . They might have come to know also the smell of wet dark earth in newly turned furrows, and the pride in first fruits, and to understand the passion of the *indio* for the *milpa* of his fathers."[21]

This passion would soon motivate the despairing Anenecuilcans into militant action. The time for Zapata's return had almost arrived. Escandón should have paid more attention to governmental affairs: other events were taking place on the fringe of Morelos which merited his concern. The opposition surge which arose during the campaign for governor was now being reflected in an even greater movement: an opposition attempt for the presidency of Mexico itself. The name of Francisco I. Madero was increasingly being heard.

Officially, Díaz's term of office ended in 1910. Under normal circumstances no complications would be expected over his automatic reelection, or over his choice of successor should Díaz prefer to retire. But the ripples from the Creelman interview still ruffled the surface of Mexican politics; the opposition campaign in Morelos for the post of governor had indicated the strength of feeling against the established order, and now Madero put himself for-

ward as successor to Díaz. Initially the eighty-year-old Díaz failed
to recognize the threat, and indeed, Madero seemed an unlikely
person to lead a revolution. Born in 1873, he was the eldest son of
Francisco Madero, a rich businessman in Parras, Coahuila state.
Young Francisco grew up on the family estate, received an excellent education in Paris and at the University of California, and then
managed one of the family plantations in Coahuila. He grew cotton, treated his employees well, and earned local respect; it
seemed he sought nothing more. But his local prominence brought
him into contact with district governmental affairs in this part of
north Mexico; gradually, filled with ideals of democracy obtained
during his Paris days, he became politically involved. By 1909 this
involvement led to Madero's being pushed into the leadership of
the anti-Díaz campaign, aiming at the presidential elections scheduled for the following year. Yet circumstances, rather than character, still dictated his career. "In appearance and manner he was the
reverse of impressive," wrote an American eyewitness, Edward
Bell.[22]

Another American provided a slightly more flattering description; according to Edith O'Shaughnessy, wife of the first secretary
at the embassy: "Madero, seen at close range, is small, dark, with
nose somewhat flattened, expressive, rather prominent eyes in
shallow sockets and forehead of the impractical shape. But all is re-
deemed by expressions playing like lightning over the shallow, fea-
tureless face and his pleasant, ready smile. . . . There is something of youth, of hopefulness and personal goodness."[23]

Contact was established between *Leyvistas* in Morelos and the
Madero movement, but Madero himself did not visit the state in
1909 and 1910, and groups supporting him in Morelos failed to undertake firm action. Escandón and his officials dismissed the activities of the *Maderistas*, even when Díaz began to appreciate the
danger. On June 13, 1910, on the eve of the presidential election,
Madero was arrested. The threat seemed over; Díaz turned thankfully back to his plans for magnificent and extremely costly ceremonies to be held in mid-September, intended to celebrate both
his birthday on the 15th and the 100th anniversary of Mexican independence on the 16th. All seemed well again. In Cuernavaca,
Escandón joined wholeheartedly in the activities at the Bella Vista,

finally opened four days before Madero's arrest. "My memory of that evening is an intoxicating blur of lights and music and perfume," enthused Mrs. King, and the governor, champagne glass in hand, proclaimed: "This is a great day for Cuernavaca!"

Over the mountains at Anenecuilco the villagers waited for Zapata and faced the prospect of starvation. Now, in these early summer weeks of 1910, as the rains continued to sweep down from the volcanic peak of Popocatepetl, Zapata at last arrived. Within hours of his return he summoned a council meeting. Zapata now declared that Anenecuilcans must act. He gathered together about eighty men from the village, most of them as young as himself; arms were distributed—old rifles, specially sharpened machetes, pointed stakes—and the group walked to the fields. The outsiders from Villa de Ayala stood from their crops to meet them. The Anenecuilcans had no quarrel with the men from Villa de Ayala, Zapata stated, and many were kinsmen and friends. All were from the same rural stock. But the Anenecuilcans would farm their land. Behind Zapata stood the armed villagers. The men from Villa de Ayala picked up their tools and left and with them went the field guard from Hospital hacienda. Zapata immediately organized men in defensive positions, armed with the best available weapons, and he drew up a rota for guard duty; at the same time he assigned land lots to the local farmers.

News of this dramatic and effective peasant action spread rapidly through the villages and haciendas of central Morelos, and Zapata prepared for his next step. Even in Cuernavaca amidst the bustle and gaiety at the Bella Vista, Mrs. King remembered the slightly inaccurate but perceptive words of her manager, Willie Nevin. "These *indios* aren't the fools they take them for," he told her. "There's a fellow over near Cuautla—Emiliano Zapata's his name—who's been stirring up the people. It seems the hacienda annexed his father's *milpa*. Later they sent him to the owner's Mexico City house on an errand, and when he saw the horses stabled there in marble stalls, it made him pretty sore." Willie Nevin also joined with those who feared the effects of the Mexican President's plans for the September celebrations. "You can bet that when the people see this *Centenario* circus they're not going to fall down on their faces and worship: they're going to ask: 'Who paid for this?' "[24]

Hospital hacienda avoided outright violence against the Anen-ecuilcans: the armed villagers seemed too determined. Instead Za-pata received a rent demand, which the village refused to pay. The hacienda appealed to the district prefect at Villa de Ayala, a move soon shown to be a mistake. A hearing took place in late summer and Zapata appeared for the village; there to judge on the case were the prefect and the municipal president. The latter was Refu-gio Yáñez, the highly respected citizen with long experience at his post who, in January 1909, had been one of the three founder members of the *Leyvista* group in Ayala. The prefect, José Vi-vanco, was an Escandón appointee, raw to this type of adminis-trative position and with inadequate knowledge of the area. Now both men acquiesced to Zapata's view and the Hospital hacienda emerged defeated. Zapata and his fellow villagers returned to An-enecuilco, having been told by the municipal authorities that they need pay no rent at all in 1910—Zapata had pleaded that the har-vest would be insufficient—and only as much as they felt able in 1911.[25] Yet Zapata was still unsatisfied. He wrote to the President himself, seeking to obtain a definite ruling over the right of the vil-lage to the land. Díaz, surprisingly, obliged. This additional suc-cess forged an added link between Vivanco, Yáñez, and Zapata, and the trio extended their activities: other villages followed the Anenecuilco example and Zapata was automatically asked to advise and lead, backed by the municipal authorities at Ayala. The hacien-das, faced with the possibility of peasant action against their vul-nerable irrigation networks, and even with the possibility of a full-scale uprising, could merely arm themselves in return and seek of-ficial support from Cuernavaca.

But the governor and his officials remained preoccupied with other matters. September brought a month of festivities in Mexico City, centering on the long-awaited celebrations ordered by Díaz for the 15th and 16th. Escandón left Cuernavaca for a two-month holiday at the beginning of September and his leading officials also departed from the state capital, together with all others who could afford the expense. "By the 14 September all of us who could possi-bly contrive it were up in Mexico City to see the pageantry," wrote Mrs. King. "We saw the plenipotentiaries, representing the vari-ous nations, driving up in their gorgeous dress uniforms to the Na-tional Palace to pay their respects to Porfirio Díaz, permanent

president of Mexico. They rode in luxurious carriages drawn by the
most beautiful horses that could be bought, the horses whose price
had shocked Willie Nevin. Escorting the ambassadors was a squad-
ron of hussars in gala dress, who galloped ahead of the coaches to
clear the streets. . . ."26

Full-scale celebrations began on the night of the 15th, with
banquets, dances and receptions throughout the capital, topped by
a huge feast in honor of Díaz. The next evening, Independence
Day, Díaz stepped onto the balcony of his palace and rang the bell
which Father Miguel Hidalgo had tolled on September 16, 1810,
to begin the Independence Revolution. Earlier in the evening "the
most brilliant ball of the epoch" took place, according to Mrs. King
—"a gathering of the aristocracy of Mexico, and an exhibition of
the gorgeous gowns and precious jewels for which the women of
Mexico were famous. Such a display had not been seen since the
days of the Emperor Maximilian."27

Nor would such sights be seen again. With the last parades
ended in Mexico City, the last bull killed, the last reception finished, the name Madero suddenly appeared again in the newspapers. Madero had been kept at the town of San Luis Potosí during the summer, charged with inciting rebellion; his arrest had
revealed to his supporters that Díaz could only be removed by
force. Reluctantly, Madero agreed. On October 6 he jumped bail
and fled to Texas disguised as a railway worker. He established his
headquarters at the unpretentious Hutchins Hotel, San Antonio,
where he was joined by his brothers Gustavo, Raúl, Alfonso, and
Julio, and by Roque Estrada, who had been arrested with him.
Madero planned to announce the formation of a revolutionary junta
as soon as sufficient followers had been gathered; meanwhile he
worked on his political manifesto—his summons to the people to
rise and fight.

And Zapata, with his entirely separate activities, had already
prepared the ground in the mountains and valleys of central
Morelos.

2

• • • • • • • • • • •

Season of Revolt

News of Madero filtered south during late October and early November 1910. Almost immediately the attidude of the haciendas changed. "The foremen didn't do anything to us anymore," commented one Morelos peasant. "They were afraid now, and besides we didn't take it anymore."[1] As the rains dwindled and the dry season began and the last hog plums were picked in the orchards, the peasants gradually began to stir. Zapata rode from village to village in his immediate area, organizing local defense groups and even supervising the ripping down of hacienda fences where these encroached on village lands; at the same time he ruled on titles and peasant land holdings.[2]

For the moment the planters in the Villa de Ayala region offered no resistance: they believed they could afford to wait. Other local leaders had emerged before, only to fade into obscurity; the Madero movement, while sufficient to cause apprehension, remained far to the north and Madero himself still stayed out of the country. The landowners adopted a cautious policy, treating the peasants with greater care and believing that soon these peasants would once more be lulled into customary political apathy. Meanwhile, they soothed their own fears with optimistic forecasts from Mexico City experts that the next sugar harvest would be the largest ever. Escandón returned from his two-month holiday in mid-November and installed new machinery at his own plantation in anticipation of this record crop.[3]

Also by mid-November copies of Madero's manifesto reached

Morelos. The document was issued from San Antonio, Texas, but to avoid accusations that the United States encouraged a Mexican rebellion, the publication was backdated to October 5, the last full day Maderos had spent in Mexico, and the announcement bore the title "The Plan of San Luis Potosí," named after the Mexican town from which Madero had escaped. Madero declared void the recent farcical presidential elections—in which Díaz had been automatically returned, unopposed—and he promised a free election as soon as the country could be controlled by "the forces of the public"; meanwhile, Madero named himself provisional president. The document then stated his attitude toward the leading problems facing the nation, including the agrarian question.[4] Díaz now moved to meet the threat. On November 16 federal troops began rounding up *Maderistas* throughout Mexico; forty-eight hours later the first shots of the revolution were fired. Contrary to the hopes of the Morelos planters this violence erupted in the city of Puebla, a capital of the state neighboring Morelos to the southeast.

A *Maderista* named Aquiles Serdán had managed to arm over 400 followers in the Puebla City area. But his organization was crude and amateurish, and secrecy had been neglected. At seven o'clock in the morning, November 18, the Puebla police chief led a detachment of his men to Serdán's house in the center of the city. The police surrounded the block and moved in. Serdán opened fire, killing the police chief, Miguel Cabrera, only to die himself in the subsequent fighting. Remaining *Maderistas* in the house, totaling about 20 men, held out for almost twenty-four hours, and slaughtered 158 men before being eliminated.[5] Despite this appalling loss, the police in Puebla seemed in firm control on the 19th, and on the same day Madero suffered a *débâcle* on the Texan border far to the north. An attempt to link with a force from Mexico failed dismally when the Madero group lost its way crossing the Rio Grande frontier, and the "provisional president" scuttled back into the safety of Texas.

For the moment the revolution seemed to have crumbled; in Morelos no attempt had been made to join the brief uprising. All remained outwardly quiet. "The political situation in Mexico does not present any danger," boasted Díaz on November 24, "and the lives and interests of all foreigners are absolutely secure. All that has occurred to disturb order is a few mutinies of small importance in Puebla, Gómez Palacio, Parrá and the city of Guerrero. These having been suppressed, at this moment order is complete in the whole of the Republic." Díaz stressed that the uprising was "a thing of no importance" and he joked: "If they, the rebels, ever reach 5,000 I shall take the field myself, despite my years."[6] Mrs. King, feeling "a little alarmed" by recent events, asked her friend the governor of Morelos if the situation might become serious. " 'Oh, certainly not serious,' said Don Pablo, laughing at my fears."[7] Escandón failed even to take the opportunity offered by the would-be revolution to arrest Zapata among other *Maderista* suspects. Vivanco, the prefect at Villa de Ayala, resigned in mid-November, but hopes by the planters that he would be replaced by someone more respectful of their interests were disappointed. The new-comer, Eduardo Flores, felt nervous and uncertain in the face of Zapata's determined stand and the *Maderista* threat.

In late November Flores rode out with ten armed men to question Zapata—only to find himself confronted by Zapata with an armed escort of over a hundred. Faced by this firepower Flores could only accept Zapata's glib denial that he favored Madero, and ride thankfully away.

Despite the depressing beginning, the *Maderista* movement remained in being and inevitably Zapata was drawn in. Within days of his hollow assurances to Flores, Zapata began to make regular journeys to Villa de Ayala. There he joined with other activists at Pablo Torres Burgos' house on the outskirts of the town, and although Torres Burgos acted as nominal head of this hard-talking and potentially explosive group, Zapata soon emerged as the real leader. The experiences he had already accumulated; his successful policy in the fields so far; his close connections with the land and therefore with the peasants; his strong personality and family background—all stamped him as the natural man to follow. Yet Zapata never spoke much, preferring to sit silent when others talked, his eyes watching their faces with disconcerting attentiveness. But when he did speak his words were incisive. He spoke softly, to the point, and stressed his statements with decisive movements of his hands; he had an intense appeal. And in the automatic selection of Zapata as the decision maker, the fundamental but unconscious move was begun by the Villa de Ayala group to place the Morelos revolutionary campaign on an active military level, rather than on a purely intellectual and abstract plane. Instead of mere high-flown talk, there would be action.

But the revolution required a nonmilitary base upon which to build—no one was more conscious of this fact than Zapata. This foundation must provide an ideal to be followed and a message for the peasants. The obvious platform was being provided by Madero, presently discredited and beaten back into Texas, but nonetheless essential as a means of providing unity. Without a unifying factor such as a *Maderista* label, any revolution would be threatened by splits among the participants. Almost from the start the Villa de Ayala meetings therefore discussed ways of establishing contact with the *Maderista* movement and Madero himself.

Yet Zapata always remained cautious. The conspirators at Villa de Ayala, normally numbering about six to eight men, had before them a tattered copy of Madero's illegal Plan of San Luis Potosí, containing his basic revolutionary aims, and Zapata insisted that this document should be closely studied. First, Madero must be judged on the words he had written, then, if these proved satisfactory, contact should be made to hear Madero in person and to judge his character and sincerity. Such caution, a prime characteristic of Zapata's method, was crucial: the next step by these highly vulnerable plotters at Villa de Ayala could be a matter of life and death: Madero must offer sufficient to balance the danger involved. Zapata and his colleagues therefore paid close attention to the third article of Madero's plan, which seemed to cover their main interest —the land question. "Through unfair advantage taken of the Law of Untitled Lands," declared the manifesto, "numerous proprietors of small holdings, in their majority Indians, have been dispossessed of their lands—either by a ruling of the Ministry of Public Works or by decisions of the courts of the Republic. It being full justice to restore to the former owners the lands of which they were dispossessed so arbitrarily, such dispositions and decisions are declared subject to review. And those who acquired them [the lands] in such an immoral way, or their heirs, will be required to return them to the original owners, to whom they will also pay an indemnity for the damages suffered. Only in case the lands have passed to a third person before the promulgation of this plan, the former owners will receive the indemnity from those to whose profit the dispossession accrued."[8]

This statement appeared clear enough. Madero's plan seemed to offer sufficient and not too much; the question would be solved by legal process, under the law as it already stood, and therefore Madero avoided the excesses demanded by others. Such a reasonable policy was seen by the careful Zapata as a point in Madero's favor. The peasants respected the law administered fairly and Madero's policy would thus be more realistic, popular, and durable than the frantic urgings of those extremists who merely shouted that the peasants should take the law into their own hands. The conspirators at Villa de Ayala voiced their approval. But all depended upon Madero's sincerity and this could only be judged through a personal meeting.

The small Ayalan group also discussed other urgent matters: encouraging reports were seeping through the mountains of events elsewhere. Madero himself had left San Antonio for New Orleans, still discouraged, but small gatherings similar to Zapata's were meeting in other southern states of Mexico, and in the northern states a few courageous men acted in even more positive fashion. In Chihuahua the city of Guerrero fell to rebels under Pascual Orozco in late November, and at the same time San Andrés was occupied by Doroteo Arango, soon to be famous and feared under the name of Francisco "Pancho" Villa. Outbreaks were reported to the meetings at Villa de Ayala—fighting in Sonora, Durango, Parral, Coahuila, often uncoordinated, spasmodic, and soon extinguished, but nevertheless indicative of the revolutionary undercurrents. So, in early December, the Morelos conspirators reached their decision. They collected money in secret and with this finance to pay expenses Torres Burgos slipped north in an attempt to see Madero. No time could be lost. The flurries of fighting which gave heart to the conspirators correspondingly alarmed the planters and the government in Mexico City, and almost daily the reaction increased.

The government attempted to induce the American authorities to take sterner steps against Madero, still safe on United States soil: the American ambassador, Henry Lane Wilson, sent reports to the State Department which were probably designed to help

Díaz's protests to Washington, but which in fact were most likely a hindrance. Wilson played down the revolutionary outbreaks, informing his superiors on November 26 that the "recent disturbances" had been quieted, although he added that the movement had been "remarkable for its intensity and bitterness."[9] The United States government in turn replied to Díaz that since the "attempted revolution" had failed, no state of war existed, and Madero's continued freedom could not be considered a breach of international law regarding neutrality in time of war or armed rebellion: Díaz must provide more evidence that Madero constituted a serious threat. This Díaz could not do without exposing his own weakness.

Madero remained unmolested, returning from New Orleans to San Antonio at the end of December or the beginning of January 1911, before leaving for Dallas. The Mexican authorities could attempt to take measures only within their own territory, but for the most part the revolutionary movements stayed intangible and thus hard to combat. In Morelos, with overt rebellion yet to emerge and no targets therefore presented, the planters took what practical steps they could. Arms and equipment were stockpiled on the haciendas; men were formed into semimilitary units; vulnerable parts of the plantations were increasingly patrolled; Escandón received financial help from the planters with which to reinforce the police.[10] The federal authorities arrested as many suspects as possible, increased their surveillance, and waited to pounce.

These tense weeks of early 1911 were the most difficult and dangerous for the Mexican revolution as a whole. In this context it is useful to see the Mexican upheaval in the light of other revolutionary movements. Broadly, any revolution or guerrilla conflict passes through three basic stages.

First, the groundwork has to be prepared, in strict secrecy. Groups must be organized, recruits found for both the political and the military aspects of the coming uprising: in a Communist struggle this initial stage marks the formation of the cell structure. The better this basic underground preparation, the better the chances of ultimate success.

Next comes the emergence of the revolution into the open, with increasing guerrilla action and military measures. The original groups form the basis for expansion, for further training and overt organization; the revolution declares itself with a full call to arms. Now, with this second stage, the revolution stands or falls on the success or failure of the first. The counterrevolutionaries have a target against which to operate: if the secret build-up in the first stage has been insufficient, if the transition to the second stage has been too hurried, then the revolution will prove unable to withstand the impact of the counterrevolutionary measures, and will not survive for the third and final stage—the switch from limited guerrilla warfare to full-scale military measures.

The latter sometimes reach the status of a complete conventional campaign waged by guerrillas who have developed into a regular army. During the first stage the revolutionaries are vulnerable, lacking power but enjoying the benefit of secrecy; during the second stage they have acquired more power but are easier to locate; during the third period they should have built up sufficient strength and momentum to combine forces in the field and eliminate the opposing army. A revolution stands most chance of success if each stage is fully completed before the next is attempted— if, for example, pitched battles are avoided in the second period until the guerrillas are adequately trained and experienced enough to meet regular troops in open combat. Above all, the organization and leadership of the revolution must be sufficiently strong and flexible for a reverse to be absorbed: the movement must be able to shift back from the second to the first stages if necessary. Zapata's experience would underline the importance of this point. It would also reveal that the precise moment of most danger for revolution is the point of transition from first to second phases—the emergence into the open.

These general principles lay behind the difficulties now encountered by Zapata in Morelos. During the first weeks of January and February 1911, he had to move through the first stage, building his organization in secret, establishing his authority over other revolutionaries, training and equipping his men. Problems loomed large: above all, Torres Burgos had still to return from his mission to Madero. With the planters preparing and Torres Burgos still absent, Zapata faced a critical decision. Daily the hacienda stockpiles accumulated and federal troop strength increased; revolutionary moves must soon be made or the power of the opposition would be

overwhelming. Extremists around Zapata demanded a switch to
the offensive before too late. But once again Zapata displayed caution, sound military sense, and an instinctive grasp of the basic revolutionary principles: first, he decreed that no overt move would
be attempted until adequate preparations were completed; secondly, from a personal standpoint, Zapata himself preferred not to
assume a position of dominance before the arrival of Madero's authority, for either the emissary Torres Burgos or Zapata to take
command. There is no evidence that Zapata, at this time, held any
objections to being officially subordinated to the original chairman
of the Villa de Ayala meetings; conversely, his actions now and
later emphasized his belief that the military aspect of the revolution must be coordinated with the political aims, and in early 1911
these stemmed from Madero.

So for the moment Zapata's activities remained low-key. He organized men around him in the Villa de Ayala region, appointing
lieutenants and supervising training among a small band of fighters. The whereabouts of available weapons were noted, ready for
collection and distribution; frequent meetings were held in the
outlying towns and villages such as Tlaltizapán and Anenecuilco;
his spies closely observed the movements of hacienda men at Hospital, Buenavista, Cuahuixtla, Tenextepango, and Temilpa. Messengers constantly climbed through the high mountain passes and
along the twisting tracks among the foothills. But these preparations affected only a minimum number of people: for the vast majority of peasants in Zapata's area life continued as usual. They harvested their corn, sold their produce, and cleared brush from their
plots for next year's crop. The dry season reached its stultifying climax. The ground cracked, dust drifted in heaps against the shim-
mering stone walls, day after day the air hung heavy and the blue
shapes of the mountains trembled in the haze. It seemed the
wrong season for war. Zapata took care to leave the age-old routine
of the villages undisturbed; the time had still to come for massive
upheaval. Nor did he attempt to extend his influence beyond the
region immediately surrounding Villa de Ayala. He kept his own
men under tight control, refusing to listen to those who clamored
for action, while others nearby made their bid for revolutionary
glory. One rebel burst into the open in the neighboring Yautepec

valley, over the mountains to the west, and his operation, compared with Zapata's, demonstrated the latter's superior military judgment and leadership.

Gabriel Tepepa was seventy years of age. Tough as old leather, he had fought in the War of Intervention and in the struggle for power by Díaz in 1876. Now, in 1911, Tepepa again took up his weapons. Superficially he enjoyed considerable advantages: his employment as a foreman on the sprawling Temilpa hacienda, two miles upriver from Tlaltizapán on the east bank of the Yautepec, provided him with intimate knowledge of the planters' outlook on the one hand and the grievances of the peasants on the other. He had gained strong local respect, through age, experience, and employment; he found no difficulty in recruiting a tough, militant group of small local landowners and villagers. Zapata would have welcomed Tepepa as an ally. But, unlike Zapata, Tepepa refused to await the return to Torres Burgos: he dismissed Madero's political philosophy declared in the Plan of San Luis Potosí, and the need for *Maderista* approval before acting. On February 7 Tepepa began his military revolt, prematurely, foolishly, and without Zapata.

With Tepepa worked Lucio Moreno, the Jojutla extremist who had been thrown into jail the previous year. Moreno aimed to use Tepepa as a military tool with which he, Moreno, could win political predominance in Morelos. Together they planned to operate first from Jojutla, then advance north up the Río Yautepec, taking Tepoztlán and Yautepec itself, before thrusting northwest for the prize goal, Cuernavaca. With the state capital seized, Moreno reckoned he could declare himself provisional governor: any rival move by Torres Burgos or Zapata would come too late. Now, at the end of this first week in February, the move north began. Other small-time chiefs joined Tepepa's company, each bringing his own group of followers, and initially the operation showed success. Revolutionary riders made rapid progress up the Yautepec valley, bypassing the well-armed haciendas; they skirted Yautepec but rode triumphantly into undefended Tepoztlán ten miles farther north. Soon they pulled out of the town and into the hills, placing themselves in a position to strike for either Yautepec or Cuernavaca should an opportunity occur.

But such an opportunity never arose. Zapata refused to act in

support, staying quiet and successfully ordering his followers to behave likewise. Tepepa and Moreno failed to spark a general uprising. The state authorities reinforced the cities and town, the
most important haciendas were alerted, and Tepepa and Moreno
stagnated in the hills. Unity began to collapse among the various
militants who had ridden with them and Tepepa himself soon quit
the camp to travel aimlessly south. His operation had been grossly
mistimed and his status barely rose above the classification of mere
bandit. Moreno stayed in the hills, joined by another extremist,
Bernablé Labastida, but apart from occasional murders and outbreaks of fighting the campaign ended. Still Zapata waited.

Then, in mid-February, Torres Burgos returned at last. He immediately conferred with Zapata: Madero seemed sincere, Torres
Burgos claimed, and he produced documents outlining the proposed leadership of the revolution in Morelos. Patricio Leyva, the
former would-be governor in rivalry to Escandón, was named as
chief revolutionary; should Leyva be unwilling to assume this dangerous responsibility, as seemed almost certain, then Torres Burgos would assume command. His saddlebag also contained commission forms which he could hand to subordinates; and one of
these appointed Zapata to the rank of colonel. Zapata apparently
made no protest at being listed with the others under Torres Burgos. Simultaneous with the return of Torres Burgos, events quick-
ened in the north. News took time to reach Morelos, but when the
information was obtained it proved a mixture of good and bad, and
both had direct effect on the situation in the Villa de Ayala region.

First came optimistic reports: Pascual Orozco managed to concentrate his Chihuahua revolutionaries and in early February
seemed ready for a successful offensive against the important city
of Ciudad Juárez, immediately over the Mexican border from El
Paso. Madero prepared to return to his country at the moment of
this expected victory. But the Mexican government rushed reinforcements north: Orozco attacked in the first week of February,
only to be defeated and forced to flee. Madero canceled his plans
for a triumphant return—but then received warning that the
American government had at last responded to the Díaz protests
with an order for his arrest. So, on February 14, Madero slipped

across the border west of El Paso, obliged to restart his revolution in person whether he liked it or not. News of Madero's return traveled south while he maneuvered for position in the north, aiming to restore the hold in Chihuahua, and throughout Mexico the revolution again began to simmer. Fighting broke out in various areas, including Guerrero, the southwest neighboring state to Morelos. Once again Zapata and his leader Torres Burgos had to decide whether they too should move into the open. And once more Zapata urged delay—but this time for only a few days.

Zapata used this last quiet before the storm to undertake further preparations. Final plans were drawn up and men recruited; now the hidden weapons were uncovered from adobe walls, pits in the fields, cracks in the rocks, and were cleaned, oiled, and handed out. Precious ammunition was carefully allocated. Subordinate leaders were told the plan for the coming campaign. This revealed considerable subtlety and far-thinking—and probably originated from Zapata.[11] It also marked a sharp contrast to the amateurish efforts of Tepepa. The revolutionary call would be made in Villa de Ayala. Then the rebels would proceed south, not north into direct conflict, and would cross from the Cuautla valley into the state of Puebla, where groups could gather and forces organize in the shelter of the hills. Only then would the revolutionaries begin to maneuver northward, with a firm base behind them and consolidating each area as they marched.

Meanwhile, the activities of *Maderistas* in upper Mexico would draw police and army units away from Morelos. The revolutionaries in the south aimed to make use of this weakening of federal power by holding a strong line running from Jojutla to Yecapixtla. Jojutla was to be an important target, but Cuautla marked the primary objective, situated at the strategic heart of the state. This would be attacked after Jojutla. From Cuautla the state capital of Cuernavaca could be threatened, lying northwest, and a route also ran northward through the mountains to Mexico City itself. Moreover, these mountains offered perfect protection and a sanctuary should the plan falter. And indeed, despite the logic and sound reasoning displayed by the strategy, numerous difficulties remained. Jojutla, the first major target, was still the headquarters of the fiery but unsound Gabriel Tepepa—a potential rival who must be won over.

Above all, the essence of the scheme lay in the cautious policy upon which it was based, and which Zapata advocated so vehemently. He argued that pitched battles must be avoided until the revolutionaries were fully ready and reserves accumulated; targets must be carefully chosen and overambitious objectives rejected. Events would prove Zapata correct, but not before he was forced to oppose plans put forward by extremists—and by the leader of the southern rebellion, Torres Burgos.

On March 8 Escandón ordered the expansion of the state police force; hacienda owners strengthened their own private armies, both as a reaction to the fighting in the north and as added protection for their property during the coming weeks of the cane harvest. Torres Burgos believed the moment had come. Zapata still retained doubts. His men remained raw material and without further training he doubted their ability to fight police detachments, even less the regular government troops. Zapata most likely voiced his objections and urged greater caution at a secret meeting held in Cuautla on Friday, March 10: he had taken advantage of the bustling Lenten fair in the city to slip in and join Torres Burgos and a fellow Anenecuilcan, Rafael Merino. All Zapata's objections were cast aside. Torres Burgos decreed that operations must now begin.

Torres Burgos and his supporters could find ready evidence to overrule Zapata. Further delay might be disastrous; the people were ready; the opening of the campaign in the north must find an echo in the south. Moreover, the standard of military skill likely to be displayed by the opposing regular forces was expected to be low. The federal army was riddled with corruption, especially regarding fictitious muster rolls: senior officers claimed they had more men under them in order to indent for additional pay and equipment which they immediately took for themselves. Nominally 30,000 strong, the army therefore probably numbered no more than 18,000. "The army was honey-combed with padded muster-rolls and petty larceny," wrote an American journalist in Mexico City. "More than half the roster were men of straw who were clothed and armed at regular rates but from whom no bugler,

not even Gabriel himself, could bring forth an answering 'Here.' "[12]
Those soldiers actually present were usually poor quality; their officers often cared more for their uniform trappings than for military
expertise.

Torres Burgos scorned this opposition: determined peasants,
hard as the land from which they eked their living, accustomed to
toil, motivated by revolutionary zeal, would surely overcome the
puny and unwilling regular soldiers. Zapata saw further: he noted
the lack of unity among many revolutionary chiefs in the field;
helped by his own experience with army service he knew the firepower available to government forces; he was fully aware that rifles
and horsemanship, no matter how skillfully employed, could not
win battles in the face of heavy cannon, machine guns, grenades,
and barbed wire.

Nonetheless, Torres Burgos made his decision at the Cuautla
meeting on March 10, 1911. Twenty-four hours later, on a hot,
sticky Saturday night, the revolution began at Villa de Ayala.

3

••••••••••••

Revolution

Two or three men burst into the small police office near the center of Villa de Ayala. Within moments the police were disarmed, surrendering without a struggle. Zapata and Torres Burgos shouted to the gathering crowd that a meeting would be held in the square and there, as dusk fell on this Saturday, March 11, the townspeople collected. Torres Burgos stepped onto a low platform. The listeners remained quiet, perhaps bewildered and uncomprehending, as he read the long, legalistic Plan of San Luis Potosí, Madero's guide for the disaffected to follow in the imminent campaign. The sober declaration seemed a strange method of announcing the arrival of blood and destruction. Articles 1 and 2 contained the refutation of the elections and the pronouncement that government officials were no longer recognized as legally holding office. The plan then dealt with Madero's position as provisional president; an election would be held once Mexico City had fallen and when at least half the states were in the hands of the insurgents. Article 8 declared that strict military discipline was to be exercised by the revolutionary forces, and the armies were to operate within the framework of the recognized laws of war . . . . And so the sensible sentences continued.

Occasional voices shouted from the Villa de Ayala crowd: "Down with the haciendas! Long live the pueblos! *Viva Madero!*" Torres Burgos ignored the interruptions and most of the townspeople listened in silence. He put down his copy of the document and told of uprising elsewhere, especially in the north. And only then did Torres Burgos display emotion. *"Viva! Viva! Viva!"* he shouted, and the people roared in reply.[1]

About seventy men crowded into the revolutionary headquarters after the meeting. These rebels formed the first military group from Villa de Ayala, most of them Zapata's trained core. Other men rode into the surrounding countryside and southward down the valley, to summon waiting revolutionaries and to prepare the way. In villages and scattered settlements the peasants collected to hear the declaration; in twos and threes they moved from their farms, their *milpas*, their homes, and their hacienda hovels, and began to surge toward Torres Burgos and Zapata. The latter's preparations, although considered by him incomplete, ensured that this recruitment took place in minimum time; the campaign began on Sunday, March 12, less than twenty-four hours after the Villa de Ayala proclamation. The seventy rebels and the latest arrivals left Villa de Ayala and rode south along the fields by the Cuautla River, and along the way other groups came down from the hills to join the ranks. By Sunday evening this embryonic revolutionary army had swollen into the hundreds, and the flames from the multitude of fires flickered over a wide area as the *Maderistas* camped in the rolling hills north of the Puebla border. The army crossed the border during Monday, still keeping away from towns and haciendas, and then, in the greater safety of Puebla state, the revolutionaries paused to consolidate and organize for the offensive.

The original plan now entailed the establishment of control over the area south of the Jojutla-Yecapixtla line, prior to surging north via Jojutla to seize Cuautla. Much still needed to be done. Day after day groups of revolutionaries rode up from the lowlands to join the swelling army in the Puebla mountains, and each arrival brought fresh cries of *"Viva Madero!"* and *"Muera Díaz!"* Yet most of the newcomers were ill armed and virtually untrained. Zapata's invaluable team of lieutenants worked hard to mold some semblance of an efficient fighting force from this fresh material, but this would take time. One day a dust cloud heralded the arrival of another band of volunteers, and this brought forth especially boisterous *Vivas*—Gabriel Tepepa had decided to quit Lucio Moreno, still inactive, and now joined the more promising army under Torres Burgos. Yet there were drawbacks to his support, stemming from Tepepa's own unreliable personality, and most of all from the reaction to his arrival shown by Zapata's nominal superior, Torres Burgos. Flushed by the response so far shown to the revolution, Torres Burgos believed Tepepa's extra strength enabled the offensive to begin immediately. Arguments between Zapata and his leader broke out at the mountain camp. Zapata continued to insist upon caution, Torres Burgos was supported by Tepepa, and Zapata found himself shouted down. Orders were issued for the assault on Jojutla, twenty miles to the north.

Tepepa expressed his customary confidence: Jojutla, boasted this veteran, would fall without trouble. The town lay in the area over which he had previously enjoyed virtually undisputed control, and many of his men originated from the region; strong local support would surely be forthcoming. Torres Burgos seemed blind to the danger contained in Tepepa's claims: if his words were true, he would obtain *de facto* predominance with operations in the Jojutla area. Torres Burgos, the officially appointed *Maderista* leader in Morelos, would find himself overshadowed by the old rebel who cared little for the Plan of San Luis Potosí, and who already had shown himself scornful of the careful preparations for revolution which Zapata repeatedly urged. Unseeing and unwisely, Torres Burgos made his plans for the actual assault on Jojutla. Perhaps because of his declared attitude, Zapata would not play a direct part in the operations against the town, but would lead a subsidiary group of men to patrol the Puebla-Morelos border while Torres Burgos struck north with Tepepa and his men.[2]

Militarily, the offensive justified all Tepepa's optimism. But events also showed the wisdom displayed by Zapata in keeping military matters closely connected, and even subordinated, to the political aspect of the revolution: fighting must never be an end in itself. Governor Escandón, at last prodded into practical activity, left his Cuernavaca base to meet this threat in the south. He remained confident of his ability and of the strength of the Porfirio Díaz government, telling the anxious Mrs. King: "Our Porfirio, with his army and his strength of character, will make short work of this revolt."[3] Escandón rode into Jojutla on March 22 at the head of a picket of cavalry from the Cuernavaca garrison. But his confidence rapidly evaporated during the next forty-eight hours.

Other federal commanders would soon share the fears which now gnawed him: the feeling of being slowly encircled, escape routes gradually severed by this amoeba-like revolutionary army which crawled everywhere. Jojutla felt increasingly claustrophobic. Few locals seemed prepared to help the wavering Escandón: no one hindered the rebels when they entered Tlaquiltenango on March 24, six miles north of Jojutla and almost astride the escape road to Cuernavaca. Escandón could stand the strain no longer and raced back to the state capital with his cavalry and with local official and police units trailing in panic behind. Late on the 24th Tepepa and his men clattered in bloodless triumph through the streets of Jojutla.[4]

Almost immediately success turned sour for Torres Burgos. Tepepa and his men reverted to mere bandits: contrary to the dictates of the Plan of San Luis Potosí, carefully contained in Article 8, the so-called revolutionaries went wild. Smoke and flames gushed from stores owned by the unpopular Spaniards, contents of houses and shops were strewn about the streets, and the soldiers from the area used the opportunity to seek revenge against tradesmen for personal grievances. Objections voiced by Torres Burgos were drowned in the din and he appealed for help to Zapata and to another Villa de Ayala colonel, Rafael Merino, who had been undertaking diversionary operations around Jonacatepec. Zapata and Merino hurried to Jojutla for a tense meeting—at which Torres Burgos threw down his resignation. This, he shouted, was no way to fight the people's revolution; Zapata agreed but made no move to share his chief's sacrifice. Next day Torres Burgos left Jojutla with his two sons, on foot, walking along the road to Villa de Ayala twenty miles to the northeast. Within a day the trio was captured by a federal police patrol: Torres Burgos and his sons were thrown against a wall, and summarily shot.[5]

The course of the revolution in Morelos had reached its most critical moment. The move from secret to overt operations, from phase one to phase two, had been made—too soon, believed Zapata; the revolutionary army now offered itself as a target for governmental forces, especially after the capture of Jojutla and, despite Escandón's humiliating retreat, stiff opposition must soon be expected. Yet the revolutionary forces still lacked efficiency, ex-

perience, and practical power—and, in this last week of March, a
single leader. Acute divisions existed between the *Maderistas* and
those who followed Tepepa. This in turn confused the means to be
adopted in the immediate future: Tepepa sought battles; Zapata refused to alter his cautious policy regardless of the military victory at
Jojutla.

In this dissension the dangerous likelihood existed of the revolutionary army's degenerating into a rabble, either staying together
as a weak, quarreling force easily dealt with by the disciplined regular army, or splitting apart into marauding bandit groups which
would be eliminated one by one. Neither of these equally disastrous paths was taken, owing solely to Zapata and the hard-core
revolutionaries whom he had gathered about him. Zapata depended primarily upon his own personality; nor was this as ex-
trovert as later accounts described. Always shy and reserved, he
preferred others to come to him, rather than making the first approach either with threats or exhortations. So, once a decision was
taken at Jojutla for a temporary withdrawal to the sanctuary of the
Puebla hills, he adopted a waiting policy, and this proved successful. Others clamored to be heard at planning meetings, and although Tepepa's voice rang louder than most, it remained insufficiently strong to quiet the rest. About fifteen village chiefs or
presidents enjoyed the status of colonel in the revolutionary army;
most of them felt qualified to present their opinions and in the resulting hubbub no decisions were possible. Tepepa realized this
soon after the withdrawal to Puebla began, and with the recognition of his own failure to sway the rest came an appreciation of
the only possible solution if they were to survive: Tepepa and a
powerful party of rebels gathered to elect Zapata as leader, with
the title of "Supreme Chief of the Revolutionary Movement of the
South."[6]

Zapata thus gained greater authority, but his status as commander remained weak. Moreover, he still attempted to link the
military revolution in Morelos with the political *Maderista* movement as a whole, and he now sought official *Maderista* approval for
his succession to Torres Burgos. As March closed Zapata left the
Puebla camp, despite the danger of rivals undermining his leadership during his absence, and he rode north deep into Morelos,

dodging police patrols, to seek means of strengthening his position in the state. Traveling mostly by night and with only a small group of men, he crossed through the mountain passes west of Cuautla, splashed through the upper Yautepec river, and disappeared into the hills around Tepoztlán.

Zapata's primary concern was to make contact with Tepepa's old ally, Lucio Moreno, still in these mountain ranges. But his journey north also provided greater opportunity for an approach to Madero or his officials, and in this Zapata found himself fortunate. A rebel from Mexico City, Octavio Magaña, came into his mountain camp, and agreed to carry a message to Madero's men in the Mexican capital, who in turn would transmit the message to Madero himself. Through this tenuous link, Zapata attempted to inform the revolutionary leader of the death of Torres Burgos and that he, Zapata, was provisionally taking command in Morelos pending orders from Madero. The meeting with Octavio Magaña brought further benefit. Magaña belonged to a revolutionary group in Mexico City, the Tacubayans, who, although advocating a more extreme line than the Plan of San Luis Potosí, nevertheless supported Madero. But the Díaz authorities discovered this Tacubaya conspiracy, moved in, and shattered the metropolitan network. Among the survivors was Rodolfo Magaña, Octavio's brother, who fled to Zapata with about 10,000 pesos from the coffers of the ruined revolutionary group. Zapata accepted the money and thereby gained a financial advantage over potential rivals.

By now Zapata had achieved a reasonable working relationship with Lucio Moreno in the Tepoztlán hills, although Moreno never proved of significant value, and he hurried south again to join his stub of an army on the Puebla border. His mission north had been worthwhile: his presence so far in federally held territory brought him greater renown among the peasants who heard of his journey. One result of this emerged on April 4, when Zapata reached the small, poor village of Tepexco, a few miles over the Puebla border. A young man approached him and introduced himself as Juan Andrew Almazán, from Puebla City, a former medical student and previously with Madero in San Antonio. There, said Almazán, he received authority from Madero to act as *Maderista* plenipotentiary in the south, and he showed Zapata documents and official papers to back his claim. In view of Zapata's name and provisional position, this Maderista "ambassador" said he would recognize the young rebel from Villa de Ayala as the rightful military leader.

Almazán could not be considered entirely trustworthy: he seemed shifty, with a doubtful reputation, and the papers he produced might be forged. But Almazán had certainly been with Madero in San Antonio and this alone provided him with an impressive standing among the peasants. His recognition of Zapata, giving the semblance of Madero's stamp of approval, therefore contained value. It would have made no difference to Zapata had he known that Almazán had quarreled with Madero, who had criticized him for being unruly and unreliable.[7]

Zapata's methods of gaining ascendancy were reaping rewards. His quiet assumption of power won him respect. Once the process of recognition began it rapidly accumulated. Almost daily more petty leaders brought their small groups—twenty, fifty, perhaps as many as a hundred men—to his camp in the Puebla hills. These individual chiefs embraced all types of men—hacienda foremen, preachers, textile workers, shopkeepers, and, inevitably, the occasional bandit or cattle rustler. The very diversity of membership added strength to Zapata's army, always provided he could weld the men together with firm leadership. Zapata received his most valuable help so far, with an event displaying all the irony and unexpected twists which so often emerged during the Mexican revolution.

Realizing too late the nature and extent of the revolution in Morelos, the Díaz authorities were now attempting desperate measures to avert an imminent bloodbath. Among these measures, all of them largely ineffective, was the effort to replace unpopular officials by more acceptable persons, and included in the latter was the state's first governor, seventy-five-year-old General Francisco Leyva. His son Patricio received the offer of Escandón's position; ironically, the former contender for the post of governor now refused and Escandón tottered on for a few more weeks at Cuernavaca. With the failure of this offer, the Díaz representatives then successfully persuaded the old General Leyva to accept a commission as state military commander, hoping his presence at the head of the troops would convince the rebels that the old days were ending. The plan collapsed; the revolutionaries were incensed by General Leyva's apparent betrayal of the anti-Díaz cause and the whole Leyva family lost credit. Potential *Leyvista* rivals to Zapata were rendered impotent.

During the first days of April an invitation reached Zapata as he continued to train his men and welcome new recruits. General Leyva proposed a meeting. Further, the aged Leyva showed himself willing to honor Zapata by traveling to the border of Morelos for this conference, almost to the rebel leader's own territory. The general sought Zapata's advice over the appointment of a new governor in Morelos. Zapata agreed to the proposal and the meeting took place at Jonacatepec, five miles east of the Morelos state line. He was accompanied by his brother Eufemio, by Gabriel Tepepa as his principal military subordinate, and by Manuel Asúnsulo, who represented rebels gathered in the neighboring state of Guerrero. For Leyva the meeting proved completely abortive. He sat at one side of the table, flanked by anxious aides, the revolutionaries sat at the other side, swathed in their bandoliers; Zapata conceded nothing. No common ground could be found and Leyva rode north again. Zapata rode south, well satisfied. No better approval of his leadership could have been provided than this recognition by Leyva, who had to depart completely emptyhanded.

Zapata intended to adhere to the original plan worked out with Torres Burgos: consolidate a hold in Puebla and southern Morelos, then strike north toward the primary target of Cuautla. He retained his cautious approach, but now judged the moment opportune to display himself and his army. Personally, he adopted the appearance which later became familiar throughout Mexico and, in newspaper photographs, throughout America and Europe. His dress gave him the largely false reputation of a dandy among those who failed to realize the full significance of his thick rings and glittering buttons. These, and his waistcoat, tight black trousers, and white shirt, formed a uniform: Zapata dressed as a typical village chief wearing his best clothes for the local fair. He therefore retained his peasant appearance while setting himself slightly above the ordinary people. Zapata's attitude in this respect contrasted with Pancho Villa, the other great revolutionary figure, who stressed the military aspect of his role by dressing himself and many of his troops in khaki, and by doing so placed himself apart from the villagers and the popular basis of the revolutionary movement. Zapata's dress, gaudy and dandified as it may have seemed to foreigners, was immediately indentifiable and representative for those whom he commanded, and proved symbolic of his natural aptitude for leadership. Now he would rely more then ever before on this talent as commander. His army, still inexperienced, would be split and sent in various directions to perform different tasks: no longer would Zapata be able to exert close supervision.

Early in April Zapata sent Tepepa and Almazán to operate farther south along the Puebla-Guerrero border. He then gathered the rest of Tepepa's previously independent men around him, together with the bulk of his remaining forces, and made ready to mount his first major offensive. This would be directed against the Puebla towns of Chietla and Izúcar de Matamoros, lying in the eastern half of Puebla close to the Río Balsas valley; Matamoros held especial importance as a railroad junction. Soon after dawn on April 5 the orders were given to move.

Down from the hills surged Zapata's army. Men rode in rough formation, with the *guerreros*—warriors—closest to Zapata. Most of the rebel soldiers wore the typical peasant clothing of coarse white cotton cloth, cut in traditional pattern, and consisting of *calzones*—pajama-type trousers, tied with string at the waist and ankles, a loose, collarless shirt, and a collarless jacket knotted together at the front. Their feet were shod with heavy *huaraches* (sandals), and over their shoulders or across their saddles were slung their sarape blankets, worn as capes on cold or rainy days. They rode an ill-assorted multitude of mounts: some fine horses, many hags, and many mules. Among them traveled the women, with more following, most of them short and stocky and with the same medium-dark complexions as their men. These women, some soon to be warriors as fierce as the men, had clothing consisting of a slip, an ill-fitting cotton dress, and perhaps a shawl (*rebozo*). They parted their black hair in the center, combed it back, and fashioned it in a single braid. Many walked behind the army, mile after dusty mile, in a seeming horde. In fact, this throng of women had an organization of its own, with the mass divided into the lowest, the *guachas*, who performed most of the routine work in the camp, slaving to provide water, food, fuel, and clothing for the men, and the *soldaderos*, many of whom were armed and fought side by side with the men as well as supervising the crude commissary department formed by the *guachas*.[8]

Zapata trotted near the front of his army with his staff of about twenty men. Chief of his staff was his brother Eufemio, with the rank of general. Most of the others were colonels, commanding the various sections of the army. This force probably totaled about 1,500 men when the campaign began, organized into groups of between 200 and 500 soldiers. Often these sections split apart during long marches, to spread over the countryside, foraging for food and attacking isolated government posts, and converging again for battle; this method helped solve the problem of provisions, and proved most effective in striking maximum terror. News of the approach of "the Horde" spread far ahead: faint-hearted federal opposition faded away. And so it proved now, in early April 1911.

Zapata's force formed a frightening contrast to previous ill-organized and independent guerrilla bands in the south, and the Puebla authorities lacked courage to oppose this well-directed advance. On April 6 the federal troops and police pulled out from Chietla and Izúcar de Matamoros, and within twenty-four hours Zapata and his men moved in. Zapata exerted tight control over his troops, who caused only minimal damage and therefore retained the support of the local people, Zapata's most valuable weapon. But his enemy had even more powerful weapons: on April 8 federal reinforcements were rushed down to Matamoros from the garrison at Atlixco, twenty miles to the north, and these regular troops brought with them artillery pieces and machine guns, against which Zapata could form no defense. He withdrew from Matamoros, ordering only brief delaying action. Instead, he regrouped around Chietla, retaining his hold on the town and on the surrounding countryside.[9]

For the moment Zapata rested, with no wish to clash yet against the enemy in full battle. Meanwhile, his men were gaining experience and his limited action assured him revolutionary authority over central Puebla. His area of influence over rivals now spread north from central Puebla over the Morelos border into the center of his native state. But elsewhere, to the west, lay other rebel groups; Zapata, adhering to his policy of gaining strength for the revolution by establishing unity between the various factions, therefore sought control over or at least alliance with the chiefs established in this direction.

Greater difficulties than ever before faced Zapata in this search for an alliance, despite his military success in Puebla and his greater political success in achieving *Maderista* recognition. The principal chiefs with whom he now had to deal were powerful, well established in the important state of Guerrero, and disputing Zapata's claim as *Maderista supremo* in southern Mexico. Comprising the leadership of the Guerrero revolutionary movement were two brothers, Ambrosio and Francisco Figueroa, with two more brothers from this influential family giving support. Head of the group was Ambrosio, a successful farmer from Jojutla and an ex-officer in the local army reserve. His friend Lieutenant Colonel Fausto Beltrán had just been appointed military commander in the Jojutla district—and Beltrán's value as a friend to Figueroa was further enhanced through his position as General Leyva's chief of staff. Beltrán arranged a deal whereby local planters paid protection money to Ambrosio; armed with this advantage the Figueroas opposed Zapata's pretensions to leadership in Morelos.

Zapata worked at the delicate problem of obtaining an alliance during the days after the capture of Chietla; by the end of the third week in April contact had been made with the Figueroas, largely owing to the courageous efforts of a *Maderista* agent recently arrived in the area, Guillermo García Aragón. This official arranged a conference between Zapata and Ambrosio Figueroa, and on April 22 the two men met at the small town of Jolalpan, situated in the neutral area of Puebla. They brought few followers with them and these bodyguards sat in the street, hostility barely concealed, while the discussion continued. Yet the talks were less tense than expected, suspiciously so. Ambrosio Figueroa agreed to a compromise which in fact favored Zapata, who rode away apprehensive over the reason for the others' apparent cooperation. Both men agreed to take the status of revolutionary generals in command of separate columns, able to operate independently; then the agreement specified that when joint operations "take place in the state of Morelos, the supreme chief will be Señor Zapata; when the column is to operate in the state of Guerrero, the supreme chief will be Señor Figueroa; and when the [joint] column is to operate in other states, it will be previously agreed who between the said chiefs will assume the supreme command." Added to this solution was a plan for a joint attack on Jojutla six days hence, April 28.[10]

Zapata's suspicions now saved him from almost certain destruction. Preparations for battle at Jojutla went ahead, with Zapata moving his men northward over the Puebla border and sending scouts to reconnoiter the federal strength and positions at the objective. These scouts slipped into Jojutla and mingled with the locals as they sat drinking their *mezcal* in the town's bars. They brought back disturbing reports to Zapata. Firstly, these confirmed the friendship between the military commander, Beltrán, and Ambrosio Figueroa, and provided full evidence of the protection money being paid by the planters in the Jojutla area. Why, then, should Figueroa agree to attack Beltrán and his planter benefactors? Zapata's fears were confirmed only one or two days before the April 28 target date for the offensive. Scouts and agents returned with further information: of a deal fixed between Figueroa and his friend Beltrán. Figueroa would lead his men forward with Zapata, as arranged, but at the last moment would desert his ally, leaving Zapata to plunge on unsupported against the prepared federal defenses. With this news arrived a final reconnaissance report: scouts observed Beltrán's artillery being concentrated in the sector which the joint plan laid down as Zapata's area of assault.[11]

Zapata ordered his men to pull back. He sent word to Figueroa requesting another meeting. Figueroa wisely refused, then said he intended to go ahead with his own "attack." Zapata turned south to the shelter of nearby hills. Figueroa moved forward with his men against the western outskirts of Jojutla, which were completely undefended by Beltrán. After occupying a few houses Figueroa retired with his friend to a nearby hacienda to negotiate an armistice; Zapata declined an invitation to attend these talks. He planned an infinitely better move. His dealings so far with the dubious Figueroa brothers had underlined his caution; now he displayed another of his attributes as a leader—his ability to strike with maximum speed when he judged the moment right. So Cuautla would be Zapata's target, ignoring the valuable but less significant Jojutla. He intended to move while Figueroa talked. By securing the place of the greatest strategic worth, Zapata would outflank Figueroa in the fight for revolutionary supremacy in the south, and at the same time would push the true *Maderista* cause to the forefront in the event of Díaz-Madero talks, which daily seemed more likely. Moreover, Zapata intended to seize advantage of the growing chaos in the administrative affairs of the state, caused by the virtual abdication of governorship by Escandón. The latter abandoned the struggle in April. Although stopping short of formal resignation, he obtained a six-month leave of absence and fled the state and the country, sailing for his second home and first love, England, to attend the coronation of King George V in May. For the moment the governor's chair remained empty.

Zapata now struck. Over two dozen of his principal officers rushed to Jantetelco, eastern Morelos, in answer to an urgent summons from their leader. Their forces followed them through the mountain passes and along the fertile valleys, while in Jantetelco the chiefs heard Zapata's plan. The offensive on Cuautla would be waged on a large-scale swinging line, sweeping toward the objective in indirect fashion from the south and east: this would draw off federal forces and also avoid the better-defended towns and haciendas along the Río Cuautla. Speed was stressed as a most important factor: the chiefs must avoid being entangled or trapped in positions against which the federals could move superior forces and artillery. Thus briefed, and presented with their individual objectives, the chiefs joined their respective sections of the army. As May opened the campaign began.

One revolutionary force stabbed south from Jantetelco over the easy five miles to Jonacatepec, where the federal garrison fell with only minimum opposition. Simultaneously another, larger, rebel group swung north around Yecapixtla, then west over the railroad from Amecameca to Cuautla, and hooked farther westward along the upper valley of the Yautepec valley to Yautepec itself. This marked the most ambitious target so far. The ancient city, scene of a desperate clash between Cortés and the Indians centuries ago, lay close to the mountains and surrounded by low hills. It offered a prosperous, plump prize, famed throughout Mexico for its sugar, oranges, chirimoyas, corn, mameyes—and beautiful women; about 8,000 inhabitants enjoyed the apparent security offered by the well-defended garrison situated in the broad central *plaza*. During the first days of May sections of Zapata's army filtered into the nearby hills: by the end of the week the city lay ringed. Zapata relied upon speed to crack the garrison defenses, and also upon a ruse. Small boys were sent into the *plaza*, unsuspected by the guards at the garrison. The American journalist H. H. Dunn, sometimes unreliable but providing the atmosphere, wrote an eye-witness description of the next step.

"Suddenly the little fellows reached inside their ragged shirts. They withdrew small, round, bright objects, tin cans with a short piece of string dangling from each. The boys touched these strings to the burning ends of their cigars, then hurled the round, bright objects at the *cuartel*—guard-house. Two threw their cans on the tiled roof. Four pitched them into the narrow windows, from which the muzzles of machine guns peered. The boy at the centre threw his toy into the open door. All ran. . . . A section of the roof rose in the air. The great door leaned forward, split down the centre, and fell. The two guards disappeared. . . . Fragments of other men came through the gaping doorway. . . . A human head came through a window, bounced, rolled across the road and into the *plaza*. . . ."[12] The explosion acted as a signal: before the roar had died down Zapata's men struck the city from all sides, racing along the streets leading to the center before the garrison could recover. "Two machine-guns, hurriedly replaced in the windows, met them," wrote Dunn, "but the fire was so badly directed that the horses suffered most. While they screamed in pain their riders leaped from their backs and continued the charge. Others coming behind saw the situation, left their mounts, and swept, a second wave, on to the *cuartel*. The federals, half their number dead or wounded, and others smothered in the fumes of the dynamite, fought desperately, hand to hand, bayonet against *machete*."[13]

Within an hour the simple shock tactics brought total success. The garrison buildings lay gutted, federal bodies sprawled in the streets, and Zapata's troops celebrated their victory. But contrary to later reports, these revolutionaries were probably kept under reasonable control: a few rioted, mostly when drunk, some houses were looted, some women raped, but these excesses were exceptions. Alienation of the local people would be counterproductive for Zapata, and his discipline remained strict—although, with amateur junior officers and with such a diverse composition of other ranks, this discipline could never be complete. Some prisoners were doubtless shot in the heat of victory, other regular soldiers, the majority anyway reluctant to fight for Díaz, joined the rebels.

Zapata's army stayed in Yautepec for four days, long enough to levy forced loans from the rich merchants and obtain provisions and equipment, but allowing insufficient time for federal forces to concentrate. During this period other units from Zapata's forces were operating over to the east, in Puebla, occupying the towns of Metepec and Atlixco, where more arms and equipment were seized. Zapata needed as much strength as possible for the next, final, stage in his offensive: the attack on Cuautla. He pulled back from Yautepec and organized his forces at Yecapixtla about twenty-five miles northwest of his target. By May 12 he judged that the attack must begin. Zapata knew the battle would be extremely difficult and bloody: his scouts informed him of the arrival of the 5th Regiment to reinforce the Cuautla garrison, and the city—called the Place of Eagles by the Aztecs—lay in an excellent defensive position. Roads to it were few and vulnerable, and the stout walls of the houses offered strong protection for a trained and determined enemy. The federal armory included dozens of machine guns.

But Zapata, normally anxious to avoid pitched battles, knew he must make the attempt. Time swung against him. Reports revealed that Ambrosio Figueroa had emerged successful from his negotiations in the Jojutla region, establishing a private truce which would enable the enemy to rush more men northward. Moreover, emissaries from Díaz and Madero were discussing a possible truce. Ciudad Juárez had fallen to the *Maderistas* in the north on May 10, largely through pressure from troops under Pancho Villa, who was rapidly becoming Madero's most useful general—in contrast to the other northern commander, Orozco, who revealed signs of untrustworthiness. Now, with the seizure of Ciudad Juárez, the remaining federal garrisons in the north were wavering in their support for Díaz; the aged president began to seek peace, sending his negotiators to Ciudad Juárez as Zapata prepared to attack Cuautla in Morelos. Zapata therefore considered that he must seize the city as a bargaining counter for the *Maderistas.*

At sunrise on Saturday, May 13, Zapata gave the signal for advance. His army began to sweep down the narrow valley through which ran the Cuautla River. Zapata was fully aware that his force was still inexperienced and only capable of the simplest tactics: deployment, taking cover, charging in open formation, rear-guard action, and withdrawal—all basic moves. Against the revolutionaries would be ranged far better drilled regulars with their machine guns and cannon. Zapata therefore relied heavily on sheer weight of numbers, concentrating all possible rebel bands for this win-or-die assault until the proportion of attackers versus defenders reached about 4,000 to 400. These revolutionaries looked impressive as they swarmed down the Río Cuautla valley this Saturday morning: column after milling column, a sea of sombreros under a thickening cloud of dust which rose up into the mountains on either side of the plunging river. They would need all the confidence and all the numbers they could muster.

By mid-day rebel detachments were drawing up around the city. Across the fields federal troops could be seen manning machine-gun posts. These were positioned on the outskirts of the city, placed with interlocking arcs of fire to command street entrances and the outlying approaches through the cornfields. More rebel groups rode up: Zapata arrived and almost immediately ordered the attack. The first wave formed a line and charged; their horses flattened the corn as they swept forward, thundering toward the waiting machine guns. Most of these men managed to cross the fields, some reached the backyards of the houses on the outer rim of the city; but there they met the concentrated fire of the multiple clattering federal guns. Horses were slaughtered in scores, men struggled to their feet and some attempted to rush on, only to fall sprawling over the walls and fences. Survivors fled back across the corn amidst the careering, riderless horses and mules. Perhaps three hundred rebels were killed in this first failure—three quarters of the total enemy strength opposing them in the city. Dusk dropped with no further attempts being made to break the defensive ring.

But as dawn broke over the mountains next day, Sunday, Zapata tried again. This time he selected one point, concentrating his men in a tight wedge to batter a way through the Cuautla suburbs. Hundreds of foot soldiers crowded behind the horsemen as they advanced over the fields again; wave after wave of *Zapatistas* washed against the defenses and were broken by murderous machine-gun fire, but more men ran forward, again and again, climbing over the bodies to reach the red-hot federal weapons. The slaughter continued throughout the morning and the mounds of dead steadily rose before the stubborn federal positions.

But by mid-afternoon weight of numbers at last began to tell. *Zapatistas* flooded over one enemy machine-gun nest, hacking down the surviving defenders with their swinging machetes, then another position fell; the rebels ran down the outlying streets, doorway to doorway, and behind them teemed hundreds more, like ants. By nightfall part of the Cuautla suburbs had been taken, but at fearful cost. Firing continued throughout the night; early next morning Zapata ordered his men onward again. Street by street they clawed farther into the city throughout this day and the next.

Zapata rode among them; the battle was taking too long; events threatened to overtake him. Negotiations between envoys from Díaz and Madero were continuing at Ciudad Juárez, and closer at hand Ambrosio Figueroa seemed likely to recover his initiative while Zapata remained engaged at Cuautla. Leading planters and merchants in Morelos approached Figueroa at Iguala in Figueroa's Guerrero territory, on May 17, as Zapata's men still struggled and died at Cuautla, and this delegation asked the Guerrero leader to save Morelos from Zapata. Figueroa hesitated, but a subordinate officer, Manuel Asúnsulo, enthused over the advantages of riding into Cuernavaca before Zapata, and he persuaded his leader. Figueroa dispatched Asúnsulo with 800 men and orders to march for the Morelos capital, while another force occupied Jojutla. Zapata, on his fifth full day of the Cuautla siege and with the city still resisting, could do nothing to stop Asúnsulo's advance.

Simultaneously, the situation deteriorated further. General Leyva, still military commander in Morelos, received instructions from Mexico City to arrange a truce in the state. Figueroa, with one force now in Jojutla and Asúnsulo at Xochitepec, closer to Cuernavaca than Zapata, believed his position to be stronger than Zapata's and he readily agreed to this cease-fire—thus placing Zapata in an extremely difficult position. To refuse the truce would be to risk condemnation as a man seeking merely to destroy. To accept a temporary cessation of hostilities before Cuautla fell would be to render useless the sacrifice already made in the fight for the city: the federals could claim a victory; Díaz could claim the revolution had been defeated in Morelos and thus could force Madero to accept less favorable terms at Ciudad Juárez.

A messenger reached Zapata amid the smoking ruins of outer Cuautla. Ahead, toward the center, the chattering federal machine guns and the heavier, irregular crackling of *Zapatista* rifles still sounded. Dead and wounded from Zapata's army totaled about 1,000—almost a quarter of the original force—yet the federals had still to be prized from the inner defenses. The messenger from General Leyva brought the offer of a truce. Zapata reacted with frustrated anger. He refused to abandon the Cuautla struggle and even continued to look ahead at the next target, Cuernavaca: military victory at Cuautla would almost certainly result in the collapse of opposition at Cuernavaca, and with the state capital in his control he could claim Morelos for Madero. "You are no channel of authority for me," he replied to Leyva, "for I take orders only from the Provisional President of the Republic Francisco I. Madero. . . . If you do not turn over Cuernavaca to my men, and if I take you prisoner, I will have you shot."[14]

Leyva reported this answer to the secretary of war in Mexico City, and resigned, impotent in the face of his orders to secure a truce on the one hand and Zapata's refusal to accept his offer on the other. The dreadful battle continued at Cuautla. But Zapata, through his obstinacy and his refusal to be diverted from his original intention, had almost won the city—and in doing so would win the campaign in Morelos.

"Dynamite boys" ran forward across the central *plaza* in Cuautla. Most were cut down by machine-gun fire. But some reached the walls of the main federal defenses, and as their crude bombs twisted high in the air to land with shuddering explosions, Zapata's horsemen and foot soldiers poured into the square, cheering, screaming, firing volley after volley at the crumbling federal positions. The city fell at sunset on Friday, May 19, after almost a week of the fiercest fighting of the entire revolution. Barely a handful of federals survived from the original garrison; almost one in every three *Zapatistas* had been killed or wounded.

But Zapata's success, no matter how bloody or crippling the cost, pushed him into the greatest revolutionary prominence in Morelos. Cuautla, torn and glutted with dead, marked the real beginning of Zapata's fearsome reputation: his ruthless determination struck panic into the planters. Here, they feared, was a modern Attila who thrived upon terror and would stop at nothing. This reputation spread throughout Morelos and Zapata did nothing to stop it: yet the assessment was grossly exaggerated. Zapata still believed in more than military victory; he still clung to the political aspects of the *Maderista* revolution. Even as his weary, cordite-scorched troops celebrated among the ruins of Cuautla, Zapata dispatched important orders to local village presidents: he promised full backing for their reoccupation of lands seized by the plantations, and he authorized this reclamation to start immediately. Peasants entered their former fields, sometimes supported by *Zapatista* detachments, just in time for the opening of the planting season and before the rains reached full force.

Reports of this initiative by Zapata were also exaggerated. Story fed upon story, until Zapata was believed to be taking over plantations, burning down the haciendas and leaving a smoking trail of destruction. Confiscation of the plantations in fact formed no part of the Plan of San Luis Potosí; nor did Zapata attempt to introduce such a drastic measure. The original aims remained: to build upon the existing law; to return to the agrarian system which had functioned for centuries, having righted the more recent injustices. Zapata, with his close links with the soil, had no wish to disturb the traditional pattern of life in which both planters and peasants could play their part.[15]

Outwardly the situation therefore seemed promising for Zapata immediately after his painful capture of Cuautla on Friday, May

19. But beneath the surface, factors still worked against this young Morelos leader. Ambrosio Figueroa remained strong, in possession of Jojutla and with Asúnsulo close to Cuernavaca. The planters, realizing that the Figueroas best offered a compromise, supported this movement as a means of forestalling Zapata. All might still have been well if the very foundation of Zapata's revolution had not been suddenly shaken. Madero began to defect from his original cause. At ten o'clock on the night of Sunday, May 21, a mere forty-eight hours after Zapata took Cuautla, signatures were put to the Treaty of Ciudad Juárez.

Six basic conditions were contained in the treaty document, which should have constituted a victory but which nourished the seeds of disaster. The treaty stipulated that President Díaz must resign by the end of the month, May; an interim president was to be appointed, and the treaty named the ex-ambassador to Washington, Francisco León de la Barra, for this caretaker post—he would supervise the holding of a full presidential election. Fourthly, "public opinion in the states" was to be satisfied; in return, indemnification was to be made for destruction directly attributable to the revolution. Finally, a general amnesty was to be proclaimed.[16]

The long Díaz regime ended. According to the *London Times:* "The Cabinet Council at which President Díaz's resignation was announced was most pathetic. The aged President lay in bed in an anteroom, with swollen face, suffering with great pain from an ulcerated jaw. Señor Limantour, Minister of Finance, was the only member of the Cabinet who entered the sick room. President Díaz spoke the fewest possible words."[17]

But one major flaw existed in the treaty: too much depended upon de la Barra and those in the provisional government. The caretaker president lacked a firm personality. Although considered a moderate, and recently brought by Díaz into his cabinet as Foreign Minister in an attempt to assuage revolutionary opinion, his aristocratic background made him lean toward the planters; nor would he have sufficient strength to withstand their pressure. He was, reported the American ambassador, "an absolutely honourable and honest man, cultured and trained in diplomacy and the gentler arts, but . . . also a sentimentalist and lacking in the firmness and grasp of affairs so essential to one in his position in these critical times."[18] A Mexican reporter described the new president in more explicit fashion—"a marshmallow covered with white icing." Now this frail figurehead would have the task of supervising fair representative elections—in the face of revolutionaries flushed with supposed victory and planters maneuvering to regain their initiative. Díaz, who officially handed over to de la Barra on May 25, is reported to have commented: "Madero has unleashed a tiger; let us see if he can control him." With this, the ex-President sailed away to exile in Europe.

On the same day as the official transfer of the presidency, the darker implication of the treaty became evident. Already the planters had begun to challenge the authority of local revolutionary leaders in Morelos, and desperate infighting broke out. On this Thursday, May 25, Federico Morales, who had led the *Figueroista* force into Jojutla on May 18, captured the old guerrilla fighter Gabriel Tepepa. Morales, a favorite of the planters, immediately had Tepepa shot. The planters, in alliance with the Figueroas, clearly intended to bludgeon themselves back into power, and they received valuable support from the Treaty of Ciudad Juárez. More through omission than through specific declaration, the document in effect reinstated as legitimate the state governors, administrators, and police chiefs, most of whom belonged to the plantation party before the revolution. Also, on May 25 Zapata received orders from *Maderista* authorities in Mexico City, dated the 24th: any "act of hostility against . . . haciendas" was considered "an act of war" which Zapata was instructed to "suspend absolutely."[19]

The success of the revolution sagged. Fatal compromise seemed likely, under which the planters would regain predominance. Madero was turning away from his Plan of San Luis Potosí, devaluing his previous promises. But one hope existed for those who adhered to the original aims. Zapata remained strong at the head of a battered but powerful army. And now, on Friday, May 26, Zapata prepared to enter the final objective of his campaign plan—Cuernavaca, capital of Morelos.

When facts are sifted from fiction, Zapata (seated center) emerges as a highly skilled guerilla leader, a born leader of men—a man who could, if he had wished, have seized even greater power.

Pancho Villa (center) stressed the military aspect of his role by dressing himself and many of his troops in khaki, and by doing so placed himself apart from the villagers and the popular basis of the revolutionary movement.

Zapata's own revolution had been defeated by its allies. (Pancho Villa, upper left, Carranza, lower left, and F.I. Madera, third from left front.)

Porfirio Díaz, the eighty-year-old dictator (seated) said in 1910, "If they, the rebels, ever reach 5000 I shall take the field myself, despite my years."

Around the gentle
dove Madero (seated)
hovered the hawks.

Porfirio Díaz at the
height of his power

Villa was tall, robust, weighing about 180 pounds, with a complexion almost as florid as a German.

The guns of Pancho Villa's adherents captured by Carranza forces

4

•••••••••••

Barren Harvest

Zapata's fame flew before him with inflated terror. Soldiers from Cuernavaca had been dispatched to reinforce the federal defenses at Cuautla, and the few survivors returned with their tales of horror. Mrs. King witnessed their arrival. "Wounded, on foot, tied up in old rags they came—the remnant of Cuernavaca's invincible garrison. Most of the men would never have made the thirty miles from Cuautla if it had not been for the help of their women, who had pushed them and dragged them along."[1] They told of endless waves of screaming *Zapatistas* who came on despite death mowed by the machine guns, who swarmed over the countryside in a vast marauding horde. And now, on May 26, Zapata and his forces approached Cuernavaca.

Zapata halted a few miles from the city for a meeting with General Manuel Asúnsulo, leader of the 800-man *Figueroista* force dispatched toward Cuernavaca nine days earlier. The confrontation between the two men, each commanding rival rebels, promised to be tense. Instead it proved amicable. Zapata and Asúnsulo were opposites: the first retaining his peasant origins and now with a terrifying reputation which he made no effort to contradict; Asúnsulo was an aristocrat, a trained mining engineer educated in America, with sophisticated tastes, a private income, and a passion for ragtime. But these two young men had met before, at the useless discussion with General Leyva in April: they had presented a common front then, and now found they could do so again. Despite his present position, Asúnsulo was by no means a fervent *Figueroista:*

79

he served merely because he happened to be working in Guerrero when Ambrosio Figueroa's revolution flared in the area. Politically, he remained uncommitted; according to Mrs. King, who would soon meet this courteous young aristocrat: "He had joined the Revolution for the adventure, I think."[2] The two leaders agreed to ride into Cuernavaca together this Friday. Their armies streamed behind them from the jagged dark mountains, down into the rich central valley of Morelos in which Cuernavaca rested. The city lay just beyond the wild *barranca* (ravine), and the white houses caught the sun. Cortés' palace still stood on the highest ground in the city, at the point where the valley started to drop into the vast gulley carved by the mountain torrents of countless rainy seasons. Across the roofs of the surrounding houses rose the twin towers of the cathedral, built by the monks and priests who came with Cortés to convert the conquered Indian people. Now, on this spring day in 1911, hundreds of Cuernavacans crowded into the cathedral for sanctuary or jammed the yard outside, and the first *Zapatista* horses thudded over the bridges into the city. An American mining engineer, an acquaintance of Asúnsulo named Robinson, hurried to meet Zapata and his new ally before they entered: he insisted that Cuernavaca would be undefended and he pleaded for a peaceful occupation by the rebels.

Mrs. King stood at the window of her Bella Vista hotel to witness Zapata's entrance. "No Caesar ever rode more triumphantly into a Roman city than did the chief, Zapata, with Asúnsulo at his side, and after them their troops—a wild-looking body of men, undisciplined, half-clothed, mounted on half-starved, broken-down horses. Grotesque and obsolete weapons, long hidden away or recently seized in the pawnshops, were clasped in their hands, thrust through their belts, or slung across the queer old saddles of shapes never seen before. But they rode in as heroes and conquerors." Some citizens soon forgot their fears. "The pretty Indian girls met them with armfuls of bougainvillea and thrust the flaming flowers in their hats and belts. There was about them the splendour of devotion to a cause, a look of all the homespun patriots who, from time immemorial, have left the plough in the furrow when there was a need to fight."[3] The army continued to pour into the city throughout the early afternoon and evening, and the occupation formed a complete contrast to all the tales which had come before. Zapata and his officers forbade boisterous celebrations; bars were shuttered; no riots erupted. The prison doors in the old palace were thrown open and the political captives freed. The citizens of the state capital relaxed, and their relieved reaction to Zapata's behavior, so different from the propaganda, resulted in a rapid rise of support for him among these urban Mexicans.

Backed by this support Zapata sought another alliance. Already he had established a working relationship with Asúnsulo; immediately on his entry into Cuernavaca Zapata hurried to meet another potential rival newly arrived in the city. Genovevo de la O originated from Santa María, in the mountains just north of Cuernavaca, where he was a respected village leader. He had provided early support for Patricio Leyva in the struggle for governorship, barely managing to escape capture in February 1909 when his family had been seized as hostages. For months he remained in hiding, until in November 1910 he led a band of 25 men from the mountains in response to Madero's call for revolt—of this group, only de la O carried a gun, a .70-caliber musket. His force grew and his fame spread during early 1911. Contact was made with the *Zapatistas*, but the two men now met for the first time. Zapata discovered the other guerrilla leader among his troops: short, stocky, squash-nosed, and abrupt-mannered, with fast, animal-like reactions. Zapata was especially impressed by the way de la O made no attempt to distinguish himself from his men: like them he wore a peasant farmer's white work clothes. Zapata and de la O met with the traditional Mexican embrace, arms thrown wide around each other; *Maderistas* from north and south Morelos were thus united, and Zapata gained the ally who would prove most valuable throughout his revolutionary career.

Zapata's situation seemed excellent, for the moment. On May 29 he conferred with de la O, Asúnsulo, and another pro-Figueroa rebel, Alfonso Miranda, and all agreed that rivalry should end. Cuernavaca yielded new recruits, supplies, and money—between May 29 and June 2 the Bank of Morelos and the wealthy Cuernavaca branch of the National Mexican Bank issued Zapata 20,000 pesos.[4] Rebel soldiers could receive some payment and immediate bills could be settled. The revolutionaries continued to live in and around the city in reasonable peace. Occasional acts of ill discipline were reported, but these were only to be expected: most of the men in Zapata's army had never previously experienced anything approaching the relative luxury of Cuernavaca living, and some behaved badly as a result. Yet the account given by Mrs. King, despite her natural tendency to be pro-federal, confirms the general lack of unruliness: one young Indian revolutionary pulled a pistol on her, and was immediately arrested by his officers, who apologized profusely. "I realized that what the boy had done," wrote Mrs. King, "had been occasioned simply by his elation over the glory of his troops. The victories had gone to his head. After he was released he came to me to apologize, and was soon made happy by the present of a little money."[5]

But despite his success, on a wider scale Zapata was still seriously threatened. The planters continued to maneuver for the initiative. Madero deviated still further from the original revolutionary program. Friday, May 26, the day Zapata entered Cuernavaca, also marked the issue of the first *Maderista* manifesto since the armistice, and the content caused consternation in Cuernavaca when news of it arrived in the last days of the month. The manifesto weakened the vital paragraph 3 of Article 3 in the Plan of San Luis Potosí, which promised a judicial review of land exchanges and the eventual return of lands to rightful owners. This had been the clause most closely studied by Zapata and his colleagues at the Villa de Ayala meetings, and the reason why Torres Burgos made his journey to Madero to assess the leader's sincerity. Now Madero's declaration of May 26 stated that "aspirations contained in the third clause of the Plan of San Luis Potosí cannot be satisfied in all their amplitude."[6] In the same message Madero renounced the provisional presidency he had assumed the previous November, pending full elections, and he urged his supporters to obey de la Barra's interim administration. But almost daily de le Barra showed himself to be basically pro-planter; Madero, through his desire to introduce a policy of honesty and fair dealing into the murky Mexican political world, opened the way for more determined and unscrupulous manipulators.

As Madero struggled with his problems at his home in Parras, Coahuila, and prepared to make a supposedly victorious journey to

Mexico City, seven hundred miles away in the capital the various politicians and bureaucrats battled for position. Farther south in Cuernavaca a subsidiary struggle developed over the appointment of governor: the absent Escandón had to be replaced. Inevitably Zapata's name sprang forward as a likely candidate. "It was rumoured that Zapata would now be appointed governor of Morelos," wrote Mrs. King, "and I for one was quite content with this prospect. Rough and untaught as his followers were, they had treated us with true kindness and consideration during their occupation of the town, and I had come to have a confidence in their natural qualities."[7]

But Zapata was deserted by his *Maderista* superiors in Mexico City, not only over the possibility of his own appointment—which, typically, he never actively sought—but even over the selection of any candidate whom he might recommend. Zapata, as *de facto Maderista* chief in Morelos, sought permission to name a governor; he still clung to his policy of gaining official approval for his actions rather than taking local dictatorial steps on his own account.

Within three days of his arrival in Cuernavaca he wired three telegrams to Mexico City, suggesting individuals as Escandón's successor. These messages were addressed to Alfredo Robles Domínguez, Madero's principal agent in the city: no evidence exists that Zapata even received a reply.[8] Meanwhile the planters, still in league with the Figueroas based on Jojutla, were trying to gain the attention of Robles Domínguez through their eloquent and persistent spokesman, Tomás Ruiz de Velasco—upon whose family estates Ambrosio Figueroa had previously been employed as rice-mill manager. But while Zapata struggled in vain for a response from Mexico City, his partner Asúnsulo also attempted to negotiate for a governorship candidate, and his choice found more favor. First he suggested Manuel Dávila Madrid, but this respected Cuernavaca hotel owner refused. Then Asúnsulo recommended Juan Carreón, chief of the Cuernavaca bank since 1905. Carreón was seen by Asúnsulo as a compromise: the bank manager had cooperated with the rebels since the entry into the state—but he was also a friend and business associate of the planters. Zapata had doubts, but was obliged to agree to Asúnsulo's suggestion in the absence of any reaction from Mexico City to his own telegrams, and in view of the pressure being exerted by Ruiz de Velasco. This time Robles Domínguez signaled his approval: on June 2 Carreón took office as provisional governor.

Zapata's fears remained, but his freedom of action was limited. He could either act alone, using his power as military leader, or submit to Carreón's appointment. His reasons for declining the first drastic step were probably twofold. First, it was by no means certain that his army would follow him *en masse*. Many believed the revolution to be over; daily, men drifted from Cuernavaca, heading back to their villages for the planting season—Zapata's troops always remained farmers as well as fighters, and these weeks were among the most important of the agricultural year. Zapata never enjoyed total, automatic control over his soldiers and instead relied upon his own quiet yet strong personality to keep them together, and without an obvious military cause this might prove difficult. In a revealing letter to Robles Domínguez written two days after Carreón's appointment Zapata admitted he had to treat his troops carefully: they followed him not because they were ordered to, but for less tangible reasons of respect and regard.[9] Secondly, Zapata even now believed he must work through the *Maderista* movement as a whole; Carreón's appointment was considered temporary; Madero, when he assumed full power, would right the wrongs.

But around the gentle dove Madero hovered the hawks. Despite optimism among those nearest to him, he remained incapable of dealing with this complex situation. Disaster lay hidden beneath the trappings of victory. On June 3 Madero set out for the rail journey to the Mexican capital, a journey which took four days because of the constant interruptions. Thousands gathered at each station, railway halt, and level crossing, jamming the tracks in their efforts to greet him and even to touch his clothes. Women held up ailing babies, believing their infants would be cured by the laying on of his hands. A quarter of a million people flocked into Mexico City to sleep in the streets ready for his arrival on June 7. Suddenly, just before dawn on this triumphant day, a shattering omen struck the city. For just under fifteen minutes the strongest earthquake in living memory rocked the area, splitting open the streets, tumbling walls, snapping power cables like cotton, and killing 207 people. It seemed either the climactic end to one way of life—or the herald of fresh agony to come.

But the earthquake failed to smother the enthusiasm surrounding Madero's reception. His train pulled into the ornate station and crowds burst out from the nearby streets; hundreds perched upon rooftops, leaned from balconies, and massive *"Vivas"* filled the air together with chants of "Who wins? Madero!" The American journalist Dunn described the scene. "Out of the train at the Mexican Central station stepped an undersized man, with the wide, pale forehead of the student, his face pitted with the sunken, remote eyes of a dreamer. His pointed beard concealed the almost absent chin." Among those on the packed platform was Emiliano Zapata, just arrived from Cuernavaca and neatly dressed in black trousers, black jacket, white shirt, and pointed, polished black leather shoes. Despite his smart appearance he seemed out of place among the pinstriped politicians who clustered around Madero. So too did Madero himself. "The face turned upward," wrote Dunn, "to the sun of that brilliant June morning, was full of faith without works, confidence without strength, hope without power, a vision of victory with no ability to meet the responsibilities of its owner's triumph. . . . That peering, half-disbelieving gaze of credulous astonishment went with the little president to his grave."[10] It took four hours for Madero's cavalcade to cover the two miles from the station to the National Palace: an estimated 100,000 people lined the boulevards. But at last the procession pushed through the magnificent arch into the palace: above, one keystone of the arch had been cracked by the early-morning earthquake. Madero, his head throbbing and his voice hoarse, stayed only a few hours at the palace before slipping away to his parents' home on Berlin Street. And there, the next day after dinner, Madero conferred for the first time with the Morelos military commander. Zapata, suspicious as always, brought with him his carbine.[11]

Also present in the unostentatious dining room in the Berlin Street house were leading politicians in the provisional de la Barra-Madero coalition. Zapata paid them scant regard. He sought urgent answers and reassurances from Madero over the agrarian policy in Morelos. Madero began by pleading with Zapata to avoid conflict with the *Figueroistas;* Zapata shrugged and agreed. Then he declared his position, with none of the diplomacy to which Madero was accustomed. "What interests us is that, right away, lands be returned to the *pueblos,* and the promises which the revolution made be carried out." Madero prevaricated: the problem was delicate, he replied, and proper procedures must be followed. Meanwhile there must be an end to violence and Zapata must prepare to disband his troops—with the revolution won, no more need existed for revolutionary armies.

Zapata quietly disagreed. Carreón, he claimed, favored the planters; the planters were becoming belligerent; federal forces might break the armistice bargain. What, Zapata demanded to know, would happen "when we turn ourselves over to the enemy's will?" Madero repeated his soothing assurances. Zapata suddenly stood up, picked up his carbine from beside his chair, and walked abruptly over to the startled Madero. He pointed at the gold watch chain which lay across Madero's waistcoat, and he declared: "Look, Señor Madero, if I take advantage of being armed and seize your watch chain and keep it, and later we met again, both of us armed the same, would you have a right to demand that I give it back?" Madero nodded. "Well," continued Zapata, "that's exactly what's happened to us in Morelos, where a few planters have seized by force the villager's land. My soldiers—the armed farmers and all the people in the villages—insist that I tell you, with greatest respect, that they want the return of their lands to be started immediately."

Zapata repeated his fear that nothing progressive could be expected from the Carreón governorship, and he stressed his unwillingness to demobilize his forces before a consolidation of revolutionary gains. At the same time he emphasized his support for Madero and his willingness to cooperate once his suspicions had been proved groundless. Madero could make no real reply to this blunt logic. Instead, he promised to visit Morelos four days hence, June 12, despite his crowded schedule, and there he would see the situation for himself.[12]

Zapata hurried back over the mountains to prepare for Madero's arrival. Much depended on the visit. If Zapata could per-

suade Madero to see his point of view, then the planters would be
outmaneuvered, and Zapata would benefit from having the most
powerful ally. But Zapata now proved no match for the opposition.
Immediately when the news of Madero's impending visit became
known, the planters reacted with customary political skill. Before
Madero left Mexico City a number of leading merchants and planters reached the capital in order to escort him on the forty-seven-
mile journey, among them Tomás Ruiz de Velasco, pro-planter ally
of Ambrosio Figueroa. And as Madero reached Cuernavaca railway
station just outside the city on this Monday, June 12, he was
handed a written protest claiming that Zapata's men refused to lay
down their arms; the protest was signed by Antonio Barrios, president of the Association of Sugar and Alcohol Producers and Escandón's campaign manager in the rigged 1909 elections.[13] And with
Madero as he drove into the town from the station sat Carreón,
who immediately rushed the guest to a sumptuous banquet. This
celebration formed part of the plan to push out Zapata. The feast
took place in the magnificent Borda gardens, a delightful area of
the city landscaped the century before in formal Italian style, with
two lakes and showering fountains which bubbled in cool glades.
Zapata, always awkward and especially reserved when away from
his own people, knew he would fit ill into such surrounding and
with such elegant guests; he refused to attend. His attempt to win
over Madero had completely collapsed. The most that Zapata could
accomplish was to organize a review of his men for the revolutionary leader. Even this seemed pathetic.

"Surely, all the strength of the *Zapatistas* was kept for action,"
commented Mrs. King, witnessing the parade, "for they wasted
none on uniforms or martial drill. Poor fellows, in their huge straw
hats and white cotton *calzones*, with cotton socks in purple, pink,
or green pulled outside and over the trouser legs. They were
equipped with rifles of all sorts, and one poor little cannon. But
even the cannon looked proud of being a follower of the brave
leader, Emiliano Zapata." Mrs. King noticed that one woman soldier kept riding past again and again, and she realized that "the
troops were merely marching around a few squares and appearing
and reappearing before Don Francisco Madero. The pathetic

attempt to please Madero by seeming stronger in numbers than they were was funny, but it was sad too. Behind that sham was indomitable spirit."[13]

Behind the pretense might have been another motive. Zapata, failing in his effort to enlist Madero's support, found himself obliged to disarm his men, and this began the next day, but it seemed the guerrilla leader continued to practice deception over his troop numbers. Demobilization took place at La Carolina factory on the northwest outskirts of Cuernavaca under the supervision of Gabriel Robles Domínguez, brother of the senior *Maderista* official, Alfredo. Madero himself left early on this Tuesday morning to visit Iguala as part of a rapid tour of inspection. Domínguez stipulated that each rebel soldier should hand over weapons to state officials at one table before passing on to another, at which Zapata and his chief of staff, Abrahám Martínez, sat with Domínguez. Here, the men received discharge papers before moving to a third table where they received payment: 10 pesos to each man from around Cuernavaca, 15 for those with farther to travel home, and an extra 5 pesos for each man who handed over two weapons.

The operation continued smoothly throughout the day, but according to the American journalist Dunn, who claimed to be present, the disarmament was by no means as effective as Domínguez believed. The *Zapatistas* brought with them old, discarded rifles picked up from garrison towns, or old muzzle-loading muskets and shotguns collected in the campaign. All were relatively useless. Moreover the *Zapatistas* appeared twice. Each man "strolled round the corner and down the street to a warehouse, where he picked up another useless gun and fell again into line. . . . Every man of this organization threw away three guns, instead of one, yet retained his own good rifle hidden in the outskirts of Cuernavaca. Every man was paid 60 pesos instead of the 20 Madero agreed to pay."[14] Even allowing for Dunn's likely exaggeration, the official figures for the amount of money handed over seem to indicate his report contained some truth. Officials paid out 47,500 pesos; this gives a manpower total of 2,375, if each man came from beyond Cuernavaca and if each surrendered two weapons. The total of 2,375 is probably high—men had already left to return to their farms, and a sizable contingent must have come from the immediate Cuernavaca area; if so, then a swindle took place of which Zapata was fully aware. Madero's officials left Cuernavaca with a wrong impression of numbers of disarmed *Zapatistas*.

The pretense might help Zapata in the continuing struggle for power. Nor were the planters content with their successful maneuvering at Cuernavaca. Before leaving the state capital for Iguala, Madero had promised Zapata that he would be appointed commander of the police in Morelos: it was in return for this promise that Zapata finally agreed to the disbandment of his army. But while the disarmament took place on the 13th, Ruiz de Velasco rushed after Madero to protest the appointment, pursuing the politician from Iguala to Chilpancingo next day. On his way to Chilpancingo, Madero passed through devastated Cuautla, which the *Figueroistas* in his party showed him as evidence of Zapata's barbaric behavior. Further pressure was exerted on Madero by *Figueroistas* at Chilpancingo, and by the time he returned to Mexico City on the 15th, he seemed ready to believe the worst.

Although the promise of the police command had still to be retracted, neither was the appointment made formal, and on Sunday, June 18, Ruiz de Velasco took his opposition to Zapata a further, dramatic step. He called a protest meeting in Mexico City, attended by hacienda owners, rich merchants, and their supporters. The assembly flung down a challenge to Madero: either he must meet their demands and extinguish Zapata's remaining power, or there would be war. Ruiz de Velasco told his audience: "The advice I give is that you tighten your belts. Since Madero won't attend to anything, since nobody listens to us . . . the road we must follow is that of defiance." The rowdy meeting, reported by the pro-planter newspaper *El Imparcial* on June 19, forced not only Madero but also Zapata into action. Zapata, uncertain over the amount of support he might receive from Madero in the event of planter hostilities against him, and fearful that these hostilities might start at any moment, attempted to take the initiative during the afternoon of the 19th: he used his promised position as commander of police to request 500 rifles and ammunition from Carreón, to be taken from the police armory, and when the provisional governor refused Zapata seized them anyway. His decision seemed justified by a telegram received from Gabriel Robles Domínguez during the day: "I fixed appointment for chief state police in the form which we agreed."[15]

But the words in the telegram proved worthless, and Zapata's unilateral action in taking the arms at Cuernavaca played perfectly into the planters' hands. Carreón telephoned the news to Mexico City, where the authorities immediately leaked the information to the misnamed *El Imparcial* newspaper: next morning, June 20, the newspaper appeared with banner headlines proclaiming "Zapata is the Modern Attila," and with false stories describing the supposed atrocities committed by Zapata and his men. Armed with this "evidence" Ruiz de Velasco and his supporters protested strongly to Madero and de la Barra: Zapata was accused of starting a new revolt in Morelos, and the planters insisted that he and his ruffian peasants must be destroyed. De la Barra agreed, with a remark revealing all the snobbery of his class. He found it "truly disagreeable that an individual with antecedents such as his [Zapata's] should be permitted to maintain such an independent attitude."[16]

Zapata received a telegram from Madero during the 20th ordering him to travel to Mexico City immediately and explain his behavior. Zapata obeyed, still retaining some faith in Madero's basic good intentions, and arrived late this Tuesday. They met in the house on Berlin Street. Zapata emerged subdued, and filled with final disillusionment. Madero had abandoned him for the sake of compromise, knowing that the towering number of political problems would be rendered intolerable with Zapata continuing in power, and knowing that Zapata must therefore be sacrificed. Madero told reporters waiting outside his home that the trouble in Cuernavaca had been exaggerated and was now settled.[17] Zapata spent the night in Mexico City, then went to the railway station to board a train for Morelos. While waiting on the platform he gave a sad interview to a journalist from *El País* newspaper. "It can't be said of me," he declared, "that I went off to the battlefields because of poverty. I've got some land and a stable . . . which I earned

through long years of honest effort and not through political maneuvering, and which produce enough for me to live on com-
fortably." Zapata told the sympathetic reporter of his plans. "I'm
going to work at discharging the men who helped me, so I can retire to private life and go back to farming my fields." He attempted
to justify his enforced retirement. "The only thing I wanted when I
went into the revolution was to defeat the dictatorial regime, and
this had been done."[18]

On board Zapata's train as it left the hostile metropolis and
twisted into the familiar mountains were fifty men, the only force
allowed to Zapata for his entry into retirement. Zapata, thirty-one
years of age, had apparently ended his revolutionary career.

5

•••••••••••

Return to Revolt

Pigskins of tequila, kegs of aquardiente, and wet canvas bags crammed with bottles of wine lay on the trestle tables and on the stone shelves in the Villa de Ayala house. Outside in the shaded garden stretched a freshly dug barbecue pit. Clay jars of beans and chili, the openings covered with banana leaves, stood in regimented rows. Emiliano Zapata, a month away from his thirty-second birthday, was getting married. He had courted the girl in the days before the revolution, and his decision to wed her now marked the firm step to be finished with warfare and to return to farming. Marriage signified entrance into the local community, to raise heirs, put down roots. Zapata's bride Josefa fitted perfectly into this scheme, young and sober, daughter of a reasonably successful Ayala livestock dealer who had died in early 1909. So, on June 26, merely six days after Zapata's shattering meeting with Madero in Mexico City, the two young people were married by the Ayala municipal president amid showers of rice powder and blossoms. This civil ceremony would be followed by the more restrained religious service later in the year.[1]

Meanwhile Zapata and his wife settled into a small house near Villa de Ayala, and the former revolutionary chief planned with evident pleasure to return to his old occupation of horse training and tending a few acres of land. Yet some revolutionary tasks continued. As he had told the newsman at the Mexico City station five days before his marriage, Zapata must discharge his fighters: this time the disbandment would be more honestly undertaken. The procedure continued throughout July, while the rainy season swept Morelos and farming activity dwindled.[2]

But also by the close of July an atmosphere of rebellion had re-emerged. Zapata's retirement already faced threats; horses just bought for training and rearing would have to be resold. The uncertain state of Mexican affairs in general resulted in a dangerous vacuum in Morelos. Officially, the *Zapatistas* were disbanded, and the absence of this organized force, combined with Zapata's retirement, meant that inadequate authority existed to preserve law and order: the police system, shaken by the upheaval of the revolution, proved insufficiently strong, and federal troop strength had been depleted. Banditry increased. Beyond this problem lay another: the basic agrarian issue remained unsettled and had even been intensified by the demobilization of Zapata's army—his men returned to their scattered villages filled with confidence over their military successes, and these former freedom fighters proved even less willing to bow down to the planters. Reports accumulated of local unrest and of direct peasant occupation of disputed land. The promised free elections had still to be held and farmers and villagers expressed their impatience. A movement again stirred for Zapata to be named as a governmental candidate: Zapata apparently ignored this call, together with suggestions from Mexico City that he might resume discussions with Madero over the future of the state.[3]

Madero continued his attempted policy of compromise, and in doing so found himself outwitted by his political opponents. On July 11 a group of *Maderista* generals attempted to push him into action by issuing a demand for de la Barra's compliance with the Plan of San Luis Potosí. Zapata declined to add his name to this protest. De la Barra proved obstinate; the officers appealed to Madero, who replied that they must refrain from questioning the authority of the government. But six days earlier unrest between the *Maderistas* and federals had broken into violence in Puebla City; and when reports of this reached Zapata he began to involve himself in new militant schemes. Reluctantly, he shed his farmer's role. The Puebla City incident arose from a planned visit by Madero to the area on the 13th; twenty-four hours before Madero's arrival, reports of an assassination plot reached the commander of

Maderista troops garrisoned in the city—this young commander, Abrahám Martínez, was Zapata's former chief of staff. He arrested a number of suspects, including two state officials and a federal deputy, only to be thrown into jail himself for violating their parliamentary immunity. Fighting broke out between the federals and the *Maderistas,* with over fifty people killed.

Messengers rushed to Villa de Ayala with the news. Zapata immediately hurried orders to his former officers: they must reassemble their troops and converge on Cuautla prior to marching to Puebla City. His motives were simple—and sadly mistaken. Zapata believed the assassination plot might still be attempted, and he aimed to move in support of Madero. But Madero, reaching Puebla City as scheduled on July 13, at once blamed Martínez and his *Maderistas* for the outbreak of fighting, and he even praised the federals for their "loyalty and courage"—despite clear evidence that reports of the plot were correct. News of Madero's reaction reached Zapata before he could lead his men from Cuautla; clearly any move to support Madero would now be completely misconstrued, especially as the plotters had decided to abandon their assassination attempt; Zapata stayed where he was. But this time he kept about 1,000 men mobilized and armed, and on July 22 he signed a second protest drawn up by discontented *Maderista* officers against the de la Barra regime.[4]

Daily the tension mounted. Madero continued his hopeless policy of moderation and the federals manipulated for increasing power before presidential elections could take place. On August 2 the planters won a further victory with the appointment of Alberto García Granados, present governor of the federal district, as Minister of the Interior, replacing Emilio Vázquez. The latter, whom Zapata had met briefly during his first conference with Madero on June 8, had at least shown himself unwilling to answer Carreón's request for more troops to be sent to Morelos; now the Morelos governor could expect greater support following Vázquez's departure: Granados, a planter originating from Puebla, treated Madero with contempt and demanded the second demobilization of Zapata's force. "The government does not deal with bandits," he declared, and he threatened to send in federal troops if his orders were ignored.[5]

Zapata refused to obey, yet his belligerent attitude remained limited. He refused an invitation from Madero to discuss the situation at a meeting in Tehuacán, a spa town in southeast Puebla, but agreed to send his brother Eufemio instead. Although the talks failed to make progress, on August 6 the newspaper *El País* printed a letter from Zapata pledging his continued loyalty to Madero. Zapata, even at this late stage, seemed reluctant to embroil himself again in military matters and apparently preferred his retirement. He started clearing his fields, and he traveled to horse dealers in the district to examine possible breeding mares; his neighbors found him friendly, if reserved, and he seemed happier discussing local farming matters than revolutionary politics; he made plans for his second wedding ceremony, the religious service, to take place at Cuautla on August 9, and although his men remained mobilized, they were instructed not to involve themselves in disputes nor to adopt a warlike stand. Nothing should be done to precipitate action against them. If the situation had been allowed to continue unchanged for only a short while longer, then it is probable that the rebels would have started to drift back to their villages: they could ill afford to spend long away from their fields unless urgent revolutionary actions were imminent.

Zapata's religious wedding celebration went ahead as planned on Wednesday, August 9. His family and friends handed around the slopping tequila skins; accordions, guitars, and violins provided music for the fiesta, and the scarred houses in the surrounding Cuautla streets, evidence of Zapata's battle in May, failed to dampen the wedding atmosphere. But while the guests enjoyed themselves and Zapata lost some of his normal reserve, the shadow of war suddenly fell across Morelos. A messenger burst into Zapata's wedding festivities: over 1,000 federal troops were pushing into Morelos from the north. Commander of the federals was Brigadier General Victoriano Huerta, bold, bullet-headed and half blind, and with a saturnine calm matched by a ferocious military record. His entry into Morelos stemmed from orders issued by the War Department in Mexico City the previous day, August 8: troops would be rushed to Cuernavaca and Jonacatepec while police under Ambrosio Figueroa massed at Jojutla. The state would be threatened from east, west, and south: Zapata would be surrounded at Cuautla in the center, and eliminated.

Zapata hurried from his wedding guests and wired an urgent

signal to Madero from the Cuautla telegraph office. "Do you have
any complaints against me?" he demanded: he insisted the federal
troops should be halted immediately. Madero refused to reply.
And during this Wednesday afternoon Huerto marched into
Cuernavaca, over the mountains from Cuautla, at the head of his
elite 32nd Infantry Regiment. Soldiers already in the city welcomed the arrival of reinforcements with an overenthusiastic
fusillade of bullets; Mrs. King watched from her Bella Vista hotel
and wrote later: "Looking out from a place of safety, I saw a man
conspicuously apart, sitting on a very fine forse. He sat as though
made of iron, without a smile, almost without expression, as care-
less of the bullets flying around him as though they were feath-
ers. . . . I said to my manager: 'Who is that man of that beautiful
horse, who sits there in a shower of bullets with no more fear than
if they were raindrops?' 'That,' said Willie respectfully, 'is General
Victoriano Huerta. There's nothing he's afraid of.' "⁶

Zapata's position seemed hopeless as he received a succession
of depressing reports during the Wednesday night. A statement issued by de la Barra claimed that the federal troops being sent to
Morelos were not designed to repress a revolt, but only to provide
security while the *Zapatistas* demobilized. Also on the 9th a new
governor was planned for Morelos—Ambrosio Figueroa, who
would combine the governorship with being state police and military commander. Next day, Thursday, August 10, the state elections scheduled for the 13th were suddenly canceled. Nor could
Zapata glean any hope from Madero, who apparently endorsed de
la Barra's actions; indeed, unknown to Zapata at that time, Madero
recommended to Figueroa on the 9th that he should "put Zapata in
his place for us, since we can no longer stand him."⁷ A determined
move by the federals against Zapata would almost certainly have
brought the destruction of his force. But at this last moment Zapata
received unintentional help from a completely unexpected source
—from Huerta.

Militarily, the choice of Huerta as commander of the additional
federal troops might have seemed the best possible; politically, it
was accompanied by considerable problems from which Zapata
now obtained advantage. Huerta, born of peasant Indian stock at
Coatlán on December 23, 1854, was renowned for his ruthless suc-

cess in quelling revolts in Guerrero in 1895 and 1901 and in Yucatán immediately afterward. While in the Yucatán peninsula he
befriended General Bernado Reyes, at one time a possible heir
to Díaz, who had withdrawn from the political scene in 1909 at
the time of Madero's emergence. Reyes had recently decided to
become a presidential candidate in the elections scheduled for
October; Huerta's private secretary was one of Reyes' most
active agents. So, although Huerta's previous success in stamping
out revolts obviously pleased the planters, his politics were viewed
with suspicion by both Madero and de la Barra. Francisco Figueroa
realized the danger of being implicated in this tangle and persuaded his brother Ambrosio to refuse the offer of state governor.[8]

The resulting confusion provided Zapata with brief breathing
space: the Figueroas declined to cooperate with Huerta; Huerta in
turn failed to establish a satisfactory relationship with the existing
governor, Carreón, complaining to de la Barra on Friday, August
11: "The political situation of the state is bad, bad, very bad. . . .
I am in accord with the Governor of the state, but I respectfully
permit myself to declare to you, without failing in respect for the
deserving governor, that he is lukewarm."[9] Squabbles soon broke
out between the two men at Cuernavaca, hampering military planning. Elsewhere the rebels struggled to organize and take to the
field. Zapata remained at Cuautla, but his old colleague Genovevo
de la O struck at one of Huerta's columns. Using this action as a
pretext, de la Barra suspended the state's sovereignty on Saturday,
August 12, by declaring martial law, and with problems of civil liberties therefore removed, Huerta prepared to start his offensive.[10]
But the slight delay allowed Madero time for second thoughts over
the desirability of eliminating Zapata, who had pestered the revolution leader during the previous two days with further pledges of
loyalty. These messages would doubtless be made public: Madero,
in the throes of his presidential campaign, would appear in an
unsatisfactory light. On Sunday, August 13, Madero arrived in
Cuernavaca and notified de la Barra of his intention to negotiate.
The news was received with alarm in Mexico City: conservative
members in the cabinet urged that the suggestion of mediation by
Madero should be rejected, but de la Barra, also with his thoughts
on the autumn election, could hardly prevent Madero's attempt—

especially as the latter had wisely delayed seeking official approval until after his arrival in Cuernavaca. Any move by de la Barra would come too late; by now Madero had spoken over the crackling telephone line to Zapata at Cuautla.

Zapata proved obstinate. Superior forces virtually surrounded him, intent on his destruction; Madero's support had previously been sadly lacking. But at this crucial time Zapata's eyes stayed fixed on his permanent aim—an agrarian reform. He shouted down the telephone line to Madero that he still wished to retire, but now he demanded that a select revolutionary force should remain in being, "to take custody of the state's public security while a legislature is elected, which, in accord with the executive, and under the law, will settle or solve the matter which occupies us—the agrarian matter." Zapata also insisted that federal troops should be pulled from Morelos, and that a governor must be appointed able to guarantee the revolution land policy. As a result of this telephone talk, Madero sent two messages to de la Barra during the night, dated August 14. He strongly recommended to the caretaker president that part of Zapata's force be maintained as an effective security force, under the command of a revolutionary from outside the state, and he begged that federal troop moves should be at least delayed.[11]

De la Barra rejected the proposals. Instead, on August 15, a coded sign reached Huerta from the War Department. Federal forces were pushing forward from Puebla to Jonacatepec, and Huerta was instructed to inform Madero that if Zapata refused to disarm immediately, his troops would advance from Cuernavaca toward Yautepec. The latter lay less than ten miles from Zapata at Cuautla.[12] Huerta made no mention of this message to Madero, who remained ignorant of the military plans. Huerta requested extra artillery ammunition from de la Barra late on the 15th. Madero left Cuernavaca for Mexico City at nine o'clock next morning, Wednesday, August 16, believing that Huerta "thinks as I in everything" and anxious to persuade de la Barra in person that Zapata's proposals should be accepted. As the politician's car drove the few miles to Cuernavaca station, Huerta issued his orders; precisely sixty minutes after Madero's train left the station and headed toward the mountains, the leading detachments of Huerta's col-

umn tramped from the Cuernavaca suburbs, heading down the
narrow valley toward Yautepec. Behind the infantry and the cavalry rumbled the federal artillery, including powerful 75-milli-
meter guns.

But the situation suddenly changed. De la Barra received a
telegram from Madero, dated the previous day and delayed in
transmission, which provided a clear foretaste of the arguments
Madero would use when he reached the capital. "I think it indispensable that it be resolved peacefully," the telegram stated, "for it
would be dangerous to resort to arms. . . . Zapata now has over a
thousand men ready, and a large number could be raised and the
revolution could then spread to Puebla. . . . Moreover, for these
military operations the former revolutionaries could not be counted on, since in no case will they fight against Zapata, but make
common cause with him. For this reason I think it would be a very
serious mistake to have recourse to arms, since this conflict would
not be ended in a few days and much blood would be spilled."[13]
Madero's firm attitude placed de la Barra in an extremely perilous
political position—only the extremists wanted a return to prolonged, debilitating war. He therefore sent an urgent signal to
Huerta, ordering the commander to halt the advance while he
conferred with Madero. Huerta's reply seemed vague, and de la
Barra tried again—but this message also displayed ambiguity, as
a defense against later accusations that he had made the wrong
decision: all military operations "which can be considered offensive" should be suspended. Huerta took the hint, with another
message to de la Barra now describing his military movements not
as an offensive operation but a maneuver, a demonstration to press
Zapata into submission.[14]

De la Barra "cordially praised" Huerta's attitude: he had made
his political gesture for peace and whatever happened now would
be beyond his jurisdiction. But Madero reached Mexico City during the afternoon, and his plea for a complete avoidance of aggres-
sive action found favor among politicians anxious to avert a clash.
The Council of Ministers recommended a suspension of operations
for forty-eight hours, during which time Madero would make another conciliation attempt. Madero therefore hurried from Mexico
City early next day, August 17, in a brave bid to negotiate with Za-

pata at the latter's Cuautla headquarters. He risked assassination *en route:* nor could he be certain of the reception he might receive from the Morelos rebel, angered by Huerta's advance. Huerta, now ordered definitely to halt his march, nevertheless continued to creep into excellent positions and his engineers went ahead to prepare the Yautepec road for artillery passage. By August 18 the federal commander had established himself at Tejalpa, halfway between Cuernavaca and Yautepec.

Also on the 18th Madero reached Cuautla. A crowd of sullen *Zapatistas* confronted him. Madero walked to them and began to speak; his small, dapper figure seemed overshadowed by the huge sombreros. He insisted on his faith in the people, and he repeated his belief in the *Zapatista* demands; he blamed others for stirring up disorder in the state, upholding the "valiant General Zapata" against the "slanders of our enemies." The crowd remained quiet. Madero walked with Zapata into one of the houses, and the two men talked for most of the day. Perhaps because of the federal threat looming only a dozen miles away, they found themselves closer than ever before. Zapata condemned Huerta and de la Barra; Madero sympathized. They discussed a possible solution acceptable to Zapata. First, a candidate for governor in Morelos must be chosen: Zapata favored the Morelos-born Miguel Salinas, presently the director of state education; Madero suggested Eduardo Hay, one of his loyal lieutenants in the north and his chief of staff before Ciudad Juárez—he had lost an eye in the fighting. Zapata finally agreed. Zapata also concurred with the choice of Raúl, Madero's brother, as commander of the state police. In turn, Madero agreed that the federal troops should return immediately to Cuernavaca, prior to complete withdrawal from the state, and Raúl Madero would bring in 250 former *Maderista* fighters to replace the federal garrison. Zapata promised that demobilization of his own men would commence the next morning, within the forty-eight-hour time period specified by the Council of Ministers in Mexico City. As proof of his good intentions, Madero said he would remain in Cuautla until the federal force returned to Mexico City "because otherwise it is very difficult to overcome the distrust which people have for them, and which is newly justified by the stand assumed by General Huerta." He praised Zapata again, describing him as that "most upright soldier of the revolution."[15]

Disarmament began as arranged next morning, August 19, even though Huerta's force had still to start its movement back to Cuernavaca. Even worse, Huerta resumed his advance during the afternoon—and de la Barra ordered Ambrosio Figueroa to threaten towns in the south and west of Morelos, while federal forces in Puebla moved on Jonacatepec. Reports of these operations reached Cuautla late in the evening, together with news that Huerta had arrived outside Yautepec—his troops fired on the municipal president attempting to approach under a white flag. "It can't be said that a column like that marches in peace," exclaimed Madero. "It's war." Zapata ordered those troops yet to hand over their weapons not to do so. Appeals left Cuautla for Mexico City and for Huerta's headquarters during the night and early next morning, August 20, with no effect. Madero, increasingly desperate, decided on the afternoon of the 20th to confront Huerta himself.

This courageous personal intervention by Madero once again altered de la Barra's attitude. Informed of Madero's intention in a signal from Cuautla late on the 20th, the caretaker president immediately called a cabinet meeting, which resulted in a new forty-eight-hour truce. Madero, now in Yautepec, was also informed that all federal troops would cease forward movements; Huerta agreed to this since, as he signaled the War Department, he would need longer to prepare the next stretch of mountain road for artillery.[16] Zapata made a rapid visit to Yautepec on the 21st and conferred with Madero, who gave repeated assurances that all would now be well. Both men returned to Cuautla during this Monday, and the *Zapatista* demobilization restarted under the direction of Raúl Madero and Gabriel Robles Domínguez, while Madero and Zapata discussed a new agreement for ending the dispute. This emerged virtually the same as the compromise on August 18, except for an explicit statement that federal troops would remain in the state until the conclusion of *Zapatista* disarmament, on the firm understanding that free elections would be held for choosing a provisional governor. On Tuesday, August 22, Madero signed a statement in the name of the federal government, absolving Zapata and his men from any charge of rebellion; Zapata's permanent insistence that military activities must be linked with the political revolution, hence raising the fighting above banditry level, seemed to receive recognition in this statement: it contained the express provision that the absolution did not extend or give protection to anyone who "committed any offense against the common order."[17]

At last hopes were high that an excellent settlement had been reached. Madero's personal intervention and persistence increased his prestige, with a consequent sagging in support for de la Barra: massive *Maderista* demonstrations in Mexico City on August 20 had probably played their part in persuading de la Barra to obtain a second two-day truce, and strong chances therefore existed of Madero's winning the autumn elections. Prior to these the promised state elections would most likely result in a satisfactory successor to Carreón as governor. To Zapata the situation seemed favorable as he stood by a table in a Cuautla street while his men handed over their arms, one after another, after which he and twenty-two officers received their vouchers of loyalty from Madero. Refugees responded to the prospect of peace by cautiously returning to Cuautla.

Already, federal moves were being made to shatter all optimism. Within days Zapata would be fleeing for his life down the Cuautla valley, branded as a common bandit, his voucher of loyalty a worthless scrap of paper. Federal trickery, on a scale which made both Madero and Zapata appear extraordinarily naive, now reached its climax. Carreón provided de la Barra with his flimsy pretext for action on August 21, even while the first *Zapatistas* walked forward to hand over their arms at Cuautla. The temporary governor dispatched hysterical signals to Mexico City: he insisted that Eufemio Zapata intended to launch an imminent attack on Cuernavaca. De la Barra ignored the fact that Zapata's brother was with Emiliano and Madero back at Cuautla and ordered extra troops to make for Cuernavaca, amounting to 330 men with machine guns. De la Barra also overlooked the point that Huerta lay between Cuernavaca and Eufemio and could block the advance of any rebels long before Cuernavaca could be threatened. Instead, also on the night of the 21st—as Zapata and Madero concluded their agreement—Huerta advanced and occupied Yautepec.[18] News of the federal treachery reached Cuautla early on the 22nd, and threw the *Zapatistas* and *Maderistas* into chaos. Zapata heard that some of his subordinates might rebel against him in their frenzy. Madero's first reaction was complete disbelief: a mistake must surely have been made, he declared, perhaps in the transmission of orders.[19] Zapata confronted Raúl Madero and demanded the return of the weapons; Raúl refused until more accurate reports of federal activity could be obtained; Zapata retorted that these reports might come too late and they would all be massacred. Even Francisco Figueroa, whose brother Ambrosio so hated Emiliano Zapata, condemned the federal moves: he signaled Madero on the 22nd to say the actions were ill advised in view of Zapata's jealous attitude toward Morelos sovereignty.[20]

In direct contrast to the *Zapatista* and *Maderista* confusion during this fateful Tuesday, August 22, the federals displayed incisive and effective execution of their plans. The deadline for the second forty-eight-hour truce had come; Carreón at Cuernavaca still swamped the wires with grossly exaggerated reports of *Zapatista* aggression. De la Barra therefore declared that the rebels had violated the truce, rendering all agreements null and void, and Huerta echoed his sentiments when reporting to Mexico City during the day that the remedy was "to reduce Zapata to the last extremity, even hang him or throw him out of the country."[21]

Huerta's columns began to file forward from Yautepec soon after dawn on Wednesday, August 23. The road wound gently up toward the watershed between the Yautepec and Cuautla valleys. The rainy season continued and clouds hung low over the dark-brown hills; the white-uniformed federal troops sweated in the humid air as they marched along the track, the ground beneath their boots churned into white paste by recent downpours. Behind them they dragged 75-millimeter artillery pieces, and on their backs they carried the latest repeating rifles, Mausers, .44-caliber Winchesters, and machine guns. Cuautla lay less than ten miles away, over to the southeast, where Zapata still retained his headquarters and struggled to organize some defense against this advancing regular force. His men had been demobilized and many had left the area; only a few armed *Zapatistas* remained in the city, and these quarreled among themselves. One group, including Eufemio Zapata, shouted that Madero—"the little squirt"—should be shot as a traitor. Emiliano protected the shattered politician while he boarded a train for Mexico City, almost in tears. Zapata stayed in Cuautla, still hoping for a last-minute agreement before Huerta reached the city. The most he obtained was a slight delay. Huerta halted to allow his artillery to catch up with the leading infantry; Madero reached Mexico City and hurried to de la Barra seeking an interview—only to be told that the President must attend a cabinet meeting and could spare no time. Madero stayed in the capital a few hours more, pleading with officials and sending a long, bitter letter to de la Barra on the 25th. Carreón should have been thrown out and Hay appointed, he declared: Hay had publicly stated that as provisional governor he would honor the wishes of the majority. Madero accused Huerta of being the primary instigator of the renewed conflict, and he blamed Huerta's actions on Reyes' influence. The letter complained at the government's refusal to fulfill any of the provisions contained in the agreement with Zapata, and Madero especially resented the reflection on his own honesty which the failure implied. Having made this last, futile gesture, Madero wiped his hands of the affair and left the capital to begin electioneering in Yucatán.[22]

Meanwhile Huerta, the past conqueror of rebels in the Yucatán peninsula, continued his threatening move on Zapata at Cuautla. But Huerta could only advance slowly: de la Barra's concern with his presidential image still dictated that a last attempt should be made to secure Zapata's unconditional surrender without bloodshed. Meanwhile another federal force advanced on Cuautla from Jonacatepec under General Arnoldo Casso López, and Ambrosio Figueroa moved his forces into Jojutla: Cuautla was being threatened from three sides. Zapata refused to surrender. On August 27 he issued a defiant declaration from Cuautla, addressed to the People of Morelos, in which he placed heavy blame on the government for the agony which the state now had to endure. These troubles for the people of Morelos were daily increasing, bringing with them murder and atrocity. Ambrosio Figueroa arrested about 60 local *Zapatistas* during the first four days of his move on Cuautla: all of them were thrown against walls and shot. More were being

held for court-martial and would doubtless suffer the same summary fate. So too would Zapata if he were caught: Minister of the
Interior García Granados ordered "the active pursuit and arrest of
Zapata" and branded him as a common criminal, wanted dead or
alive.[23] The full hunt was on: Huerta stabbed forward, past the
Casasano and Santa Inés haciendas, and by Thursday, August 31,
the federals surrounded Cuautla. The city streets were deserted;
shutters were secured over windows, making the houses seem eye-
less and abandoned. Scouts rushed into the town with news for Zapata that troops were advancing through the sugar fields at Guadalupe hacienda, less than two miles up the road. Zapata walked to
the telegraph office, and one more signal clacked from Cuautla to
de la Barra: Zapata insisted he had no intention to lead a rebellion
and said that only a small bodyguard, assigned to him by Madero,
remained in Cuautla; he declared that the government would be
responsible for any bloodshed. De la Barra scribbled the notes for
his reply on the back of the telegram. "I lament that the disarmament of your forces has been ineffective and that parties of
bandits have appeared." Then the president rushed a signal to Huerta, informing him of Zapata's whereabouts and weakness as revealed in the final protest from Cuautla.

Before nightfall both Huerta and Casso López ordered their
troops into the city. The two federal commanders met on Galeana
street facing the central *plaza*. Each eagerly asked the other for
news of Zapata's fate. Zapata had slipped away. Minutes before the
federal ring closed around Cuautla he galloped south, outflanking
Casso López's advance from the east along the tracks from Jonacatepec, and veering to the west of Ambrosio Figueroa's leading
patrols probing from Jojutla. Keeping to the low hills along the
lower Rio Cuautla valley, Zapata passed through his native village
of Anenecuilco, and helped by his intimate knowledge of the area
he felt his way forward during the night of the 31st, around Villa de
Ayala and beyond Tenextepango.[24]

But Zapata might still be trapped. Ambrosio Figueroa's forces
fanned eastward from Jojutla across the southern sector of Morelos
state. If Zapata could be blocked by these detachments, he could
then be killed like a rabbit in a net by Huerta's troops beating
down behind him from Cuautla. Huerta urged his men forward at

maximum speed—and without regard for the lives, liberty, or property of the peasants in the area of advance. Peasants near Villa de Ayala who attempted to help their kinsman were brutally beaten, and Huerta explained his ruthless policy in a report to de la Barra sent just after Villa de Ayala was passed on September 1. "The facts show me the necessity to work resolutely and without consideration. These people are all bandits." The President wired that Huerta was "at liberty" to use his favorite methods.[25]

Yet once again Zapata wriggled through a hole in the net. For a few hours on this Friday, September 1, he attempted to snatch rest at Chinameca hacienda. One of his handful of remaining men stood sentinel at the plantation's front gate. A party of Figueroa's men, led by Federico Morales, galloped up the long straight drive and foolishly attempted to rush the guard at the gate: the sudden snapping of rifle shots awoke Zapata, who stumbled from his bed and ran through the hacienda rooms to the rear of the building. Knowing the plantation well, he sneaked through the cane fields and doubled down the drainage ditches until he reached cover. On foot until he obtained a peasant's donkey, he worked his way up into the hills, exhausted.and alone—but safely through the enemy lines. Forty-eight hours later he crossed the Puebla border and climbed high into the state's mountain sanctuary. Huerta thrashed his way through village after village in southern Morelos and vented his frustrated fury on the peasants—and everywhere ensured more support for Zapata through his vicious policy. On September 5 an old peasant, Isaac Narváez, revealed the nature of this support in a prophetic appeal to the journalist Juan Sarabia: he pleaded that those with access to the newspapers should "propose to the government the means for averting those calamities which are assuredly going to come in this fight to the death. Those who follow Zapata being so numerous, who knows but that these *hacendados* will regret tomorrow the hatred which they display today."[26]

Early in September Zapata established a rough base three thousand feet up in the mountains on the wild Puebla-Guerrero border. There, among the rocks and stunted pines, the outlaw made his plans. He remained determined to rescue his Morelos from Huerta, rampaging so freely throughout the state and flooding district after district with his federal troops. Zapata led no army and no staff officers were with him save Juan Almazán, the former Puebla medical student whose dubious connections with Madero first helped Zapata establish his authority back in the spring of 1911, and who now accidentally met Zapata in a small mountain village. [27] Almazán helped Zapata in the difficult and dangerous task of regrouping a fresh rebel band: Zapata's revolution had been cast back to the beginning, to the secret planning stage. But Zapata continued to enjoy the advantage resulting from the reaction to Huerta's ruthless campaign; the federal commander daily sent out his detachments from Cuernavaca into the towns and villages and his officers treated almost everyone as a "bandit"; the mountains constantly echoed with sudden volleys as his men carried out immediate executions, and peasants were herded from the villages and plantations into camps and forced-labor settlements. Outwardly, Huerta seemed in control. The American ambassador in Mexico City, Henry Lane Wilson, gave him this description: he was "a man of iron mould and courage. . . . He possessed abundant vices but was not without great qualities of mind and heart"; he was "in his own way a sincere patriot."[29] If so, then Huerta's "patriotism" at this time proved fatal. Mexico City newspapers printed glowing accounts of supposed federal successes, but the propaganda remained empty. Mrs. King at Cuernavaca gained some insight when a *Zapatista* charcoal seller whispered to her: "*Señora,* they always say we are running away and being killed, but they do not tell how many we catch and kill when we are hiding in places where we can shoot on them."[29]

Zapata himself remained free and defiant in the Puebla mountains. Previous revolutionary officers made their way to him, collecting small groups of militant peasants *en route;* the rebel army steadily swelled. Zapata's growing courier system passed on messages from the leader to restless local chiefs: on September 20 prominent men in the state of Oaxaca, to the south, were told to "revolt as fast as you can" to divert federal attention.[30]

Huerta could only batter this way and that—and drown himself in alchohol. "He himself drank heavily," wrote Mrs. King, who became acquainted with Huerta at Cuernavaca, "and nearly every evening had to be led off to bed." But she added: "He was always up in the morning bright and early, looking as though he were not even acquainted with the odor of drink." Nevertheless, his craving for the bottle affected his campaigning. One morning he ordered a large-scale patrol to be undertaken in the hills, which he himself would lead. All was prepared; the men were ready to go; Huerta remained inside the Bella Vista hotel, having a last drink, then another. "He took a drink and another drink," wrote Mrs. King. "The troops were kept standing all that day in the pouring rain. When night came on, I could stand it no longer and sent out great pots of coffee to warm the poor fellows. Finally, at daybreak, General Huerta got over his intoxication and was able to mount his horse. The troops moved off—artillery, infantry, and cavalry—to comb the mountains in search of Zapata."[31]

Huerta sent pompous messages to de la Barra: his operations in Morelos were "sowing trust, if the word fits, with the rifles and with the cannon of the Government of the Republic, preaching harmony, peace, and brotherhood among all the sons of Morelos." On September 26 he dared to boast that the state was "pacified" and his mission therefore concluded.[32] On this same day Zapata and his officers issued the first public declaration of their demands, through a defiant petition to de la Barra which made a mockery of all Huerta's claims. Although the petitioners declared their continued recognition of de la Barra as provisional President, they demanded the dismissal of provisional state governors and the election of men either freely elected by the people or selected by the "Generals and Chiefs of the present Counter-Revolution." The document continued: "We ask that the federal forces evacuate the *plazas* which they are presently occupying in the states of Morelos, Puebla, Guerrero and Oaxaca; that [presidential] elections be suspended; that to the *pueblos* there be given what in justice they deserve as to lands, timber and water, which has been the origin of the present Counter-Revolution; we ask that Political Prefectures be abolished and that absolute liberty be given to all political prisoners. . . ." The document was signed by Emiliano and Eufemio Zapata and twelve other rebel leaders, two of whom went under a flag of truce with Almazán to deliver the message to de la Barra in person.[33] The provisional President rejected all requests, except for an amnesty for political refugees—the latter would not, however, cover those charged with criminal acts, thus excluding Zapata.

The petition was clearly designed to act as a rallying call for the revolution—simple, basic, and straightforward, it could be understood by peasants and politicians alike. The message contained no more aims than the objective Zapata had always sought: agrarian reform in Morelos through legal processes. As a rallying signal, the petition was successful. But, perhaps intentionally, it also offered a target for the federals: below the text was the place of issue, San Juan del Río in Puebla. Within minutes of receiving the declaration, de la Barra issued orders to Huerta: strike for this area of southeast Puebla. In Cuernavaca, Huerta hastened to obey.

"As General Huerta said goodbye," wrote Mrs. King, "he assured me that he would be back in two or three days with the prisoner on exhibition."[34] The federal commander rushed his cavalry and infantry southward, informing de la Barra the next day, September 27, of his vigorous pursuit of the "ridiculously pretentious bandits." But now Zapata's military campaign exploded into life. After merely a month of preparation, Zapata proceeded to pinpoint federal mistakes and to display his brilliance as a guerrilla leader. His tactics and strategy during the next few days would be among the most skillful of his whole career.

6

•••••••••••

Betrayal

Each move by Huerta was immediately reported to Zapata. His spy system had been perfected: even before the federal force left Cuernavaca, messengers were carrying news of its imminent departure south to Puebla. Huerta's exact route was revealed to the rebel leader as the federals marched from village to village toward the mountains. Scouts slipped from ridge to ridge; Zapata sifted the reports at his headquarters and prepared to put his plans into operation. Leading federal patrols clashed with rebels in the hamlets and along the mountain trails, but after a sudden flurry of fighting the guerrillas appeared to flee. Huerta urged his advance to move faster; Zapata withdrew back through the high passes. Huerta speeded his offensive to outflank and catch him, but now the guerrillas made no attempt to stand and fight: as soon as they came within range of federal guns they wheeled their horses around and retreated. The federal officers believed the enemy to be panic-stricken at the sight of this superior force, and urged their troops onward into Puebla—and further from Morelos.

On about October 6 Zapata suddenly switched direction. Taking about 250 picked men, he rode at maximum speed along carefully selected mountain paths to outflank the lumbering federals, and Huerta found himself shadow-boxing with an opponent no longer there. But Zapata avoided wasting the advantage which the rebels had seized: a guerrilla commander with lesser ability would have used this surprise movement to attack the enemy forces from the rear; Zapata had other plans. Twenty-four hours later he resurfaced in eastern Morelos—far to Huerta's rear and completely out of reach. His maneuvering brought immediate success, even greater from the political point of view than the military. The peasant's idol had returned to lead the people; former *Zapatistas* rode to join him and hundreds of peasants, persecuted by Huerta, willingly lent support. By October 10 the rebel army numbered 1,500. Groups continually joined this force as it flowed up the Cuautla valley to threaten Cuautla itself on the 10th. Huerta remained too far south and federal troop remnants in central Morelos were insufficient to prevent any obstacle. Ambrosio Figueroa, given the governorship of Morelos at the start of the month, together with state military authority, found himself unsupported. Figueroa, although attractive to some sections in Morelos—Mrs. King wrote: "I liked our shy, serious young governor and believed him sincere"—was hated by the peasants for his treacherous policy toward Zapata in the past.[1]

But Zapata still preferred to threaten rather than to attack. As with the last campaign, he remained anxious to avoid pitched battle while his troops displayed inexperience and lack of adequate equipment. Show of force might succeed alone, and this demonstration of strength daily reached new proportions. Not content with proving his power in Morelos, Zapata surged north into Mexico state and reached the Ozumba area by mid-October. Recruits continued to stream forward, and Zapata's troops attacked the garrison at Milpa Alta, within the Mexico City federal district and almost at the capital's doorway. Panic increased in the capital. Metropolitan newspapers were crammed with shocked reports of *Zapatista* occupation of villages within an hour's ride from the city's suburbs. This was the man believed defeated and his movement annihilated; he now ran amok and apparently unstoppable.

Zapata's success had tremendous impact on the political situation in Mexico City. Presidential elections had taken place on October 1, with Madero easily defeating de la Barra and the far less likely Reyes. Inauguration was scheduled for December 1; now, in the uneasy interim period, Zapata acted as a counter to any potential movement against the new President. Madero's opponents found themselves tarred by Huerta's failure. The people, by supporting Zapata, were in effect showing their opposition to de la

Barra's provisional administration and the methods which the government had used. At the same time, Zapata's advance served as a warning to Madero. "Emiliano Zapata is no longer a man, he is a symbol," declared one congressman, José María Lozano. "He could turn himself in tomorrow . . . but the rabble . . . would not surrender."[2] Zapata's presence so near the capital resulted in a cabinet crisis on October 27. José González Salas, acting War Minister, was forced to resign, and two other ministers soon followed. Madero, pushed into positive action by Zapata, demanded Huerta's dismissal on October 28 and 29, and his demands brought success at the end of the month. "He is a very bad man," declared the new President. Huerta left Cuernavaca for the capital, where he would take even more to drink—and where his hatred of Madero would rapidly fester.

Zapata's operation proved beyond all doubt that this Morelos villager could outmaneuver one of the most able federal commanders; he was far removed from being a mere bandit. His army showed itself to be disciplined, and Zapata accomplished one of the most difficult military tasks for a leader of insurgent forces; he could detach sections of his army to undertake different duties, widely separated from each other, yet could retain cohesion for the conduct of his campaign as a whole. Operations in October 1911 form a classic example of the flexibility, rapidity, and decisiveness of first-class revolutionary tactics and strategy. Yet Zapata's skill reached its height not with the acquisition of this military power, but with the use he made of it: the operations were motivated to gain political rather than military victories. Only on rare occasions were clashes reported between revolutionary and federal detachments. The theme running so far through Zapata's career once again became apparent: his deep conviction of the need to link military strategy with political aims. He sought to convince the people, the political leaders in Mexico City, and Madero, that his military power must be considered a factor in political affairs.

Madero heeded this warning as he waited at his home in Parras, Coahuila state, for his formal takeover of office. He issued a public letter which amounted to a reply to Zapata, expressing confidence that the revolutionary commander would lay down his arms once the inauguration had taken place. "He knows that I will carry out the earlier aims of the government, which I believed were the only means of pacifying the state of Morelos, and which Zapata already knows because I communicated them to him in Cuautla."[3] At the same time the inauguration date was hurried forward from December 1 to November 6, in an effort to return to normalcy as soon as possible. This indirect message from Madero was apparently received well by Zapata; at the beginning of November he began pulling his troops south into Morelos again, and he rode back to his Villa de Ayala headquarters. There he waited for negotiations to begin, and he played his part in the attempt to return to a normal state of affairs by issuing orders that his men should permit repairs to railroads and telephone lines. The authorities seemed to respond to Zapata's peaceful attitude: on November 1 the governor, Zapata's long-standing enemy Ambrosio Figueroa, declared he would pardon all rebels who surrendered in two weeks.

Optimism therefore surrounded Madero's official inauguration on Monday, November 6—but so too did confusion, matching the chaos in the country as a whole. Madero might be president, yet his well-meaning but ineffectual actions during de la Barra's disastrous provisional administration cast doubts over his ability to lead the nation from the current morass. Madero had still to learn that without suitable backing a policy of "fairness and honesty with all" would merely encourage further muddle—in which the less scrupulous would seize advantage.[4] His behavior on November 6 epitomized Madero's continued attempt to act without resort to double-dealing or strong-arm tactics. He refused to have a guard at the Chamber of Deputies, where he took the oath, so ignoring the fact that this military escort would not only have provided protection, which Madero was anxious to show he did not need, but would also have helped control the screaming, pushing crowd. "There was indescribable confusion outside," wrote Edith O'Shaughnessy, "since Madero had not called out the soldiery, wishing, as he said, to show his confidence in the people. Even the band of the presidential guard was scattered; the trombones sounded from one side and the bugles from another. . . ." The German ambassador, Admiral Paul von Hintze, expressed pessimism about the effect of "so much legality in Mexico."[5]

Zapata stayed at Villa de Ayala during the celebrations. He heard disturbing news that Ambrosio Figueroa had attended the ceremony as representative of the southern wing of the *Maderista* movement, yet he apparently reckoned negotiations could soon begin for the future of the state. But another disquieting factor remained: the campaign against him and his troops, started so dismally by Huerta, still officially continued. No armistice had been arranged; according to the notices posted by Governor Figueroa, rebels would be pardoned only if they surrendered. The federals were still officially at war, even though Zapata had withdrawn and was now actively seeking ways to restore peaceful activites. Nevertheless, forty-eight hours after Madero's inauguration in Mexico City, the new President's emissary, Gabriel Robles Domínguez stepped off the train at Cuautla with instructions to negotiate with Zapata. Zapata rode the five miles up from Villa de Ayala to meet him.

Robles Domínguez had acted as Madero's representative in the south during de la Barra's administration, and had supervised the previous demobilization of Zapata's men at Cuernavaca in June. He now appeared enthusiastic for reconciliation; for three days the two men continued intense discussions to work out a suitable settlement, and these Cuautla talks were successful. Zapata agreed to disarm, provided that the authorities undertook certain promises: the Villa de Ayala faction must supersede the Guerrerans, headed by Figueroa, as the dominant party in Morelos; federal troops should be progressively withdrawn, replaced by local revolutionaries as federal police; the agrarian aims of the revolution must be guaranteed. Fulfillment of these basic aims would amply satisfy Zapata; he never sought more. In return Madero would obtain peace in Morelos, the richest state in Mexico, and prospects for his presidency would be immeasurably improved. Robles Domínguez prepared to leave for Mexico City, saying he would report to Madero and obtain presidential approval for the agreement. Zapata intended to wait at Cuautla for his return.[6]

But ominous moves were being made in the hills outside the city and on the slopes above Villa de Ayala down the valley. Zapata had withdrawn his troops too soon, partly through the difficulties of sustaining his force in the field, partly through his desire to bring about a return to peaceful progress in Morelos as soon as possible. While Zapata and his chiefs had been concentrated at Cuautla for the negotiations, federal detachments crept forward from Cuernavaca over the mountains to the west. The federal commander aimed to gain advantage from the cessation of *Zapatista* activities. As far as General Casso López was concerned, the war continued. Orders to the contrary had yet to reach him from the War Ministry in Mexico City and Arnoldo Cassso López, previously a subordinate and strong admirer of Huerta, conducted his military affairs strictly according to the textbook. He carried out his instructions to the best of his ability—and continued to carry them out until told otherwise by his superiors. An engineer by training, he was a career officer of long standing and, like Huerta, was a veteran of antirebel operations in Guerrero. To an officer of his restricted vision, the opportunity now offered seemed too good to miss. His forces surrounded the *Zapatistas* at Villa de Ayala and their leader at Cuautla; he refused to allow Robles Domínguez to come through his lines on Saturday, November 11, and speeded his final preparations for attack. Robles Domínguez managed to send an urgent wire to Madero during the Saturday evening, begging the President to have the offensive halted. "I obtained excellent conditions," he signaled Madero. "Federals want to attack only to break conferences. They refuse to say [what they are up to]."[7] The federal general further strengthened his positions during the night.

Early next morning, Sunday, November 12, Robles Domínguez managed to sneak through the federal lines, and he immediately rushed to see Madero at the Chapultepec presidential residence. The emissary revealed the terms of the agreement worked out with Zapata. But President Madero refused to accept them. And with this betrayal the President brought the final break between himself and his most powerful revolutionary general. The reasons for his decision are confused, but they doubtless stem from his permanent policy of seeking to rule through compromise means. Ironically, he remained anxious to avoid the dictatorial image of his predecessors. Zapata must be firmly dealt with because he represented the acquisition of political power through military means. Madero considered the revolution ended, and all revolutionary methods must be likewise finished. Seeking to present himself as a civilized, democratic president who did not owe his position to the continued use of force, Madero probably felt it necessary to wipe away this reminder that he had come to power through such force. Moreover, Madero hoped to win support from all sections of the community—including the plantation aristocracy, to whom Zapata was anathema. This section remained the most influential, far more so than Zapata's peasants; so, to prevent criticism that he dealt with brigands, Madero had to treat Zapata as little more than a bandit. The President made only one concession in his reply to Robles Domínguez: Zapata would be allowed to live, if he agreed to "temporary" exile from Morelos. Perhaps Madero gave Robles Dominguez some private message to be handed to Zapata which contained sympathetic, explanatory words; if so, this has been lost, and Zapata probably never received it. Instead only the cold, hostile, official answer from Madero to Zapata remains.

"Let Zapata know that the only point I can allow is that he surrenders, unconditionally, at once, and that every one of his soldiers immediately hand over their arms. If this happens, then I will grant pardon to his soldiers for the crime of rebellion, and he will be handed passports so he can travel to temporary settlement outside the state. Tell him that his rebellious stance is greatly harming my government, and I cannot allow it to continue in any way, and that if he is sincere in his pledge of loyalty to me, this is the only way he can prove it. Tell him he need not fear for his life, if he lays down his weapons immediately."[8]

Robles Domínguez hurried south again. His last attempt to see Zapata marked him as a brave man, in view of the likely reception he and Madero's reply would have received. In the event Casso López prevented him from passing through to Zapata, now at his headquarters in Villa de Ayala and preparing to meet the federal offensive. Signs that this attack would soon start were increasing hourly: Casso López acted with the excuse that since the *Zapatistas* had not disarmed, negotiations must have failed and the rebellion therefore continued—so ignoring the point that the reason for the continued state of armament by the *Zapatistas* stemmed more from his own threat, against which the revolutionaries must defend themselves. Robles Domínguez managed to send off a messenger, giving him Madero's demand for Zapata's surrender: the courier also carried a personal note from Robles Domínguez, hastily scribbled and totally inadequate.

This messenger rode down the track from Cuautla and into Villa de Ayala. *Zapatistas* surrounded him as he entered rebel territory: with guns leveled at his back he was escorted out from the town and up the slope into the nearby fields. There he was taken to the rebel leader, who was directing troops into defensive positions. Zapata remained on horseback as he read Madero's reply and his emissary's letter. Less than a mile away across the brown, sun-baked fields, he could see uniformed federal soldiers hauling artillery into line; files of soldiers were lining the rises to the west, more were concentrated for a push down the road from Cuautla. Zapata angrily told the messenger to flee for his life. The courier galloped back down the road to Cuautla, and within minutes the federal guns opened fire. The *Zapatistas* could hear the shouted orders; then smoke mushroomed from the cannon and shells whistled overhead to explode in the fields. The federals improved range and the shells began to smash one after the other into the town itself.

The odds against Zapata were hopeless, not so much in terms of manpower but in the superior federal weaponry. The revolutionaries stood no chance against those enemy guns, or the machine guns which the enemy would soon carry forward into battle; almost immediately Zapata ordered the bulk of his troops to pull back. He himself stayed at Villa de Ayala for a few more hours on this November day, waiting until evening while the barrage continued. Then, as the federals began to feel their way cautiously forward under cover of their guns, Zapata mounted his horse and used the advantages of twilight and his local knowledge to slip through the enemy lines with his small personal escort. He headed east during the night, across the Río Cuautla and into the dark mountains of south Morelos. General Casso López entered Villa de Ayala, to find the town deserted; he threw out patrols in all directions but all returned emptyhanded. Three days later Robles Domínguez let it be known that he wished to communicate with

Zapata in the hope of agreement still being arranged. He received no answer.[9]

But Madero received Zapata's official reply when the revolutionary general suddenly reappeared at the end of the month. On November 28 Zapata issued his famous manifesto, the Plan of Ayala, although the document would not be made fully public until December 15, when it appeared in a Mexico City newspaper. The Plan marked Zapata's recognition that only violence could gain justice for the peasants, not only in Morelos but throughout the nation. Zapata called his officers to him on the 28th; they entered his mountain hut situated near Ayoxustla, a small town in southeastern Puebla. So many crowded into the small room that those at the back were unable to see their leader, and Zapata stood on the rough table to read the manifesto. This relied heavily upon images of blood and destruction and damned Madero as "the so-called Chief of the Liberating Revolution."

Zapata declared: "Madero has tried with the brute force of bayonets to shut up and drown in blood the pueblos who ask, solicit, or demand from him the fulfillment of the promises of the revolution, calling them bandits and rebels, condemning them to a war of extermination without conceding or granting a single one of the guarantees which reason, justice, and the law prescribe." The present governor of Morelos was described as "the so-called General Ambrosio Figueroa, scourge and tyrant of the people of Morelos," with whom the hated Madero had entered into an alliance, together with the feudal landlords, "so as to forge new chains and follow the pattern of a new dictatorship more shameful and more terrible than that of Porfirio Díaz, for it has been clear and patent that he [Madero] has outraged the sovereignty of the States, trampling on the laws without any respect for lives or interests, as has happened in the State of Morelos, and others, leading them to the most horrendous anarchy which contemporary history registers."

Zapata read the Plan's proposals. The first choice as leader of the new revolution would be General Pascual Orozco, who had fought brilliantly for Madero in the opening days of the campaign in Chihuahua, but who now seemed disillusioned with the *Maderista* cause. Should he fail to respond to the Plan of Ayala, then Zapata would assume command. The Plan adhered to the original San

Luis Potosí declaration, apart from two notable differences. First, usurped lands would be seized immediately by the peasants, rather than waiting for the due process of law—in defense, the planters would have to plead their cases "before the special tribunals which will be established on the triumph of the revolution."

Secondly, not merely land which rightfully belonged to the peasants would be taken by the rebels. The Plan of Ayala claimed that the leading proprietors enjoyed a monopoly situation, and that this in itself was evil "in virtue of the fact that the immense majority of Mexican pueblos and citizens are owners of no more than the land they walk on, suffering the horrors of poverty without being able to improve their social condition in any way or to dedicate themselves to Industry or Agriculture, because lands, timber, and water are monopolized in a few hands. . . ." The Plan therefore declared that one third of the possession of these largest proprietors would be seized and given to the people. The document added that any landlords or "bosses" who opposed the plan, directly or indirectly, would have their goods nationalized, with the other two thirds of their possessions being used "for indemnizations of war, pensions for widows and orphans of the victims who succumb in the struggle. . . ."

For Zapata himself, the plan contained one important divergence from his previous personal aims. Officially, no longer was he fighting just for Morelos—although his state would continue to be his primary concern. If leadership of the revolution came to him, as was highly probable, then he would be fighting for peasants throughout Mexico. He had never sought such power, nor did the prospect seem to appeal to him. Now, from his platform in his crude mountain headquarters, he read the final appeal. "Mexicans: consider that the cunning and bad faith of one man is shedding blood in a scandalous manner, because he is incapable of governing; consider that his system of government is choking the fatherland and trampling with the brute force of bayonets on our institutions; and thus, as we raised up our weapons to elevate him to power, we again raise them up against him for defaulting on his promises to the Mexican people and for having betrayed the revolution initiated by him. . . . Mexican People, support this plan with arm in hand. . . ."[10]

Zapata had committed himself. He intended to stand or fall by the Plan of Ayala. If he succeeded against Madero, then the message in the manifesto would have found response among the people of Mexico. If he failed, then history would judge from the Plan his abortive aims. The declaration marked far more than a cry of defiance against Madero's recent betrayal; indeed the origins of the document, plus some of the passages, probably existed before the disastrous negotiations with Robles Domínguez. Even before the tragic events in mid-November, Zapata had reason enough to be disillusioned with Madero. Zapata probably asked for some declaration to be drawn up by his subordinates back in October, to refute claims by his opponents that his campaign aimed only at pillage. Chief among these *Zapatistas* who drafted the document was Otilio E. Montaño, the intellectual schoolmaster, and Montaño worked with Zapata on the final version during late November.[11]

The Plan of Ayala failed to merit any claim as a legal political document, but neither did it have any pretensions to be such a declaration. Despite its basic adherence to the Plan of San Luis Potosí, the two could not be compared. Politicans could—and did —scoff at Zapata's in a way which would have been impossible with Madero's smoothly worded manifesto. Yet Zapata's Plan benefited from a strength which the other totally lacked: it provided immediate appeal for the peasants, written in colorful, emotional language which they could well understand. The Plan of San Luis Potosí had to be explained to them. It was for the peasants that Zapata fought, and now, in the Puebla mountains, it was upon the peasants that Zapata relied. He refused to consider compromise, and when a group of would-be negotiators reached his camp in early December, sent by Madero, Zapata threw them out with a violent message for the President. "Tell him this for me, to take off for Havana, because if not he can count the days as they go by, and in a month I'll be in Mexico City with 20,000 men, and have the pleasure of going up to Chapultepec castle and dragging him out of there, and hanging him from one of the highest trees in the park." Zapata wrote to his chief agent in Mexico City on December 6: "I am determined to struggle against everything and everybody. . . ."[12]

Zapata prepared for the struggle during December. Nor was he the only leader of an armed rising against Madero. Bands of rebels known as *Vazquistas*, supporters of Dr. Francisco Vázquez and his brother Emilio—the first of whom stood in an unsuccessful bid to become vice-president—revolted in Chihuahua, claiming Madero was not fulfilling the promises of the Plan of San Luis Potosí. In October Emilio Vázquez had retired to San Antonio, Texas, where he met the unsuccessful presidential candidate, General Reyes, and they plotted together. When the Mexican government complained to the American President over this activity on his soil, the United States authorities arrested Reyes but released him on bail pending his trial. On December 4 he jumped bail and crossed the border into Mexico, gathering a force of about 600 around him. But Reyes lacked popular support. "The days passed and not even a single individual came to join me," he complained. On Christmas Day he surrendered, after watching his few surviving supporters flee in headlong panic from government troops. Reyes was thrown into jail in Mexico City to await his trial, still complaining bitterly over the lack of support he had received. "I called upon the army and called upon the people but no one responded, so I resolved to discontinue the war. . . ."[13]

Zapata would never have made this mistake of moving into the open as a target until the groundwork had been sufficiently prepared. This remained his primary aim during the last weeks of 1911. Reyes' attempt, although a dismal failure, illustrated the threats which Madero faced, and other opponents, like the *Vazquistas*, still survived. Such movements against Madero would be to Zapata's benefit: federal troops would be drawn off to deal with them, and Madero's position progressively eroded. Zapata could afford to wait and complete his careful, cautious preparations. These closely resembled the secret arrangements made when he organized his hard-core revolutionary force at Villa de Ayala, awaiting the return of Torres Burgos from seeing Madero exactly a year before. Despite all his success in the past twelve months, despite his recent advance to the gates of Mexico City, Zapata had to return almost to the beginning again. His ability to do so underlined his resilience. This time he could make use of the stubs of success which remained from his 1911 triumph: his name was known throughout Morelos and beyond; he had never suffered defeat in full battle; his military achievements provided confidence for all those who might join him now. Zapata enjoyed a reputation among the peasants and local chiefs as a fair, reserved, yet forceful leader; one who displayed caution, but who could nevertheless act decisively; a man who never promised more than he felt able to deliver, and who always kept his word.

Yet Zapata's fame also brought disadvantages. His presence proved harder to conceal, and he could never be safe from capture or assassination attempts. He found it dangerous—and less practical—to establish a semipermanent headquarters, and instead spent these hot weeks of the dry season traveling from one temporary camp to another in the mountains on the Puebla-Morelos border. Only a small staff rode with him, again for reasons of both security and convenience. Even one of these senior officers proved unreliable. Jesús Morales, one of those whose names were put to the Plan of Ayala and a general in the revolutionary army, tried to arrange a private deal with the federal government in early January 1912, although he still stayed on with Zapata afterward.

Nor did Zapata enjoy automatic leadership over other rebel groups in the Morelos-Puebla area. Some had still to be won over, including the most notable, Genovevo de la O, and all of them threatened to complicate Zapata's task. Nevertheless, as 1912 opened, definite progress could be reported. A system of command had been created for the army under Zapata as general-in-chief, upon which Zapata would rely heavily to keep the largely untrained troops under control and to provide overall cohesion in the fragmented fighting. This system stemmed from seven generals: Eufemio Zapata, the nominal chief of staff although owing his position more to his status as Emiliano's brother than through his military ability; Francisco Mendoza, Jesús Morales, Jesús Navarro, the intellectual Otilio E. Montaño, José Trinidad Ruiz, and Próculo Capistrán. Under them were twenty-seven colonels and numerous captains. Once again the number of troops began to rise, to such an extent that by December 20 Zapata could issue general orders to his "Liberating Army of the South." These orders revealed the peasant basis of the army: officers were instructed to allow troops to return home for harvest.

Zapata also remained fully aware of the importance of retaining

local peasant support: the army was to provide "every class of guarantees in the villages and fields and on the roads . . . to respect
and aid civil authorities who have been legally and freely elected";
revolutionary forces were forbidden to "destroy or burn the property of the haciendas, because these will be the patrimony and
source of work for the villages." Zapata summed up his policy—
directly opposite to the "Attila" image which his opponents and
later historians attempted to depict—in his conclusion to these
general orders; officers should "bring to the consciousness of our
troops that the better we behave, the more adherents and help we
will have among the people and the faster will be our triumph."[14]

Meanwhile Madero, who should have known far better, completely underestimated Zapata, and in doing so provided his opponent with invaluable assistance. In mid-December the editor of
the Mexico City newspaper *Diario del Hogar* obtained a copy of
the Plan of Ayala, and asked Madero if he could publish the document on his pages. "Yes," sneered the President, "publish it so
everyone will know how crazy that Zapata is." The newspaper
therefore appeared with the Plan on December 15, and immediately sold all available copies to avid readers. Coupled with
Madero's dismissal of the threat was an equally mistaken policy of
repression practiced by the authorities in Morelos. General Casso
López continued the methods previously used by Huerta—arrests, imprisonment without trial, acts of brutality. All played into
Zapata's hands, and made the people more receptive when the
rebel general-in-chief issued a manifesto to the "beloved pueblos"
on the last day of 1911. He warned the people against the activities
of the authorities—and of bandits who pretended to operate in the
name of the new revolution. "These persons," proclaimed Zapata,
"I ask all my partisans and the pueblos in general to throw back
with energy, for these I consider enemies of mine who try to dis-
credit our blessed cause and prevent its triumph."[15] To the peasants the message was clear: Zapata stood for law and order, justice,
and the overthrow of federal repression.

In early January 1912, Zapata moved into the second phase of
his revolution: overt guerrilla warfare. The basic flexible organization had been created, and money collected—from local
contributions, from forced loans, and from occasional donations

received from a few Mexico City politicians. The army remained extremely weak in arms and equipment, yet no more could be obtained without seizing them from the federals. The time had come to wage active war. Zapata's strength at the beginning of the new year probably amounted to about 800 reasonably trained officers and troops, with up to 2,000 immediately available semi-trained peasants who filled the ranks. Opposing them were over 1,000 federal troops and about 5,000 police. Although the enemy outnumbered the *Zapatistas,* the ratio remained far too small for effective counterinsurgency operations: to cover the state the federal forces would have to be spread far too thin, making each detachment vulnerable to sudden ambush. The only alternative, the method adopted by General Casso López and the various district police commanders, was to concentrate in garrison towns and at selected points which were considered strategically important. Moreover, although the standard of training among federal troops proved reasonably high, and far superior to that of the bulk of the guerrillas, the latter had the invaluable advantage of better local knowledge. Federal officers and soldiers usually came from outside Morelos, and knew nothing of the unmapped mountain tracks.

From the outset Zapata's campaign during January 1912 therefore proved militarily successful. He continued to handle his army with perceptive flexibility. Wisely, he concentrated almost entirely on guerrilla war, avoiding large-scale clashes and making no attempt to attack strong federal positions. His guerrilla sections gradually exerted control over the countryside, driving the federals farther back into the garrison towns. Either enemy attempts to strike from these towns came to nothing, because the guerrillas merely melted away, or, if the federal force was dispatched with insufficient strength, the guerrillas lured them from the roads and into the mountains, and subjected them to ambushes and harassment.

By mid-January the federals therefore only moved from their garrisons in battalion-strength patrols, which failed dismally, being too large to operate with any hope of remaining undetected. Zapata held the initiative. The campaign illustrated, in classic fashion, the advantages of guerrilla warfare waged intelligently against insufficiently strong regular forces. Zapata, Mendoza, and Morales operated with relative impunity in the southeast; Trinidad Ruiz moved with virtual freedom in the north while Salazar and Felipe Neri acted likewise in the center; in the northwest, around Cuernavaca, de la O held the countryside and threatened the towns. A number of these senior officers were based in their own native districts—de la O, for example, originated from Santa María, where he established his headquarters—and this deliberate policy enabled maximum advantage to be gained from knowledge of the local terrain and local inhabitants.

On January 17 Madero made a bold attempt to restore the situation in Morelos—a situation which would encourage others elsewhere to revolt against him. The policy he now adopted displayed considerable intelligence, and would confront Zapata with the greatest difficulties so far. Madero accepted the resignation of Ambrosio Figueroa, with Francisco Naranjo becoming the interim governor of the state. Naranjo, a moderate, might sap support from the *Zapatistas* with an ending of the repressive practices. At the same time Madero provided the federal authorities with sharper teeth for the persecution of the war: he declared martial law in Morelos, in Guerrero, Tlaxcala, and in thirteen districts in Puebla and Mexico, with this suspension of state rights to last for one month. All Madero's hopes rested on this combination of a more moderate state governorship and tighter control exercised from Mexico City. Naranjo took over from Figueroa with full intentions to act humanely. He explained his position in an interview printed in the *Diario del Hogar* on January 25: the government had committed "an extremely grave error" in condemning the "deep social problem" in Morelos as mere banditry which could be "resolved by artillery barrages."[16] Once in Cuernavaca the new interim governor started a conscientious study of the basic reasons for the unrest, writing later: "Morelos lacked three things—first ploughs, second books, and third equity. . . ." Madero attempted to make further use of the encouraging atmosphere generated by Naranjo's arrival by arranging the release of Zapata's former chief of staff, Abrahám Martínez, presently imprisoned in Puebla City. On January 26 Madero sent him on a secret negotiating mission to Zapata's camp.[17]

But Zapata refused to be deterred. He no longer believed

Madero's word, and he persuaded his followers to hold similar skepticism. Madero's hopes for peace in Morelos soon collapsed, and even if Zapata had wished to open talks for a possible settlement, the semi-independent rebel chiefs elsewhere in the state were flushed with the prospect of imminent victory. On January 26, the day after Naranjo's sympathetic statements appeared in the Mexico City newspaper and as Martínez left for Zapata's headquarters, about 3,000 rebels under de la O began to exert dangerous pressure on the state capital, Cuernavaca. For over a week they sustained an offensive despite all federal attempts to drive them back into the hills with concentrated artillery fire. Citizens in Cuernavaca experienced food shortages, cuts in communication to the outside world, and a rising feeling of being suffocated by the pervading guerrilla threat.

The rebels relaxed their pressure at the beginning of February, but only to regroup and gather fresh ammunition; Martínez conferred with Zapata and coolly informed Madero that he intended to rejoin his old commander; de la O publicly declared on February 6 that the rebels would soon start blowing up every train attempting to cross the mountains into the state. On the same day de la O resumed the offensive against Cuernavaca. Zapata's aims remained to flaunt federal authority, to encourage others to revolt, and gradually to undermine Madero's position. Daily, his methods seemed to be nearing total success. Madero, also threatened by the increasing likelihood of outbreak of direct rebellion by Pascual Orozco in Chihuahua, felt his control slipping; he sought desperate means to stem the paralysis creeping over his presidency. "The evidence of a weak hand and a vacillating will in the capital did not help our situation in Cuernavaca," commented Mrs. King. "The morale of the soldiers was impaired by the suspicion that the government was not squarely behind them in their campaign. Some of them deserted and went over to the *Zapatistas*. The *Zapatistas* raided with new boldness and confidence, closer to the town. . . ."[18]

Faced with this rapidly deteriorating situation the Mexican President abandoned all hope of introducing a moderate policy which might persuade the rebels to negotiate. He appointed the vicious, barbaric Brigadier General Juvencio Robles as the new military commander for Morelos, and in doing so rendered negative any chances which Governor Naranjo's enlightened attitude might have offered. Naranjo's appointment had been an intelligent decision by Madero: by contrast, his choice of Robles constituted an example of how a counterinsurgency war should not be fought. Robles' command would make Huerta's methods seem like those of a saint; all the past miseries in Morelos would be overshadowed by the cruelties now to be introduced. In selecting Robles for this post, Madero in effect admitted total failure; the terrible repression which followed could only increase Zapata's determination and provide him with even greater support from among the people. Moreover, Robles made the mistake of considering all the people in Morelos—moderates, liberals, even staunch *Maderistas*— as potential bandits. Thus the newspaper *El País* quoted him on February 4: "All Morelos, as I see it, is *Zapatista*, and there's not one inhabitant who doesn't believe in the false doctrines of the bandit Emiliano Zapata." He boasted that "in a comparatively short time" he would "cut down that mob of gangsters who scourge the state at the moment . . . with their crimes and robbery worthy of a savage."

Robles, a veteran of fierce fighting against Indian rebels in northern Mexico, reached Cuernavaca at the end of the first week in February. He immediately turned his attention on de la O's rebels still threatening the capital, and ordered the village of Santa María to be razed, five miles north of Cuernavaca. Objections from Governor Naranjo were overruled. Federal troops swarmed around the village on February 9, swooped in, and drove the rebel fighters out. The soldiers soaked the huts with kerosene, watched by terrified women and children, then withdrew; guns cracked from nearby woods and the shells touched off the flames. Woods around the village were also ignited, and within minutes the whole area was a raging inferno. The federals returned in supposed triumph to Cuernavaca, leaving a smoking, reeking mess—and implacable hatred among the peasants. The body of de la O's small daughter was found in the ashes of the village.[19]

Worse soon followed. On February 10 federal troops seized Zapata's mother-in-law, sister, and two sisters-in-law in Villa de Ayala and dragged them to Cuernavaca as hostages. With Zapata's family as security, Robles then practiced on a regular basis his policy of burning villages. In doing so he added a vicious twist to the counterinsurgency method known as "resettlement," which then and later was considered a standard operation for destroying guerrilla bases. The aim was to separate the guerrillas from the people—the most difficult task of all.

The attempted answer, already used in northern Mexico, in South Africa by the British, later by the British in Malaya and by the Americans in Vietnam under the "strategic hamlet" program, was to shift the people into areas where they could be better supervised and controlled by the security forces. These areas could be concentration camps or "pacified" hamlets. Anyone outside them could thereafter be treated as enemy, liable to be shot on sight. Robles, as an extra to this standard procedure, burned the villages in which the peasants previously lived and the fields they farmed. He explained later: "If the *Zapatistas* returned to occupy the *pueblos* and make barricades out of their houses so as to battle the federals, besides obtaining the necessities of life from the inhabitants, there was nothing more rational and logical than to destroy those Zapatista redoubts and prevent the residents from giving arms, ammunition, and food to the gangsters."[20] A succession of hamlets and villages were therefore put to the torch—San Rafael, Ticumán, Los Hornos, Coajomulco, Ocotepec, Nexpa . . . The *El País* correspondent described the scenes at the burning of this latter hamlet, situated along the Chinameca River near the Guerrero border. "The residents cried and pleaded that the pueblo which had seen them born not be destroyed . . . . In the midst of the greatest terror and consternation the flames did their work, and a dense, black column of smoke rolling laboriously up the sides of the mountain announced to the *Zapatistas* hidden there that they no longer had a home."[21]

Wretched inhabitants of these villages were taken to the nearest district seats, where they were either corralled or released but told to report each day, or they were put into special camps. *Morelenses* who were considered especially suspect—if only because they were of military age—were carted to labor camps outside the state. Many never returned. Mrs. King saw a group of them at the Cuernavaca railway station. "Never shall I forget the sight of those poor wretches standing tied together, not one uttering a word, looking like the farmers they were, caught unprotected in their *milpas.*" A colonel explained the system to her. "The only way we can quiet down Morelos," he said, "is to ship out these *Zapatistas.* If we break up families doing it—well, our families have lost their husbands and fathers too. I tell you, *señora,* when these warlike rebels find themselves a thousand miles from home with nothing to eat and no place to go, among people who speak a different dialect, they will not be so brave!" Mrs. King watched with horror as the prisoners were herded into the train, among them her own servant. "The soldiers were hustling the poor wretches into a cattle box-car, pushing them in till there was not even standing room. They boarded up the doors and nailed them shut." General Robles had previously seemed civilized to Mrs. King: he lived at her hotel, and only a few days before had ordered his military band to play sweet music beneath her window to celebrate her birthday. Now she protested to him about the inhuman treatment of the peasants. Robles replied: "Why, I am trying to clean up your beautiful Morelos for you. What a nice place it will be once we get rid of the *Morelenses!* If they resist me, I shall hang them like earrings on the trees. . . ."[22]

This Robles proceeded to carry out. Mrs. King's shocked account continued: "My daughter and I often saw the sickening sight of bodies swinging in the air. At that high altitude they did not decompose, but dried up into mummies, grotesque *things* with the toes hanging straight down in death and hair and beard still growing. . . ." Horrors became commonplace, even to Mrs. King. "We thought at first we could not live among such sights; but, as I look back, I realize that the worst part of all was that in time we grew hardened to them and they no longer bothered us."[23] Robles preferred hanging his victims to shooting them, declaring they were not worth a bullet. But shooting nevertheless proved frequent; fourteen "suspects" were put before a firing squad at Yautepec on February 13, within a week of Robles' arrival, and thereafter the executions continued steadily in hamlets, haciendas, isolated farms, on fabricated charges or no charges at all. Inevitably, the less disciplined federal officers and soldiers made use of the vicious official policy and committed atrocities on their own account, murdering, raping, stealing.

"If they found you sitting in your house, they would shoot you," wrote one peasant. "If they found you walking, they would shoot you. If they found you working, they would shoot you. That was what they called martial law. There was *no* law!"[24] Provided that the federals moved in sufficiently large patrols they could perform their brutal operations with relative impunity. Once again Mrs. King, by no means naturally pro-*Zapatista,* witnessed the cruelties. "Many of these men were surrounded by federals while thus working unprotected in the fields. They were made prisoners and driven to the nearest towns, where they were forced to dig their own graves before they were shot—if one can call 'grave' the holes into which their bodies were thrown."[25]

Zapatista activities inevitably dwindled during February and early March, with the rebels forced onto the defensive as they absorbed the impact of the federal operations. But Zapata, still in southeast Morelos within easy reach of sanctuary across the Puebla or Guerrero borders, could well afford to wait. Daily his support grew among the peasants. The villager quoted above also commented: "I said to myself, 'Rather than have them kill me sitting, standing or walking, I'd better get out of here.' And so I went to war along with the *Zapatistas.*"[26]

The people were losing their three most prized possessions: their homes, their land, and often members of their family. They had nothing else to lose, and they turned to Zapata for help. Mrs. King described one typical incident, an example of hundreds. "Long afterwards, in Cuautla, a mason who was working for me told me how the federals, in the name of the Revolutionary Government, had come unexpectedly upon the little piece of ground his father owned, and had shot his father dead before his eyes and his mother's, and then set fire to their poor hut, all to steal the corn they had planted. He and his mother fled, hiding in the fields and woods, anywhere for safety, until they could find Emiliano Zapata, the protector and the avenger. The boy was only fifteen at the time, but his father lay dead and his home was in ruins. The *Zapatistas* gave him a gun. 'With my gun in hand and hatred in my heart, I killed and destroyed wherever I could,' he told me."[27]

The atrocities in Morelos condemned Madero in the eyes of the world. His Mexico City newspapers attempted to justify the official policy, with total lack of success. *El País* agreed that the actions in

Morelos were "liberal in cruelty," but claimed "heroic remedies" were necessary, otherwise "we fear that the state of revolt might become chronic. . . . The total destruction of the shanty towns which serve as refuge for *Zapatistas*" was the only method of saving the state from becoming "the tomb of our heroic army."[28] Madero tried to defend himself to the American commentator Edward Bell on February 13. "I do not want to kill my people to make them good," he cried in a shrill voice. "I could have controlled them. I am preparing to open lands to them. I am arranging employment at good wages for all *Maderista* soldiers and many other men, on public works. Does your Government suppose that I have given no thought to conditions here, or that extensive plans such as mine can be carried out by magic in a day? I ask of no man or government anything but a reasonable chance." The hysterical outburst continued: "Why is this unfriendly effort made to force me to violate my pledges against the shedding of blood? What influence is at work secretly to accomplish this injustice? Surely the United States has nothing to gain by making me a tyrant and a madman."[29]

By mid-March it had become abundantly clear that the Morelos peasants were refusing to submit to the federal coercion. And by now federal strength was becoming increasingly overstretched, not only by a resurgence of guerrilla activity in Morelos, but also by events elsewhere. Federal troops and police were being withdrawn from the state for urgent reassignment to Chihuahua, where Orozco emerged in open opposition to the government on March 3. While Mexico City was never actually threatened, most of Chihuahua fell to the rebels before the government could check their advance. Hysteria swept through the Mexican capital, with the municipal council warning all "friends of order," native or foreign, to arm themselves as protection against revolutionaries. Henry Lane Wilson, the American ambassador, sponsored a defense league of foreigners in the capital, sending requests to the State Department in Washington first for 1,000 rifles and 250,000 rounds of ammunition and then a million rounds. On March 23 the first major encounter between the Chihuahua rebels and federal forces took place at Rellano, about 600 miles from Mexico City, with the government army suffering a crushing defeat. The federal commander, General González Salas, committed suicide during the subsequent retreat. In Mexico City the panic increased: Wilson now asked his government for 1,000 more rifles, one million more rounds of ammunition, plus service belts and military supplies.

This emergency brought a development which would soon have direct consequences for Zapata in the south. The cabinet insisted on recalling Victoriano Huerta for active service, initially against the Chihuahua rebels in the north, despite the quarrel between this general and Madero in Morelos the previous year. Huerta was now presented with an ideal opportunity to reestablish his military reputation, which Zapata had shattered, and his appointment placed him in a position to make demands on the government. Moreover, he retained his smoldering hatred for Madero.[30]

Meanwhile the federal preoccupation with the north created fresh chances for the rebels in the south. Suffering from drastically depleted forces, Robles had to restrict his main activities in the countryside and he pulled back into the larger towns; he left the peasants so far untouched by his "resettlement" program even more determined to act before the troops returned. Nor did Madero attempt to mitigate this hatred by the timely reintroduction of a moderate political policy. The President described the unrest in Morelos to Congress on April 1 as "this amorphous agrarian socialism, which for the rude intelligence of the farmers of Morelos can only take the form of sinister vandalism," and he added that agrarian reform could not even be attempted until full military control had been regained. The peasants therefore knew Madero offered them no hope; they could only rely upon Zapata and the other rebel chiefs. And on April 1, even as Madero reported to Congress in Mexico City, the rebel commanders Neri and Salazar swept into Tepoztlán in the north of Morelos. Next day Zapata's own troops emerged from the low hills around Jonacatepec over in the east, having made a rapid march from the nearby Puebla border, and the town fell after only desultory defense by the undermanned federal garrison. Zapata hurried on: four days later, on April 6, he joined with Mendoza, Vázquez, and other subordinate commanders for coordinated assaults on Tlaquiltenango, Tlaltizapán, and Jojutla, in a ten-mile line along the banks of the Río Yautepec. Jojutla, the local district seat in this southern part of the state, was occupied several times.[31]

Edward Bell described the harassed Madero during these critical days. The American journalist felt some pity for "the undersized frock-coated figure . . . dwarfed by his huge responsibilities." Bell commented: "He was greatly changed. . . . His cheeks, which used to curve smoothly from his broad forehead to his narrow chin, were now shrunken and lined; his brow was wrinkled; a dozen years had been added to his apparent age, a fair half of them in the last seven days. He showed loss of sleep and was extremely nervous, with the impatient manner of a man who is trying to do too many things at once."[32] Daily the newspapers in Mexico City printed news of fresh federal setbacks, and criticism of Madero soared. *El País*, especially hostile to the president, blazoned a banner headline after Rellano: "The Beginning of the End." The former playboy governor of Morelos, Pablo Escandón, now back in Mexico City after a brief escape to Europe, wrote: "If things go on as they are going, surely we will retrogress to our former position as A NATION OF THE LAST ORDER, A TRUE NIGGERDOM."[33]

But once again the pendulum swung. Huerta left Mexico City to campaign in Chihuahua against Orozco, sneering to Madero: "I'll whip him. I guarantee it." Final objections to his appointment voiced by Madero, on the grounds that Huerta drank too much, were overruled: a cabinet member pointed out that this handicap had never detracted from Ulysses S. Grant's effectiveness in the American Civil War.[34]

After their triumph at Rellano the rebels had stopped to celebrate outside the important city of Torreón, instead of making full use of their victory, and they were soon weakened by internal dissensions. By May 23 the federal forces had recovered sufficiently for Huerta to inflict a heavy defeat on Orozco at the second battle of Rellano, and Orozco began to retreat north blowing up railway tracks behind him to hinder Huerta's advance.

Nor was the rebel situation in the south as successful as it might have seemed by the actions at the beginning of April. Zapata found extreme difficulty in moving from phase two to phase three of the revolution—from guerrilla operations to full-scale warfare fought almost on conventional lines. The guerrilla activities had proved victorious, with relatively small bands of rebels moving rapidly and effectively across the countryside to attack federal patrols, harass communications, and generally keep the revolution pot on the boil. After Robles moved back into the major towns at the end of March, the rebels virtually controlled the rural areas. But the war had still to be won, and the correct method of bringing this about presented Zapata with a problem common to all conflicts of this type—and one which would continually plague him.

Two ways existed of bringing the final success. One was to continue guerrilla operations indefinitely, in the hope that Madero's will to resist would eventually be worn down, and criticism of him would develop to such an extent that he was either thrown out or forced to agree to rebel proposals. But this might take many exhausting months: Madero's attitude revealed in his report to Congress on April 1 indicated his continued stubbornness, which seemed to be tinged with fanaticism bred by sheer desperation. The only other method of achieving full victory was to defeat the federal forces in the field, switching from guerrilla to full conventional tactics. But this neccessitated trained soldiers—and ample ammunition, which Zapata always lacked. Zapata had been anxious to avoid premature transition in the 1911 campaign, seeking not to engage the enemy in pitched battle until it appeared absolutely vital to do so. He may have felt similar anxiety now, in spring 1912; in any event the rebels discovered that force of circumstances dictated that their activities continued on a virtual guerrilla level. Sheer shortages of equipment, especially arms and ammunition, meant battles could not be prolonged; towns, once taken, were impossible to hold for any length of time.

So, in the second week of April, the federals pushed back to reoccupy the towns seized by the rebels in the first days of the month —Tepoztlán, Jonacatepec, Jojutla. Fifty rebel captives in the last center suffered execution. In late April the rebels managed to mount another threat on Cuernavaca, and the municipal leaders in the city wanted to surrender, but the local revolutionary commanders de la O and Salazar found they had insufficient material to push home the offensive. Whether they wished to or not, the rebels had to keep to the second revolutionary phase. Zapata, given his natural caution and the preferences he had already shown the previous year, realized this fact earlier than the other revolutionary chiefs. He appreciated the dangers and difficulties of exposing his forces as a full conventional target, without the full means to tackle the federal regular army, and after his activity at the beginning of April he pulled back once more into the hills. Neri, Salazar, and de la O continued their raids for a while longer, but then these also dwindled. De la O drifted northward into Mexico state to reorganize his forces. In May Zapata withdrew into eastern Guerrero, taking with him Montaño, Mendoza, Capistrán, and other chiefs. A *Zapatista* attack on Tlapa to gain supplies resulted in failure. In Morelos the guerrilla bands continued to roam the mountains and valleys, retaining the rebel grip on the countryside, but this was the most that could be accomplished for the moment.

Stalemate followed. The rebels could only pin their hopes on Madero's gradual collapse. Zapata established his headquarters in the region south of Chilpancingo, where the terrain showed a marked contrast to his Morelos mountains. The rolling landscape lay covered with lush grass, offering excellent grazing, and the forests were filled with deer, wild turkeys, pheasants, and other game to feed his men. Farther east spread the Pacific beyond Acapulco: on May 6 a plea went from Zapata to Orozco in the north, seeking supplies to be sent by sea. Orozco, with troubles of his own, apparently never replied. Zapata could only rest the bulk of his army, sending detachments back into Morelos on a rota basis while he desperately tried to discover means of obtaining vital arms and equipment—and while he waited for some signs of collapse by the Madero government. Another reason existed for the dwindling rebel activity: these weeks were the time of planting, with the rainy season beginning in Morelos, and Zapata had to allow his farmer-fighters the opportunity to return to their fields, where they resumed their agricultural tasks under cover of their guerrilla comrades.

But with the slackening of military activity in Morelos, increased opportunities were offered for Governor Naranjo to introduce a more moderate policy: this, as a contrast to Robles' repression, might once more swing support back to Madero. In early May, as Zapata withdrew south, Naranjo sent a long protest to

Madero over the policy pursued by Robles, and by mid-May the governor felt safe enough to announce that law and order would soon be restored. State elections in the third week of May brought a number of reformers into office, largely through Naranjo's efforts. This developing situation promised both good and bad for Zapata. On the credit side, the ascendancy of influence by Naranjo and his reformers might open the way for a compromise solution in Morelos granting a substantial proportion of the revolutionary aims. If, as in 1911, Zapata had merely been fighting for Morelos, this would probably have been sufficient provided that Zapata could believe Madero would back the Morelos reformers. But the Plan of Ayala demanded more: the complete overthrow of the Mexican President. Winning the state was now insufficient. And with this far more ambitious objective a compromise in Morelos would undercut Zapata's ground for the Mexican revolution as a whole. Madero, with the south pacified, would enjoy a boost in prestige, especially if the campaign in the north continued to be successful.

For a while at the end of May it seemed these northern operations might falter for the federals, thus helping Zapata in the south. An uneasy alliance between General Huerta and Pancho Villa broke down. Villa had remained loyal to Madero and vehemently opposed to Orozco, and he had started to fight the rebel leader soon after the latter's commencement of hostilities. Villa hated Orozco and the cruelty inflicted by his rebels—the American John Reed described one example: "They cut the soles from the feet of one poor devil and drove him a mile across the desert before he died."[35] Early in May Villa reported to Huerta's headquarters in order to form an alliance, but this first meeting proved ominous. "Huerta and his staff officers did not get up from their chairs," recalled Villa later. "I was dusty and tired. All the men there were dressed in gala uniforms. But because I was not in the regular army I was wearing my usual old clothes. I never forgot the way those men looked me up and down as if I were a stray mongrel that smelled bad." Huerta in fact considered Villa to be "violent, undisciplined and refusing to take orders from anyone." On June 4, two weeks after the defeat of Orozco's forces at the second battle of Rellano, the federal general ordered Villa's arrest on charges of persistent insubordination and refusal to return stolen horses.

Only a last-minute reprieve saved Villa from a firing squad, and he found himself shipped off to military prison in Mexico City.[36]

The resulting dissension among the federal forces and the weakened state of Huerta's army promised an opportunity for Orozco and his rebels to recover, and Zapata anxiously awaited news. But Huerta pressed forward. Soldiers and gangs of levies slaved to repair the railroad tracks and the federal army surged on. The rebels retreated farther north, many of them deserting their commander. By July 1 the strength of the insurrection had waned to such an extent that Orozco shifted his base headquarters from Chihuahua City to Ciudad Juárez; Huerta entered the state capital on July 8 after a victory at Bachimba on the 6th. From that time onward the campaign basically amounted to mopping up the remnants of Orozco's army, with the rebel commander on the run and with Huerta spending part of the month back in Mexico City. He returned to the capital as a hero, his past failures against Zapata forgotten, and strong enough to snap "I am no bookkeeper" when Madero raised mild objections to $400,000 missing from the campaign funds. The President, his distrust and dislike of Huerta as strong as ever, nevertheless felt obliged to promote him to major general.

Madero had reason to be grateful to Huerta. His position had immeasurably improved in both north and south. In Morelos the moderate policy advocated by Governor Naranjo achieved further success in mid-June, when Robles was assigned to Puebla, and when Felipe Ángeles arrived as his successor a few days later. Ángeles provided a perfect military foil to the governorship of Naranjo. Rather than being a harsh veteran of previous struggles against insurgents, the newcomer was a military intellectual, trained in France, and recently the director of the National Military College. He enjoyed a reputation as a civilized and honorable officer, and he arrived in Cuernavaca publicly pledged to proceed "in accord with the new governor . . . in arranging pacts with the Zapatistas."[37] "General Felipe Angeles was slender and rather tall," noted Mrs. King, "not very dark, more of the paleness of the better class of Mexican, with delicate features and the kindest eyes I think I have ever seen in any man. He called himself an Indian, laughingly, but he was decidely the type the Mexicans call *indio triste* (sad Indian). Another great attraction was his charming voice and manners." Mrs. King, still well placed to view the leaders in Cuernavaca at close hand, commented: "From the moment General Ángeles was introduced to me, I felt in him a quality that I had missed in his predecessors, a quality of mercy and a willingness to understand. I liked him, even before I heard through the junior officers that he would not tolerate any cruelty or injustice on the part of his soldiers."[38]

Zapata and the other revolutionary commanders would now have to fight against one of the most subtle and effective forms of counterinsurgency: the undermining of their appeal to the people through the granting of the people's immediate desires by the authorities. The ordinary peasant in Morelos had restricted political vision: he saw no further than his immediate surroundings, his *milpa,* his village, perhaps his district, certainly no further than the state boundaries. His immediate preoccupations lay in the need to find food for his family and to obtain sufficient land to grow his meager crop. He cared mainly for the revolution in Morelos and little for the revolution in Mexico. Winning over the peasants in Morelos could save Mexico for Madero, and the new policy of moderation would seem even more effective coming on the heels of the previous brutality. Zapata had already experienced difficulties with Naranjo's policy, when the governor had first arrived. his difficulties had ended with the arrival of Robles; now, with the Naranjo-Ángeles partnership, they would return in greater degree than ever before.

The new state deputies, who had been elected in late May, convened for the first time in Cuernavaca on July 17, and they too formed a strong contrast to previous officeholders. Notably absent were the plantation owners—many of whom had anyway fled to Mexico City or abroad. Instead, the newly elected representatives were shopkeepers, clerks, schoolteachers—all of strong local standing rather than being career politicians; all of them started their term of office with a sincere wish to improve the lot of the local people.[39] Ángeles echoed this desire. "I would give anything to show these people [Zapatistas] the mistake they are making," he told Mrs. King. "President Madero is doing his best for them, but he needs cooperation. The conservatives, using all the tricks of politics, fight him at every step, but how can he force through his reforms if the people he wants to help will not back him?" Mrs. King believed the general, as would many others; she wrote: "Ángeles never forgot that Zapata and Madero had once worked together for the common goal—liberty, justice, and decent living conditions for the masses; and he saw it for the tragedy it was that their followers, Revolutionaries all, had turned their guns on one another. . . ."[40]

Madero now made use of the promising situation. Jesús Flores Magón, one of the original opponents of the Díaz regime whose advice Zapata and his fellow Anenecuilcans had sought in winter 1909, had recently been appointed Minister of the Interior in Mexico City, and in late July he sent a secret envoy to Zapata's camp with Madero's approval, seeking to open negotiations. Zapata, still south in the California-like countryside of Guerrero, proved stubborn; so much depended upon Madero's trustworthiness, and Zapata had ample reason to suspect the President's words. Madero must therefore go. Zapata also showed himself fully aware of the dangers which a moderate policy in Morelos threatened to the Mexican revolution as a whole. "The revolution in Morelos is not a local revoltuion," he told the envoy. "Not until Madero's downfall will we enter into peace agreements." Fighting continued, and even increased slightly as an answer to the official policy of liberalism. On July 20, three days after the new state legislature convened at the Cuernavaca, rebels under de la O attacked a train at the Parres station, a few miles over the mountain border in the Federal District. Nearly 100 casualties resulted, many of them civilians. Shortly afterward Zapata and Jesús Morales pushed troops northward from Guerrero into southwest Morelos, threatening both Jojutla and Yautepec.

But even the weather turned against the rebels. The rains which began each latter half of May were now sweeping from the mountains in full force, bogging the tracks and making movement difficult; moreover, many peasants preferred to stay at home during these weeks, to tend the green shoots emerging from the black soil of their fields. And the authorities increased their gentle pressure. The new deputies at Cuernavaca started to show their strength by ousting Naranjo from the post of governor in early August: Naranjo, although an admirable moderate, had not been appointed by the elected representatives of the state, and he was not a native of Morelos. Further, his presence reminded the people of his former colleague, Robles.

On August 5 a new interim governor was sworn into office: Aniceto Villamar, a respected Tepoztlán lawyer. He seemed to symbolize a new spirit, voiced by the legislature's president when introducing Villamar to the assembly: "Not only the so-called *científicos* [former Díaz supporters] should occupy themselves with the problems of social improvement, but also the humble representatives of the people, who know them well and have felt with them all the bitterness of life." He praised the "heroism" of the state's *Maderista* fighters of 1910-11, notably Zapata, but said the present federal government should be obeyed: he suggested Villamar should appeal to the rebels to cease fighting. The new President apparently agreed: "Those who follow Emiliano Zapata in good faith and without more designs than the improvement of their social condition . . . represent those who know civilization only by name." But Villamar continued: "It is only honest to recognize it frankly, their longings are legitimate. . . . If the *hacendados* of Morelos illegally enjoy lands and water . . . I will be on the side of the Indians, with the laborers."[41]

The state authorities pursued their policy with notable success during the summer and autumn of 1912. The year, which had begun with such gloomy prospects of war and devastation, ended in virtual peace. The legislature at Cuernavaca undertook to introduce reforms, and did their best to fulfill their promises. By the beginning of September the humane General Ángeles could tell newsmen that "inexpressible lack of tact" earlier resulted in the burning of "innumerable *pueblos*" and villagers had been given "more than enough reason . . . to consider the federal forces and police as their greatest enemies." All this had changed, he claimed, through his application of reason and justice. "There is no revolution here in the South."[42] As an indication of the improved atmosphere Zapata's family was released from Cuernavaca jail. His mother-in-law wrote to the authorities thanking them for the peaceful return to normal life and adding, "My girls don't cry any more." Fighting dwindled to occasional small-scale raids; many peasants now supported Zapata through past loyalty rather than through urgent motivation. Zapata and the other leaders received requests not to camp in certain areas—the people would rather they shifted elsewhere. Zapata spent most of the rest of the year moving from one temporary headquarters to another, in Guerrero, Puebla, and southwest Morelos, sleeping with his wife and young son in small adobe huts or cane-thatched shelters. He received a further setback on December 1, when the interim governor, Villamar, stood down for a proper governor to take office—Patricio Leyva.

Nor did it appear that Zapata could receive encouragement from events elsewhere. Orozco remained in hiding in the United States and by October the last sparks of his revolution were extinguished. Another rebellion broke out in October, this time led by Félix Díaz, nephew of the old dictator: he seized the port of Veracruz on the 16th, hoping to stimulate a nationwide army revolt, but he failed to obtain support. The port was surrounded and recaptured on October 23: Díaz was first sentenced to be shot, then, after a ruling of the pro-Porfirio Díaz Supreme Court, imprisoned in Mexico City. The other captive rebel leader, Pancho Villa, escaped to America early in 1913, but showed himself to be still pro-Madero by notifying the authorities of a plot against the President led by General Bernardo Reyes, still in jail after his abortive rising in December 1911. With the leading dissidents imprisoned or in exile, Madero seemed reasonably secure.[43]

Peasants and townspeople throughout Morelos virtually forgot about revolution. Zapata remained in being, refusing all armistice feelers, but to the bulk of the people his name receded into the background. The rains lessened in early November and the skies cleared over the mountains with the advent of the dry season: for most villages the harvest proved good: some *pueblos* had to hire extra teamsters to help carry down the corn. Men worked day and night in the fields, and their women had to be ready to serve them food whenever they came down from the hillside patches with fresh loads of sweet-smelling harvest. The future promised well— with or without the help of Emiliano Zapata. Christmas celebrations seemed especially gay. In Cuernavaca, the pretty dark-eyed Señora Ángeles arrived to join her husband, and a huge ball was held in the theater—the largest building in the city. Mrs. King mingled with the guests. "The military band played the music for the dancing; a fine band, doing their best for the general and his lovely, gentle wife, pouring out the slow rhythm and intricate sweetness of *danzas* and two-steps then in vogue as if they had never played anything harsher." Mrs. King continued: "Such a dance, I think, had never in those days been given in Cuernavaca, and the girls of the town were starry-eyed. That happy night, when all thoughts of war were pushed outside the circle of light, and soldiers and townspeople yielded to joy!"[44]

Zapata, pushed out into the dark, later admitted that during this period he felt greatest doubts about ever winning.[45] He knew the struggle remained unfinished: Madero could not be trusted. He could only wait. Meanwhile his militant activities merely amounted to burning some plantation fields when the owners refused to pay protection money; although this type of operation brought finance, publicity, and some recruits, it merely amounted to marking time. If the 1912 situation had continued through 1913, Zapata would have stood minimum chance of success. A revolution cannot succeed without an clearly identifiable aim: the aim remained to overthrow Madero, but for the moment this objective held little appeal for the *Morelenses*. Zapata's revolutionary career might soon have ended—if Mexico had not suddenly been thrown into unprecedented turmoil and bloodshed just before dawn on February 9, 1913. On this Sunday started the *Decena Trágica:* the "Ten Tragic Days."

7

•••••••••••

Ten Tragic Days

Madero's position rested upon a foundation of shifting sand. "He had posted a deaf and blind sentry at the gateway to his life to cry 'All's well,' " commented Edward Bell, "and there were times when he would hear no other voice." His brother Gustavo warned him of the plot being hatched against him by Bernardo Reyes and other dissidents—news of which Villa had already revealed. "He laughed at me!" exclaimed Gustavo when he left the President's room. Yet secret leaks of this plot also revealed an awesome number of anti-Madero names: these related to people in jail who were scheming with others outside, mostly in the army; they included Félix Días, Reyes, General Manuel Mondragón, who had recently been allowed to return from Cuban exile, General Aureliano Blanquet, who commanded the 4,000 troops at Toluca, General Joaquín Beltrán, even though this officer had recently commanded the troops responsible for the recapture of Veracruz from Díaz— he now had control over infantry in the Mexico City suburb of Tacubaya. . . . Another name, against which a question mark had been placed, was General Huerta.

Once the plot was revealed, these suspects should have been closely guarded. Former presidents would have gone further: the suspects would very likely have been shot. But Madero declined to act; he remained confident and he still pursued his policy of "civilized" behavior. The editor of a Mexico City newspaper summed up the situation in remarks made to the recently arrived Cuban ambassador. "You have come at a bad time, Mr. Minister. . . . [Madero] has not an ounce of energy; he does not know how to use cold steel; and he devotes himself to the mania of proclaiming himself a great democrat. He does not shoot, sir! Do you believe that a president who does not shoot, who does not punish, who does not make himself feared, who always invokes laws and principles, can preside?" The editor paused, then added: "Madero is good. But it is not a good man that is needed."[1]

Artillery rumbled through the dimly lit streets of Tacubaya suburb in the early gray hours of Sunday, February 9, 1913, heading toward the center of Mexico City. President Madero was sleeping at his official residence in Chapultepec Castle. But a telephone call awoke his brother Gustavo: the army plot against the President had burst into the open; the army mutineers were driving for the National Palace in an attempt to seize the seat of power. Gustavo hurried to forestall them, his hat at a jaunty angle and a fat cigar clamped tight between his teeth. He drove at top speed through the streets and through the palace gates moments before the army rebels arrived. Gustavo won over the palace garrison with a brilliant speech delivered standing on his vehicle bonnet, and then he frantically organized defenses against the approaching army officers. These defenses were entrusted to General Lauro Villar, commander of the Mexico City garrison and a loyal *Maderista*, who had climbed from his sickbed to report for duty.

The rebels had released Reyes from prison, and at 7 A.M. he advanced upon the National Palace. Machine guns posted on the roofs and in the open windows halted his cavalry column, but Reyes ran on—only to be cut down by a fresh burst of fire. The *Maderista* defenses held, but volleys from both sides cut across the open ground before the palace killing and wounding large numbers of civilians, who had stopped on their way to early Mass to see the spectacle. Other rebel groups led by Díaz and Mondragón pushed into the city to bolster Reyes' original force, now decimated, but these too were thrown back. By 8:30 A.M. the mutiny appeared almost over. Gustavo Madero telephoned his brother and went off to breakfast. Díaz and Mondragón held out in the Ciudadela barracks, just under two miles west of the National Palace, but with them were only about 600 cadets. At 9 A.M. President Madero rode on a fine gray horse into the center of the city at the head of 1,000 mounted police and cavalry. He ignored fears that he might be struck down by a sniper, even when one such rebel fired at him and killed a nearby spectator. Once at the palace he reacted to the rebellion with uncustomary firmness, deciding that the surviving ringleaders must suffer immediate execution.[2]

But Madero had another decision to make. The loyal commander of the city's defenses, General Villar, lay seriously wounded, struck down in the exchange of fire outside the National Palace. A replacement must be found immediately. Under normal circumstances the appointment would probably have been handed to General Felipe Ángeles, the highly successful military commander in Morelos. But Ángeles remained in Cuernavaca; no time could be spared for his recall. And so the post fell to General Victoriano Huerta, the only ranking general immediately available—despite the inclusion of Huerta's name on the list of suspected plotters, and despite the dislike known to be felt between Huerta and Madero.

Snatched news of the upheaval in Mexico City reached Zapata during the day. First came a brief report of the attempted takeover; on its heels arrived reports that Madero remained in power. Zapata alerted his troops. The mutiny in the capital might provide an opportunity to reexert pressure in Morelos, especially as federal troops may be withdrawn to strengthen Madero's position in Mexico City. But for the moment Zapata could do no more than send riders to local commanders, ordering them to be prepared to move.

Mexico City remained in turmoil. Félix Díaz still occupied the Ciudadela barracks; crowds milled through the streets during this Sunday, hearing one rumor after another. Madero stayed closeted in his palace. And Huerta began to act. Some say he soon conferred with the rebel commander, Díaz: one eyewitness, Jesús Uructa, swore he saw the two men in close conference. Whether or not these two leaders from the opposing sides actually concocted a joint plan, the subsequent tragic farce revealed them to be pursuing a joint aim—the overthrow of Madero. The single-storeyed Ciudadela building could have been reduced to rubble within an hour by the massed federal artillery; instead, for ten terrible days an artillery barrage continued, directed not against the respective rebel and government strongpoints but hitting totally random targets.

The object seemed an endeavor to instill terror into the citizens of the capital, so undermining Madero's position by pretending the rebels were stronger than they actually were, and thus preparing the way for Madero's overthrow. By bombarding the capital, both Díaz and Huerta were in effect battering the Madero government. Huerta shifted his guns from one useless point to another, the *Teatro Nacional,* Alameda, Jesús Nazareno Hospital, the Zocalo . . . and Díaz responded with an aimless, wanton cannonade— and neither hit the other if possible. Shells only landed on the National Palace twice and on the Ciudadela once. Business and residential quarters of the city suffered instead, day after day for a week and a half, and the numbers of civilian casualties rose into the hundreds and thousands. For the first time the outside world realized the full horror of the Mexican revolution. "Many people have been killed in the fighting," reported the London *Daily Mail,*" and dead civilians are piled up in ghastly heaps in the streets. . . ." Troops fought in an insane, uncoordinated fashion, from building to building, firing at mythical targets. Trenches were hacked across the cobbles; communications with the capital were severed. Women scuttled in search for food, frantically waving improvised white flags of sheets tied to broomsticks. Litter clogged the gutters and the doorways, drifted by the hot wind; the heavy scent of cordite hung on the air; flies buzzed black on the corpses. On February 11, after thirty-six hours of day-and-night gunfire, battalions of troops known to be loyal to Madero were ordered by Huerta to attack the Ciudadela across the open park before the barracks. They ran into the suicidal attack, met concentrated fire from the rebel machine guns, and were slaughtered.

On this Tuesday, February 11, President Madero rushed to Cuernavaca to confer with the loyal Ángeles. He arrived late in the afternoon and stayed the night at Mrs. King's Bella Vista hotel: Mrs. King agreed to a request that she should fly the British flag over the building in an attempt to provide the Mexican President with added protection. "I saw that Mr. Madero . . . seemed unhappy and depressed," wrote the Englishwoman, "quite unlike his usual self."[3] Morelos had been thrown into confusion, like most of

Mexico. News from the capital came in brief telegraph messages, garbled and often contradictory; only two newspapers in Mexico City were continuing to publish.

Zapata, still in Puebla, could only await the outcome of the strange metropolitan struggle: he still lacked arms and equipment for a premature campaign. But Madero's visit to Cuernavaca promised to speed the moment when Zapata should take the offensive. The President's plight seemed to stir the old resentment against him, offering Zapata the opportunity of greater support. According to Mrs. King: "While the president and his party were at dinner, a servant came and told me that a sullen crowd was forming outside in the *plaza*, murmuring against the president, saying that he had not kept the promises he had made to the people. The crowd grew larger and larger and the indistinguishable murmur swelled. There were hisses and cries of 'Death to Madero!'" Madero wanted to address this throng, but Ángeles intervened and spoke successfully himself—the military commander still enjoyed respect. But now Ángeles and the bulk of his troops would leave, nominally as reinforcements for the government forces in the capital. "We go to join Huerta, the new commander-in-chief," he told Mrs. King, who wrote afterward: "The sound of the name was like a bell tolling. I had a remembrance of Huerta's face when he returned from his ill-fated campaign without his prisoner, Zapata. Ángeles' eyes met mine, and he turned away." President Madero left Cuernavaca the next day, February 12, taking with him Ángeles and about 9,000 troops, and leaving the city in the care of Colonel García Lugo and some 250 men—"mere boys," commented Mrs. King. [4] Other troops were also withdrawn from Morelos; Zapata and the other revolutionary chiefs allowed them to leave unmolested, and then, with federal strength in the state crippled, they began to edge forward again.

The climax approached in Mexico City. Madero arrived back to meet the angry American ambassador, who launched into a bitter protest about the "indiscriminate hostilities" and the damage caused to American property. Wilson's car had been fired on by both sides as he drove to the National Palace; Madero blamed Díaz; Díaz, when spoken to by Wilson and other diplomats, blamed the government. The carnage continued. "Business is paralysed," reported the *Daily Mail* correspondent. "Dozens of buildings show great jagged holes. . . ." Food shortages grew with frightening speed and disease began to spread in the strickened city. People clamored for an end to the horror, almost on any terms —including the ousting of Madero.

Huerta was ready. The American ambassador cabled Washington on February 15: "Huerta notifies me to expect some action that will remove Madero from power at any moment; plans fully matured. . . ."[5] Madero hung on for three more days, suspecting Huerta but lacking decisiveness or definite proof. He ordered General Aureliano Blanquet to move his 29th Infantry Regiment into the capital to defend the National Palace. But once again he chose the wrong man: Blanquet, one of the original names on the list of suspected plotters, remained in league with Huerta.

Shortly after midday on Tuesday, February 18, one week after his visit to Cuernavaca, Madero was confronted by Blanquet at the presidential office. The general, in meticulous black dress uniform, announced that the state of the country necessitated Madero's resignation. Madero refused; the officer drew his pistol and declared: "You are my prisoner." Members of the President's bodyguard who attempted to protect him were shot down. Meanwhile Madero's brother Gustavo lunched with Huerta at the Gambrinus restaurant; a messenger rushed in to inform Huerta he was urgently needed elsewhere. The general stood, looked at his empty holster and said to Gustavo: "I've no revolver. Will you lend me yours?" Gustavo obliged and was thereupon arrested, unarmed. By mid-afternoon the coup was complete, and Huerta issued a triumphant statement during the evening.

"TO THE MEXICAN PEOPLE. The unendurable and distressing situation through which the capital of the Republic has passed obliged the army, represented by the undersigned, to unite in a sentiment of fraternity to achieve the salvation of the country. In consequence the nation may be at rest. . . . Within 72 hours the legal situation will have been duly organized. The army invites the people on whom it relies to continue in the noble attitude of respect and moderation . . . it also invites all revolutionary factions to unite for the consolidation of national peace." The announcement was signed by Félix Díaz and V. Huerta.[6]

Deep in Morelos, Zapata showed no inclination to accept this dubious invitation to unite his revolutionary faction with Huerta. One bitter enemy had merely been replaced by another. But the situation nevertheless marked an improvement for the *Zapatistas:* moderates in the state legislature would suffer a severe setback under the new dictatorial rule. Within a few hours of his triumph Huerta displayed his tyrannical attitude in a curt message to state capitals: "Accept my authority or perish." Yet despite the opportunity offered for a resumption of the rebel offensive through the withdrawal of federal troops, Zapata still proceeded cautiously. Theoretically, the basis for the revolution had been removed, since the major aim expressed in the important paragraph 4 of the Plan of Ayala was to achieve the downfall of Madero, and now Madero had gone.

But Madero still breathed. Moments before taking the oath of presidency on February 19, Huerta pulled from beneath his shirt a medallion of the Virgin of Guadalupe, patron saint of Mexico, and kissing this medal he declared: "I swear to you that I shall permit no one to make an attempt against the life of Señor Madero." But with the ex-President alive, though incarcerated, the threat existed of a revival under his name. Huerta sought advice from Henry Lane Wilson, the American ambassador: should he send Madero into exile, have him impeached, or commit him to a lunatic asylum? Wilson hesitated to answer, and anyway Huerta had his own plan. Madero had been imprisoned in a room in the National Palace, together with José Pino Suárez, the ex-Vice-president, and the loyal *Maderista* general, Ángeles. During the late evening of Saturday, February 22, Madero and Pino Suárez were informed that they were being taken to the city jail, for their own security. Madero turned to Ángeles. "*Adiós,* my general," he said. "I shall never see you again." Minutes later, just before midnight, Madero and his former Vice-president lay dead in or near the car used to take them from the National Palace, shot in an attempted rescue by *Maderistas*—or so Huerta claimed. He denied all complicity in the convenient deaths of Madero and Pino Suárez, and the two men were buried forty-eight hours later, on February 24.

Three days after this funeral Zapata revealed his intentions in a note sent to de la O, who was visiting Mexico City to assess the situation. "Take care," advised Zapata, "and attack the enemy as often as he presents himself." As usual Zapata would tread softly—but would be ready to strike. First he felt it necessary to ensure that significant numbers of rebels did not abandon the struggle on the pretext that Madero's murder completed the revolution; Zapata's own experience of Huerta taught him that such reasoning would be completely false. Yet others felt differently, including Otilio Montaño, the third- or fourth-ranking *Zapatista* general, who contacted Huerta's agents on about February 27: Montaño then visited Mexico City and informed the authorities that Zapata and the others would soon lay down their arms. Zapata replied to this lie on March 2 when he and several other senior officers formally notified Huerta that rebellion continued. Two days later they protested to Félix Díaz over "the imposition of the illegal government of General Huerta."[7] Otilio Montaño soon shuffled shame-faced back to the rebels.

Once again Zapata prepared to shift from guerrilla war to larger-scale actions. Weapons and ammunition remained in short supply, restricting the size of the offensive for the moment, but in an effort to gain more material the rebel leaders selected federal troop patrols and detachments as their primary targets. Isolated federal positions suffered increasing attacks during early March, and the guerrillas ambushed a military train *en route* for Cuernavaca through the mountains, killing 75 federal troops. Zapata made ready to threaten the towns, leading to an offensive upon Cuernavaca itself. Moreover, he would now receive support from the state authorities: Huerta's brutal takeover in Mexico City threw the legislature at Cuernavaca into confusion, and although on March 5 a vote was carried pledging "adhesion to the new government," it rapidly became clear that the moderates would break away: they saw all their hopes for political and social reform being swept aside. The state suffered increasing chaos during March, with guerrilla activities becoming more numerous and gradually moving toward open, regular warfare, with the legislature in Cuernavaca edging further to declaring support for Zapata—and with Huerta beginning his countermeasures. His actions merely strengthened support for Zapata; once again the federal instrument to put down the revolutionaries would be repression, rather than the enlightened policy pursued by Ángeles. And once again Robles was chosen for the task. Huerta decided on Robles' reappointment in March, but delayed his return for about a month: meanwhile the new dictator declared martial law in the southern states.[8]

Troubles beset Huerta from all sides. These weeks saw the emergence of opposition to the regime in the north, with the anti-Huerta movement being led by the strange, contradictory, and soon famous figure of Venustiano Carranza. "A Spaniard of pure descent, he is a man of striking personal dignity," reported the British journalist H. Hamilton Fyfe. "Clearly he is a man of resolution and enterprise. But he does not look it."[9] Carranza, born into the landowning class in the state of Coahuila, where he was governor and where he had spent most of his life, seemed a strange choice as leader of a counterrevolution. "He is a great reader," commented Fyfe. "His serious, studious face, with deep vertical lines between the brows, betrays 'the pale cast of thought.' His eyes gleam patiently and kindly through spectacles. His hair is dark still, but mouth and chin are hidden by a heavy grey moustache and beard, though the cheeks are shaved. His voice is gentle. . . . It is hard to understand how a man of this professorial student type can have gained such an ascendancy over the Revolutionists . . . he can scarcely be a man of overflowing physical vitality at any time. It must be by force of character and intellect that he has reached his present dangerously high position." Carranza, of all the Mexican revolution figures, would have most impact upon Zapata's life—and death. Meanwhile he organized his Constitutionalist rebellion against Huerta from his home state of Coahuila. Others would undertake the bulk of his fighting for him: on March 13 a small group of riders splashed through the Rio Grande shallows into Mexico from Texas, headed by Pancho Villa. In Sonora, the Constitutionalist forces were centered around Álvaro Obregón, a thirty-three-year-old rancher. During the spring and early summer of 1913 Carranza, Obregón, and Villa gradually drew in recruits and supplies for the coming campaign. Huerta's old enemy Orozco returned to Chihuahua to resume the fight. For the moment Huerta abandoned the countryside in the north and fortified the towns, while he turned his attention on troublesome Morelos.[10]

The Mexican dictator prepared drastic contingency plans to deal with the *Zapatistas*, revealed to the American ambassador on March 14. Up to 20,000 *Morelenses* would be dragged from the state and herded into labor camps at Quintana Roo. Replacements would be brought from elsewhere; these newcomers "may not be as efficient at first to perform the work required by landowners in Morelos, but they will at least be ignorant of the roads and trails of the state . . . and less apt to be tempted by promises from Zapata."[11] Zapata showed no sign of being intimidated, even when Orozco in the north defected to Huerta and dared to send emissaries south in the hope of persuading Zapata to compromise: the Morelos leader arrested these messengers and subjected them to show trials. In response, Huerta told the American ambassador at the end of March that the best means to handle the rebel chiefs was "an 18-cents rope wherefrom to hang them."[12] And, on April 14, Robles returned to Cuernavaca. He immediately informed the legislature that in addition to the post of military commander he intended to be state governor. When the elected politicians protested, they were thrown into jail and sent to Mexico City. By April 17 Robles had assumed full power in the state capital.

On the same day Zapata launched his offensive. He had moved his army eastward through the Puebla mountains during the previous night, crossing the border into Morelos just before dawn and riding hard to cover the five miles to Jonacatepec. His forces surrounded this district seat soon after first light and immediately started the attack. The *Zapatistas* probably numbered about 1,500 men; inside the town were almost 500 federal troops commanded by General Higinio Aguilar, elderly but still agile. Anxious to avoid expending too much ammunition, Zapata ordered his officers not to attempt massed charges, and instead he sent his men into the attack in concentrated jabs at varying sections of the federal defenses. The method took longer than an all-out assault, but proved equally successful: the town fell at noon the following day, April 18, after a battle lasting thirty-six hours. The victory was important on two counts: first for prestige purposes and as a sound declaration that Huerta's intimidation had no effect; second, as a means of collecting arms, ammunition, and recruits. Zapata's success netted the rebels 330 Mausers, 310 excellent cavalry horses and army-issue saddles, plus two machine guns with ammunition. Zapata also captured General Aguilar, whom he pardoned—whereupon the general joined Zapata. Added to the propaganda value to Zapata of this defection was the fact that Aguilar soon became useful as a go-between, contacting corrupt or wavering federal officers who might be prepared to supply the rebels with weapons and information.[13]

Huerta, with federal troops overstretched, could only hit back with words for the moment. "It is necessary to clean out all such people," he told a planters' meeting on April 21, "and you must not be surprised if perchance something abnormal happens, for the state of affairs calls for procedures that are not actually legal but which are indispensable for the national well-being." Like Robles earlier in the year, Huerta claimed the entire rural population of Morelos were "all *Zapatistas*" but he promised complete pacification within a month. On the day this speech appeared in the *Mexican Herald*, April 23, Zapata laid siege to Cuautla. Since his victory at Jonacatepec a week earlier, Zapata had established his headquarters at Tepalcingo, strategically placed to strike north across the lightly populated hills in the direction of Mexico City, or up the Río Cuautla, and within easy retiring distance of the Puebla mountains should pressure become too great. In drawing up his plans he obtained help from Manuel Palafox, recently arrived at Zapata's camp and a valuable addition to the rebel commander's staff: Palafox, previously an engineering student in Puebla City, then an accountant, proved an expert manager and adviser. Zapata would increasingly rely upon this short, spidery, and pockmarked twenty-six-year-old.[14]

Now Zapata and his staff decided once again that the campaign must be aimed at the heart of the state. This time a direct attempt to take Cuautla would be avoided: the object of the siege would be to cut federal communications along the important Cuautla valley and to help isolate Cuernavaca over to the west. As an adjunct to the plan to threaten Cuernavaca, the rebels paid increasing attention to the vulnerable road and rail links between Mexico City and the state capital: on May 1 the *Zapatistas* blew up a military train in a station on the Mexico-Morelos border, killing almost 100 federal soldiers.[15]

Fighting in the mountains took on a character of its own. The revolutionaries lived among the rocks, erecting straw shelters with more straw on the earth to sleep on, always ready to move at a moment's notice. Many *Zapatistas* brought their wives with them, and these women continued to render invaluable service as nurses and supply workers. Zapata's wife Josefa spent much of the time with her husband, always quiet and keeping in the background. The campaign continued night and day. The federals kept to the tracks, living with the constant danger of sudden ambush, trying vainly to seek out the enemy among the scrub-covered foothills. One *Zapatista* described a typical small ambush which took place on the lower slopes of the hills along the Río Cuautla valley. "There were no rocks to hide behind, only pine trees and brush and tall grass. We hid as best we could and waited for them. Man, it was cold! We heard the cavalry coming very close and our hearts were already jumping when the colonel gave us the signal to fire. *Caray!* They retreated because one side was a stream and the other side a steep hill. The horses couldn't run because of the chuck holes. They fell and couldn't stand up again. Then we began to go after the men but not those who escaped across the stream, because they had entrenchments on the other side. We killed about 150 before we got away. . . ."[16]

Attacks such as this intensified in the area around Cuernavaca after May 5. "All who could were leaving Cuernavaca," wrote Mrs. King. "Foreigners with sufficient income to live elsewhere moved on. The British and American companies began to recall their people. I could not leave because everything I had was tied up in the Bella Vista." Daily the *Zapatistas* seemed to creep closer to the state capital; stories circulated of federal positions being attacked at Jiutepec five miles to the southeast, at Santa María five miles north, at Temixco hacienda eight miles south. In Cuernavaca itself the people behaved with brittle, frenzied gaiety. "Anyone coming into the town," remembered Mrs. King, "would have thought we were enjoying the most peaceful days Mexico had ever known. There was music in the *plaza*, feasting in the palace of the governor, plays and dancing in the theatres. . . . The gaiety in Cuernavaca was rapidly rising to the pitch of hysteria. It hinted, too clearly for comfort, 'To-morrow we die. . . .'"[17]

Robles received added instructions from Huerta at the end of the first week in May. Despite the threats building in north Mexico, the President decided to increase Robles' strength to about 5,000 men. The extra would mainly be conscripted from the local population, which would simultaneously suffer a return to the "resettlement" program. Robles announced the barbaric details of his policy on May 9. Within seven days all inhabitants of *pueblos, ranchos*, and smaller hamlets must "reconcentrate" in the nearest district seat, or in one of the few other major towns; villages suspected of being "nests of bandits" would be razed; anyone caught in the countryside without a pass would be shot. The federal officers rode out to implement the orders. Inhabitants of villages were driven along the roads and into camps, and thousands of men and young boys were rounded up for military service, either in the area or in the north. The policy amounted to genocide: a constant line of cattle cars clanked over the mountain railroad to Mexico City, crammed with males to be churned into cannon fodder or thrown into labor camps. Many suffocated during the journey and the space in the cattle trucks was so tight that their dead bodies remained wedged between their living comrades. Within one month nearly 1,000 men were deported and the figure doubled during June. Thousands of families were left to fend for themselves without their men.

Zapata had to absorb the impact of this unprecedented counterrevolutionary measure. While Robles increased support for Zapata through the federal cruelty, the policy nevertheless caused considerable short-term damage to the *Zapatista* campaign. Village sanctuaries were drastically reduced in number; many revolutionary troops were caught in the general federal net, and movements across the countryside were rendered more vulnerable. Perhaps most important, the upheaval caused by Robles' retaliation resulted in some confusion among Zapata's subordinates and among the semi-independent rebel leaders. A close working relationship was more difficult to achieve with the federal authorities clamping a vicious hold over the villages and roads—the various revolutionary groups found themselves separated one from the others. All these factors combined to prompt Zapata's decision to redeclare the basic aims of the revolution: such an announcement would provide working guidelines for the scattered commanders, and would rally the shocked population closer to Zapata's banner. Once again, Zapata showed himself fully conscious of the need to link the military and political aspects of revolution. Finally, a fresh declaration would constitute another cry of defiance against Huerta. On May 30 Zapata accordingly published a manifesto amending the Plan of Ayala; this, drawn up by Otilio Montaño, condemned Huerta as a "usurper" whose "presence in the presidency of the Republic accentuates more and more each day his incompatibility with everything that signifies law, justice, rights and morals, up to the point that he is reputed worse than Madero." Orozco, who had betrayed the revolution, was "a social zero, that is, without any acceptable significance."[18]

This reference to Orozco performed two functions. First, it provided a warning to other would-be traitors. Second, it marked the fact that for the first time Zapata officially assumed leadership of the revolution: under the original Plan of Ayala Orozco had been accredited this position. Zapata now formally created the Revolutionary Junta of the Center and South of the Republic, naming himself president and with other members including Eufemio Zapata, Montaño, de la O, and other chiefs. These weeks also saw the issue of instructions to the revolutionary officers, designed to create a common, unified front in the campaign against the enemy and in dealings with revolutionary soldiers and civilians. These instructions are important for the light they shine on Zapata's highly professional attitude toward his revolutionary army. Thus the orders stated that officers should "pay the soldiers wages, or . . . help out the troops where possible." Local officials should be replaced "in accord with the will of the people"; forced loans should be levied on rich merchants and landlords. Indicative of the scattered nature of the campaign was the order that officers should report their operations every fortnight to their zone chiefs or to the central headquarters. Subordinate officers, probably cut off for much of the time from their higher command, were therefore allowed considerable initiative and responsibility, and this even had to extend into the political field: officers were to lend "moral and material help" to villages presenting titles and filing land reclamation.[19] Middle-range and junior officers obeyed these instructions with remarkable efficiency and professionalism, directly contrary to the image of Zapata's army as a mere horde. Zapata continued to insist that the troops should behave in a disciplined and sober fashion, and this policy, stemming from the very summit of command, extended down into the ranks. Murder, rape, and other atrocities remained infrequent. And as the historian John Womack commented: "Local chiefs had a stake in following the rules simply to prove themselves of value to the headquarters that might one day be a government. If they hanged municipal officials or merchants who would not pay their quotas, they still did not alienate working farmers and their families. In the deep and abiding respect plain people felt for Zapata, they revealed that at least they understood the suffering they did endure."[20]

People had far more to fear from the federals. "I saw how the federal troops would catch the men and kill them," wrote one peasant woman in Morelos. "They carried off animals, mules, chickens, clothes. The women who came with the soldiers were the ones who took away everything. The government soldiers, and the rebel soldiers too, violated the young girls and the married women. They came every night and women would give great shrieks when they were taken away. Afterwards, at daybreak, the women would be back in their houses. They wouldn't tell what happened to them. . . . For greater safety, we would sleep in the *corral*. . . . The *Zapatistas* were well liked in the village, because although it is true they sometimes carried off young girls, they left the majority of the women in peace. And after all, everyone knew what kind of girls they took. The ones who liked that sort of thing!"[21]

The men joined Zapata's revolution for a variety of reason. Chief among them was undoubtedly the hatred felt for the federals and the devotion for Zapata, summed up in a local folksong:

All through the South, they love him loyally,
For he gives them Justice, Peace, Progress and Liberty.[22]

One peasant wrote: "Now we knew what we were fighting for —Land, Water, Forests and Justice. That was all in the plan. It was for this reason that I became a Revolutionary. It was for a cause!" Yet his wife remembered his joining up in a different fashion. "One day Pedro appeared, carrying his rifle," she commented.

"He told me, 'Well, I've done it. I've joined up.' He had become a *zapatista* because they offered to give him food. I got very angry but he said at least he would have something to eat and further-more they would pay him. Then he told me he would have to go to Mexico City with the rebels and he promised to send me money. He went with the *zapatistas* and left me without a *centavo*. There I was with nothing and I had two children to support. . . . I cried in anguish because I didn't know what to do. My brother was angry with Pedro. He said Pedro was lazy and didn't want to work."[23]

Even Pedro admitted that "many joined just to get rich, to steal whatever they could. Their sons are rich now, because the fathers robbed. When a *plaza* was captured, they would sack the houses and give half the loot to their officers." The journalist Hamilton Fyfe questioned revolutionaries, and their answers confirmed this statement by Pedro. Fyfe wrote: "For each *jefe* among the *Insurrectos* who believes that he is fighting for a cause there must be twenty who are simply 'on the make.' As for the rank and file, few of them trouble their heads about the motives of the war."[24] Zapata's promise of payment and food for his troops, wherever possible, arrived at an especially valuable moment: the peasants were suffering drastically from the federal resettlement policy, with shortages of work, with normal means of livelihood gone, and with food running short.

But even if the patriotic motivation of Zapata's army has been exaggerated, his achievement was still extremely impressive. Simply because his men joined for a wide variety of reasons, his success in welding them together into such an efficient force was all the greater. He reduced looting to a minimum; his army, which could so easily have been a rabble, fought in remarkably pro-fessional manner; desertions were infrequent in comparison with the federal force, apart from men leaving—with Zapata's tacit per-mission—to tend their fields during sowing or harvesting time. Zapata, through the strength of his own quiet personality, spread a unifying influence over this unique military force, binding the men together and continuing to do so even after many months of cam-paign, after repeated setbacks, after repeatd successes which so rapidly turned bitter. Now, in June 1913, Zapata further strength-ened his organization and by July his force proved stronger than ever before, well able to survive the hammerings inflicted by Robles. Never before had Zapata's personal power of leadership been so effective. Yet he retained his caution. He still avoided moving too far from guerrilla warfare; rebel forces struck here and there, maintaining maximum mobility, and always darting away from the flailing federal military machine.

Zapata hoped Huerta would fall through the gradual whittling away of federal authority, and as he extended his influence in the south, Zapata received reports of similar revolutionary successes in the north. Villa, who four months earlier had entered Mexico with eight men, now commanded an army in the desert numbering almost 8,000, and in midsummer this huge marauding force began to roll south toward Torreón. Carranza preached vengeance in Sonora to all who might oppose him and to all who supported Huerta. "We shall execute anyone," he calmly informed Hamilton Fyfe, "who recognizes a president unconstitutionally elected and directly or indirectly guilty of participation in the murder of Madero."[25] Back in Mexico City, Huerta's drink consumption soared. "He was becoming so capricious in his habits," wrote Mrs. King, who sought an interview with him during the summer, "that even his cabinet ministers found it difficult to find him. The people of the city hated and feared the president."[26]

In Morelos, the federal military commander launched one repressive operation after another in frenzied frustration. Vast areas of the countryside had been desolated under the "resettlement" program. The state was "only a rough sketch of what it was two years ago," reported an agent of the White Cross in late July. "Those ample plantings of cane, rice, and so many other food products have disappeared, now converted into a sad heap of ashes, the monotony of the burned fields interrupted only by one or another deserted hamlet also half-ruined by fire."[27] Most minor targets were now mere mounds of rubble, and daily more burnings were ordered, even at municipal seats such as Yecapixtla, Xochitepec, Tepalcingo—and Zapata's local district seat, Villa de Ayala, Federal officers seized control of markets in Cuernavaca, Cuautla, and Jojutla to sever supplies to outlying villages. People in these villages were forced by the threat of starvation either to move into the hateful camps or to drift into the hills. Murders and countless arrests continued, and as in 1912 Zapata's mother-in-law and four of her daughters were seized as hostages and taken to a military prison in Mexico City. The dreadful draft went on, with nearly 1,300 men deported during July.

Still Zapata denied Robles a target. Temporary rebel setbacks were vastly outnumbered by the successes. The revolutionaries remained strong in the hills around Cuernavaca, yet when Robles ventured out to track them down they melted away on his approach—only to return when he withdrew to base. For the arrogant, brutal Robles the situation became intolerable. His personal position grew increasingly uncertain: orders from Mexico City to pin down Zapata could not be obeyed, yet Huerta voiced his impatience over the telephone line: Zapata must be destroyed. In the last days of July Robles attempted to save his career through one last farcical operation: since Zapata refused to oblige by standing still to fight, Robles intended to fabricate a battle, against a non-existent enemy, with which to impress his superiors. Huerta, no fool and experienced in the type of difficulties confronting Robles, saw through the deception, but the charade also suited his propaganda purposes.

Robles selected Huautla as his target, a small mining settlement situated in the hills to the extreme south of the state, about fifteen miles southeast of Jojutla and the same distance southwest of Tepalcingo. The target was largely mythical. True, Zapata had established a temporary headquarters in this collection of bleak, tumbledown huts, but the Puebla and Guerrero borders lay only three miles to the south, and Zapata would have ample time to escape while the federal columns blundered over the exposed countryside. Robles must have realized the bird would have long flown by the time his troops could arrive at Huautla: this made no difference, provided he could inflate sufficient importance into the operation. In the first days of August he therefore boasted of his plans to newsmen: three federal columns would advance into the hills and envelop the enemy; with Zapata blasted from his sanctuary, the rebellion would crumble. The battle, he told reporters, "will certainly be bloody, since in Huautla no stone will be left on stone." No effort would be spared, Robles proclaimed, and success would be assured. "The pacification of Morelos . . . will be a fact."

Suitably impressed, the newsmen filed their stories back to Mexico City, where they appeared in *El Imparcial* and other dailies on August 2 and 3, thus providing Zapata with plentiful warning.

The exercise began in early August. The columns advanced under General Alberto T. Rasgado and Antonio Olea, and Colonel Luis G. Cartón, troops marching in textbook fashion, guns rattling and screeching along behind. Robles fed optimistic reports to the press and to Mexico City: the rebels were being driven from their nests as the advance continued; the rebels were suffering increasing numbers of casualties; the rebels would never be able to recover. . . . Zapata and his men trotted casually over the border into Guerrero and Puebla. Onward went the federals, eager for the easy, worthless victory. Cartón went forward with too much impatience and marched in front of the other two columns; he failed to halt in time and inadvertently entered deserted Huautla. Hurriedly correcting himself, he pulled back to await the others for the nonsensical "attack" on the settlement. On Auqust 19 the signal came for this final assault, and the troops went in with rifles snapping and machine guns drumming. All they found in the village were the bodies of Pascual Orozco's father and two other emissaries from the northern leader who had betrayed the revolution, executed by Zapata after their show trials for treachery, and fittingly left in Huautla as a symbol of Zapata's continued resolve to resist.[28]

"Zapata's hordes have today been completely destroyed," signaled Robles to Huerta. "Properly speaking, the Morelos campaign has been concluded." Robles received promotion to divisional general, the army's top rank; Cartón became a general. The pro-Huerta press screamed in triumph. The President used the supposed victory as an opening shot in the election campaign, with the votes scheduled to be cast on October 26, and as an excuse to shift Robles and the bulk of his troops from Morelos to face the rebel threat in the north. This maneuvering took place in September; Huerta, through the transfer of crack troops from Morelos, virtually conceded defeat in the state. The federals would continue to hold garrisons in the towns, strong enough to prevent outright takeover by Zapata, but the countryside would be left to the rebels; the pro-Huerta press would pump out propaganda saying the rebels were no longer a force to be reckoned with; news of Zapata's continued activity would be repressed. On September 13 the President therefore replaced Robles as governor and military commander at Cuernavaca; succeeding him was Brigadier General Adolfo Jiménez Castro, who had served in Morelos the previous year under Ángeles, and who would engage in a holding operation. At the same time Huerta attempted to improve his international image, especially with America, by promising that he himself would not stand in the October elections.

Zapata worked from his new headquarters in north Guerrero to reorganize his army for intensified struggle. Directly contrary to the Huerta propaganda which made his army out to be an undisciplined horde, he sought to instill even greater professionalism into his forces. A regular rank structure was formed during late September and early October: local chiefs were issued fresh instructions on October 4 which included the order for them to name sergeants and corporals, "so that they . . . may mobilize their troops with more exactitude and rapidity." These instructions to the rebel army, now given the formal name of Liberating Army of the Center and South, covered other points designed to lift the organization from guerrilla to regular status: all troops must obey orders from officers, whether or not they originated from the same rebel band; all troops must stay in assigned positions when marching or fighting, rather than milling in confused fashion. Additional stress was given to the need to behave in sober and disciplined manner: rules and penalties regarding pillaging and committing atrocities were tightened.[29]

While Zapata continued his preparations, as fast as his cautious, careful nature would allow, others acted in more dramatic fashion. On September 29 Villa threw his 8,000 men against the federal stronghold at Torreón, garrisoned by 3,000 well-equipped and thoroughly prepared troops. Bitter battle raged for three days, but by the evening of October 1 the rebels had penetrated the federal defenses. Villa ordered the final assault: that night his troops attacked from three directions, bareheaded at Villa's command to differentiate them from the enemy in the hand-to-hand fighting: by dawn on October 2 the most important center in northern Mexico had fallen to the triumphant Division of the North.[30] The success had strong political impact in Mexico City, where *Maderista* militants still in the Chamber of Deputies became more voluble in their opposition to Huerta. In retaliation, Huerta's troops surrounded the Chamber on October 10 during a sitting, and the 110 congressmen were taken to prison in tramcars; the president declared Congress dissolved and he assumed total dictatorial powers, saying new Congress elections would be held the same day as the presidential vote, October 26.[31] But Huerta's action rendered chances of American support even less likely, and the opportunity was offered for coordination between the north and south rebel movements in an attempt to present a united front, whatever the results of the October 26 elections.

Zapata appreciated this possibility. He held a junta in the hills of southern Morelos on October 19, and the officers clustered around his table agreed to the dispatch of envoys to arrange "unification" with the main rebel chiefs in the north. Simultaneously, the effort would be made to deal with the United States for recognition of the allied revolutionary movement as a belligerent party. Twenty-four hours later Zapata published a manifesto, directed at the nation as a whole, which declared: "Victory approaches. The Struggle comes to its end." On October 24 Zapata sent a letter to Washington, addressed to Francisco Vázquez Gómez, onetime Education Minister under Madero and a powerful politician: Vázquez Gómez was asked to represent the southern revolution at the White House and authorized to seek a loan with which to buy ammunition.[32]

Congressional and presidential elections took place on October 26 as scheduled. As expected, they amounted to a farce. Few people bothered to vote. Most ballot boxes in Mexico City, consisting of receptacles varying from cardboard shoeboxes to chemists' pots, remained empty; the government reported that returns were "coming in slowly" and kept up the pretense by expressing doubt over the result. By the end of the day Huerta had been declared the presidential victor, although he had not stood as a candidate; the new Congress was filled with submissive army officers, so many that it was suggested a bugle should replace the chairman's bell.[33] News of the bogus results stimulated the rebels throughout the country, and outside Mexico convinced the American President, Woodrow Wilson, that this neighbor to the United States would find no peace until Huerta had been overthrown. On November 1 Wilson requested those European nations which had recognized Huerta "to impress upon him the wisdom of retirement." Huerta snapped to an American reporter: "I shall not retire until I am six feet underground." Wilson reacted with an ominous message to all governments: "If General Huerta does not retire by force of circumstances it will become the duty of the United States to use less peaceful means to put him out."[34] Meanwhile the Mexican President still seemed in firm control: his propaganda method of downplaying the southern revolution apparently proved successful. In Mexico City the newspapers only printed blown-up defeats of *Zapatista* groups; the planters and rich merchants believed they might soon be able to return home. Leading citizens were no longer concerned about reform in Morelos, and they approved of federal repression; the British journalist Hamilton Fyfe noted: "Dainty women talked unconcernedly about *peons* hung on telegraph poles and the 'funny way' in which soldiers spun round when they were shot. Genial Britons and Americans spoke of the execution of prisoners as a regular practice and approved of it. . . ."[35]

But by mid-November the basic planning for Zapata's military strategy had been completed. His scheme marked a considerable shift from all his other campaigns: for the first time Morelos would provide a sideline to the real activity, which would instead be centered upon Guerrero. Without massive increases in arms and ammunition, Zapata realized he could obtain only limited further successes in his native state: he already controlled the devastated countryside and many of the towns, and the remainder, including Cuernavaca, were still too strongly defended. Zapata reckoned he could achieve more elsewhere. So, while subordinate commanders continued to fix the enemy's attentions in Morelos, Zapata would launch feinting movements in Puebla and toward the important town of Iguala in Guerrero, where the railroad from Mexico City ended. Under cover of these diversions, Zapata aimed to concentrate his main forces in a strong stab southward to seize Chilpancingo. Capture of the Guerrero state capital would result in enormous prestige, and arms and ammunition from the defeated garrison would feed further advances toward the coast. There, the target would be Acapulco: the port offered excellent sea communications with northern Mexico and with the United States. After regrouping, and with the federals thrown off balance, the revolutionary army would suddenly strike north against Iguala, this time with the full intention of taking this vital town. Capture of the railhead would provide an excellent center from which to threaten Mexico City in a coordinated move with commanders pushing from northern Mexico. The plan, drawn up with the help of Montaño and Palafox, enabled all the best advantages to be gained from Zapata's experienced and highly mobile army. It revealed a flair for strategic thinking which utilized the strategy of indirect approach: rather than plunging headlong at the principal objective, which would be extremely risky in view of shortages of military supplies, Zapata would outmaneuver the enemy.

Yet vital time had to be spared for establishing Zapata's influence over subordinate chiefs of Guerrero. While he enjoyed undisputed leadership in Morelos, the same had still to be achieved in the neighboring state; alliances had to be formed, forces incorporated, a common system of command established. So, while this essential groundwork was being prepared, Zapata's military activity went into temporary decline. The main spotlight continued to be centered upon Pancho Villa.

Villa's Division of the North attempted to take Chihuahua City on November 5, but found the federal defenses too strong. Instead Villa made a lightning dash northward to the town of Juárez, just across the border from El Paso, and taken completely by surprise on the 15th. Tourists from the United States flocked across the Rio Grande next day to see the triumphant *Villistas* in possession, and also across the frontier flowed weapons from America. Huerta ordered 5,500 troops north to battle the rebels; Villa led his army out to nearby Tierra Blanca to meet the enemy. The two forces lined up for battle during the night of the 21st. Huerta seemed confident that this opportunity to destroy Villa would be successful: also on November 21 he addressed the recently "elected" Congress in Mexico City. Next day the London *Daily Mail* reported his confident appearance. "Through the crowded Chamber of Deputies . . . there stepped lightly, with hand upraised to acknowledge the cheers which greeted him, a . . . thickly built soldier whose briskness belied his fifty-nine years. . . . His dome-like

skull gleamed bald under the light. Closely-cropped gray hair covered back and sides. His complexion was dark but it was only when
you noticed the hand against his shirt cuff that you realized his
pure Indian descent. Clearly his sight was very weak: he added another pair to the spectacles he already wore before he began to
read his message to the new Congress." This message spoke opti-
mistically of events in Mexico: the rebels would soon be completely crushed in north and south.

Villa's army and the federal forces faced each other in sullen
silence over the desert no-man's land on November 22, each
waiting for the other to move first. The federals obliged at dawn on
the 23rd. For the next forty-eight hours battle spread along a wide
front, almost reaching the American border. The rebels began to
give way. Then Villa concentrated his forces for his favorite tactic
—un golpe terrifico—a terrific blow by cavalry charge into the
enemy's heart. Two cannon shots signaled the advance, and Villa's
men careered forward to smash through the opposing lines: the
federals started to retreat and the rebel cavalry hacked them down
as they ran. Villa reported to other rebel commanders: "I have
completely routed the enemy. They are in full and shameless
flight." One thousand federals lay dead or wounded and the survivors threw themselves on trains to steam back to Chihuahua
City. Three days later, November 28, Villa took the city after the
commander fled with his decimated garrison. The rebels ruled
Chihuahua state.

A relative calm dropped on all fronts before the holocaust. During the scorching winter months of 1913 Villa prepared for a spring
drive through the center of Mexico, aiming at Mexico City itself.
Obregón's forces prepared to thrust down the Pacific coast: in the
northeast an army under Pablo González moved into position to
threaten the oil-rich Gulf Coast. Carranza, the "First Chief" of all
these Constitutionalist forces, remained in Sonora and plotted to
take over supreme command when the moment seemed right. Zapata continued to build up his forces and his system of alliances
with the Guerrero leaders: on January 18, 1914, he signed a treaty
with the important Guerrero chief, Julián Blanco, whose area extended along the Pacific coast below Acapulco.[36] In Mexico City
the President scraped together all available forces to meet the mul-

tiple threats, and conscription reached new heights: 700 men were netted while watching a bullfight; so too was a crowd which gathered to watch a fire in the capital; men who protested when the film they had paid to watch at a cinema turned out to be religious, not pornographic as expected, were arrested and thrown into the army. The capital seemed to revolve in dizzy turmoil. So too did the alcoholic Huerta. "I have been told by one who visited him in the early morning," commented Hamilton Fyfe, "that his breakfast consisted of a beaten-up raw egg, a glass of claret, and a glass of brandy." "There has been some little trouble," said the President's doctor one day. "The General has not been able to walk [properly] for two months from rheumatism. . . . And sometimes he is in great pain and comforts himself with *aguardiente*. . . . Tonight he tried to shoot his mother. He always tries to shoot his mother . . . because he loves her very much." The doctor peered at his reflection in the mirror and tweaked his long mustache straight. "This revolution. Do not mistake. It is a fight of the poor against the rich. I was very poor before the revolution. Now I am very rich."[37]

8

• • • • • • • • • • •

To Mexico City

Zapata's struggle approached its third anniversary. The years had resulted in minimum changes to either his appearance or his character. He still dressed in dark trousers and dark jacket and usually a white shirt, even during rough campaigning periods in the hills and mountains. His face had become slightly rounder. His character remained reserved: he drank only small amounts of alcohol and disapproved of those who consumed too much, including his brother Eufemio. Reporters who visited him at his various camps found him polite, but uncommunicative: he would only start to talk freely when his natural shyness had worn away. He felt uncomfortable in the presence of politicians and preferred the company of ordinary villagers. His staff meetings were usually orderly and well conducted, although younger members such as Palafox tended to speak too loudly and too long in their effort to make a good impression. Zapata sat quietly and allowed them to talk. Disputes were settled fairly, and usually amicably. Although quiet, Zapata was by no means dour: he had a ready sense of humor, and if a joke pleased him he wanted to hear it again and again, insisting that others be told it even if they knew it already. Zapata also seemed tireless: few could match his ability to ride long distances over appalling terrain, and few could equal his skill as a rider. The gift of a horse pleased him more than any other.

March 1914 brought day after day of scorching sunshine and searing winds. The dry season would last another six weeks in southern Mexico. Across the Atlantic the European nations were drifting toward World War during these spring months; in Mexico, the temperature of revolution had steadily risen. And now revolt burst into fire to curl and burn the four corners of the map of the country, and the flames crept closer to Mexico City.

Zapata moved first. Preliminary operations began in late February, with subordinate commanders striking rapidly to seize a number of towns and large villages in Puebla and northern Guerrero, aimed at drawing off federal troops from the primary objective—Chilpancingo, "Place of Wasps." These diversionary moves proved successful, and barely necessary: the War Department in Mexico City lacked troops to send to southern Mexico. Zapata accelerated his program. On March 9 allied revolutionary detachments under Blanco, Jesús Salgado and Heliodoro Castillo moved into positions to the south, west, and north of Chilpancingo. Three days later Zapata rode up at the head of nearly 2,000 men from Puebla and Morelos, and established his headquarters in an adobe house at Tixtla, a few miles to the northeast. Spies sent a constant flow of accurate reports on the enemy positions inside the city. Only about 1,400 federal troops defended the state capital, under General Cartón—whom the rebels knew well for his part in the farcical operation on Huautla the previous August, *Zapatistas* and their allies numbered nearly 5,000, confident, primed, and anxious for battle to begin.

And on March 14 Zapata and the other commanders shifted their forces forward, out from the rolling hills and green gulleys, to snap shut their ring around the city. The federal defenders stood no chance of surviving the siege; reinforcements, always doubtful, had been rendered impossible by a mutiny at the Jojutla garrison forty-eight hours earlier, which threw the federal defense of southern Morelos into confusion and panic. And while the siege continued at Chilpancingo, the federal forces far to the north were threatened by another revolutionary general: Pancho Villa made his move on March 16. In greatest secrecy Villa advanced his army from Chihuahua City toward Torreón, reoccupied by the federals during the previous weeks and once again Villa's target. With him rode Zapata's former antagonist, General Felipe Ángeles, as commander of the artillery of Villa's Division of the North. Ángeles had been freed by Huerta after Madero's murder and sent on a study

mission to France, but he made his way back to join Carranza in
Sonora. Carranza, for whom Villa still officially fought, appointed
Ángeles his Secretary of War. Villa soon requested, and received,
his services and the two men became close friends. By March 17
they had maneuvered the Division of the North into positions at
Yermo, only seventy miles north of Torreón. Before them lay
strong federal defenses at Gómez Palacio, to which they now lay
siege; each day Ángeles pounded shell after shell into the enemy
positions, and each night the sickly smell of scorching flesh drifted
back over the lines as the federals burned their dead.[1]

Zapata reckoned his siege of Chilpancingo should last twelve
days. In the event the end came three days earlier, on March 23,
when the subordinate Guerrero chief Encarnación Díaz found he
could curb his impatience no longer and led his troops forward in
attack. Others followed in the wake of his charge, and the revolutionaries battered through the federal lines. Soon after dawn the
next day, March 24, the first cheering rebels reached the city center and tore down the federal flag from the municipal buildings.
"The fall of Chilpancingo," wired the American consul, Edwards,
to Washington, "was the result of the most decisive action yet
fought in this region."[2]

Cartón and forty-three officers managed to flee from the city
with about 600 men. Revolutionaries under Blanco and Ignacio
Maya hurried after them in pursuit. Night allowed the federal commander to escape farther down the road south, but next day he
found himself surrounded at the village of El Rincón about forty
miles from Chilpancingo. Cartón surrendered. The terrified federal troops found their captors to be lenient: they were merely told
to hand over their weapons, and then they were set free. Many
immediately joined the revolution. But Cartón and his officers received far stiffer treatment: they were taken to Zapata's headquarters at Tixtla, where the revolutionary leader decided they should
be court-martialed. The trials took place during the next week;
some officers were released, but those identified as having helped
with the burning of villages in Morelos were sentenced to death.
Firing squads took up position in Chilpancingo's public square and
the executions began. On the morning of April 6 the "victor" of
Huautla, General Cartón, was led out and shot.

Already Zapata had started to take his next steps in his campaign. And as he organized his forces and issued fresh orders from Tixtla, he received excellent reports from the north. Villa took Gómez Palacio on March 26, although at fearful cost of nearly 1,000 dead and 3,000 wounded in the three days of battle; he entered Torreón on April 2 after the federal commander skillfully withdrew his men under cover of a dust storm. Villa's troops were weary and hungry; no food could be found locally, and in Torreón the civilians dredged through horse manure in the streets to find partially digested grain for tortillas. But Villa pressed on toward the next federal strongpoint at San Pedro de las Colonias, helped by fresh supplies of military equipment from over the American border.[3]

While Villa maintained his threat in the north, Zapata rode back into Morelos to direct the southern operations. He took with him all the weapons and ammunition captured at Chilpancingo and El Rincón, but these soon proved insufficient for the size of campaign now being conducted. Some of these precious stores had to be dispatched to the Guerrero revolutionary companies: Blanco threatened Acapulco and Salgado thrust north from Chilpancingo to take Iguala on April 8, and both urgently required more matériel to keep up their pressure. Zapata, operating from headquarters at Tlaltizapán, anxiously watched his stocks dwindle. The greater the success, the greater the requirements to maintain the offensive, and one victory followed another. During these hectic days of early April de la O probed into southern Mexico state, and Mendoza and Eufemio Zapata raided far and wide in southeastern Morelos and Puebla, gradually spreading north toward Cuernavaca. The state capital still held out, but by the middle of the month Zapata's forces controlled the majority of small towns in Morelos and were constantly attacking the district seats.

Panic reached new heights in Cuernavaca; the remaining wealthy citizens stabled horses and mules hidden in upstairs rooms, ready for flight. "We found ourselves more and more shut off from the outside world," wrote Mrs. King. "The telegraph wires were down and the continual destruction of sections of the railroad track interrupted the running of the trains while the track was being mended. Newspapers and magazines seldom reached us."[4] But for the moment the city remained safe. Zapata's lack of ammunition increasingly crippled his campaign; frustrated and desperately seeking more supplies, he still planned his drive on Mexico City itself, but lacking arms and ammunition he constantly had to delay this ultimate march forward. His letter to Vázquez Gómez in Washington, sent on October 24 and asking this exile to obtain a loan to buy ammunition, brought no response; similar lack of success resulted from Zapata's effort to negotiate with John Lind, President Wilson's special envoy to Mexico, who returned to the United States in early April. Lind told Zapata to seek charity from the Red Cross.[5]

Villa, on America's doorstep, fared better. His area of operations included the vast cattle ranches and cotton plantations, the produce of which could be exchanged for equipment from the American munitions dealers. On April 15 Villa's forces entered San Pedro de las Colonias, after the two federal commanders in the town quarreled and one withdrew with his troops in a fit of temper. But then even Villa had to pause and rest. "Some of our horses had carried saddles so long," he reported, "that their blankets were stuck to their backs." Yet the pressure on Huerta remained: beyond Villa's position the road to Mexico City lay open, and other Constitutionalist forces were also reporting their successes. Taking advantage of Huerta's preoccupation with Villa, Obregón's Division of the Northwest made swift progress down the Pacific coast, placing the port of Mazatlán under siege; in the northeast Pablo González pushed south toward the oil port of Tampico, reached on April 9. Carranza, the Constitutionalist first chief, established his headquarters in Chihuahua City. This opposition leader, upon whom so much would soon depend, remained a strange and almost eerie figure. "As our eyes became accustomed to the light," reported the American newsman John Reed, "we saw the gigantic khaki-clad figure of Don Venustiano Carranza sitting in a big chair. There was something strange in the way he sat there with his hands on the arms of the chair as if he had been placed in it and told not to move. . . . I noticed with a kind of a shock that in that dark room he wore smoked glasses and although ruddy and full-cheeked I felt he was not well. That tiny dark room where the First Chief of the Revolution slept and ate and worked and from which he hardly ever emerged seemed too small, like a cell. . . ."[6]

Suddenly, on April 21, all participants in the struggle—*Zapatistas*, Constitutionalists, federal—received a shattering shock. On this Tuesday the Americans invaded the beloved soil of Mexico. The news made Zapata's "blood boil," even though the American action stemmed from a similar objective to his own, to bring about the downfall of Huerta. Direct intervention came after two weeks of futile exchanges. The Americans had for many years maintained a considerable number of warships in the Mexican Gulf, with massive oil interests at stake in the area. On April 9 a party of sailors went ashore at Tampico, including their captain, in order to purchase oil for the gunboat *U.S.S. Dolphin*. But by now the revolutionaries under Pablo González were pressing in from the northern suburbs of the town; the federal commander in the town decided to hold the Americans, more for their safety than for security reasons, and after warning them of the dangers of being in this battle area, he escorted them back to their whaleboat. The commander of the federal garrison apologized for the incident, and considered it closed. Rear Admiral Henry T. Mayo, commander of the U.S. Navy's Fifth Division off Tampico, thought otherwise: he demanded a formal expression of regret from the federal commander, plus a promise that the American flag would be hoisted "in a prominent position on shore" and given a twenty-one-gun salute. Within hours the incident escalated. Huerta refused to order the salute to the American flag, adding that in any case the United States was demanding a salute from a government it refused to recognize.

Both Huerta and President Wilson believed the situation could be turned to their respective advantage. Wilson was joined at this moment by his newly returned emissary John Lind, who brought back with him from Mexico a grandiose scheme for a small raiding party to "possess" Mexico City. While this seemed far-fetched, the American President nevertheless considered that the Tampico incident had blown up at a most fortunate time, allowing extreme American pressure to be exerted on Huerta: on the afternoon of the 14th he ordered the rest of the U.S. Atlantic Fleet to Tampico. Huerta, for his part, believed the threat of foreign intervention might unite the dissidents behind him and his tottering dictatorship might be preserved. "Is it a calamity?" he declared when he heard the news of the U.S. fleet move. "No, it is the best thing that could happen to us."[7] Both Wilson and Huerta therefore remained intractable. The crisis rapidly deepened. Wilson declared on April 15: "For some time past the Mexican government has seemed to think mere apologies sufficient when the rights of American citizens or the dignity of the United States government is involved"; one member of his audience, Senator Chilton of West Virginia, responded enthusiastically to the President's tentative plans to seize Veracruz and Tampico: "I'd make them salute the flag if we have to blow up the whole place."[8] And at 11 A.M., April 21, the first boatload of U.S. marines approached the Veracruz dockside; by mid-morning the next day, the port was firmly in American hands at a cost of 19 dead and 70 wounded. Mexican casualties ran into the hundreds.

"Federal bullets will no longer spill brothers' blood," cried the newspaper *El Independiente* on Thursday, April 23, "but will perforate blonde heads and white breasts swollen with vanity and cowardice!" The intense wave of patriotism generated by America's violation of Mexican sovereignty threatened to fulfill Huerta's hopes: the country might now unite behind him against the *gringos*. From the opposite camp Carranza sent a warning to Washington: "The invasion of our territory . . . may indeed drag us into an unequal war," and one of his commanders, Obregón, announced that his troops were prepared to fight alongside the federals "until they have exhausted every effort to resist." Huerta attempted to reap the benefit by declaring: "In the port of Veracruz we are sustaining with arms the national honour." President Wilson further aggravated the situation by suspending shipments of arms to the Constitutional forces; on April 24 he authorized the mobilization of the regular army, 54,000 strong, and the 150,000 National Guardsmen. Throughout Mexico, American citizens ran the risk of being murdered; the American Club in Mexico City was set on fire three times; in Morelos, mobs roamed the streets chanting "Death to *gringos*" and burned down American property.

But two men refused to be diverted from the real purpose. "It is Huerta's bull that is being gored," commented Pancho Villa in Torreón when he heard the news. Similar reaction emerged from

Zapata's headquarters in Tlaltizapán, southern Mexico. Proposals from Huerta that the rebels should ally with the federals to repel the "pigs of *Yanquilandia*" were rejected by the revolutionary commanders in Zapata's area, and Huerta's emissaries never even reached Zapata's headquarters. Despite the anger he felt over the American action, Zapata reacted strongly against those who might desert the revolutionary cause. Two revolutionaries who turned pro-Huerta, Joaquín Miranda and his son, were tried as traitors and shot, together with Jesús Morales, who had defected from the *Zapatistas* at the time of Huerta's takeover and who acted as Huerta's go-between.[9] Both Zapata and Villa realized that the American intervention helped the revolutionaries, provided that the temptation by other rebel leaders to join with the federals could be overcome. George Carothers, the American consular agent attached to Villa's headquarters, reported to the State Department that Villa believed: "We [the Americans] could keep Veracruz and hold it so tight that not even water could get into Huerta. . . . He said no drunkard . . . was going to draw him into a war with his friends."[10] American occupation of Veracruz, Mexico's principal port, would cut supplies from overseas to Huerta; federal troops would suffer even greater overstretch in having to guard against an American advance. Zapata would have even less opposition in Morelos, and this weakening of the enemy's strength might compensate for his own lack of arms and ammunition.

Within days of the American occupation of Veracruz, Zapata issued fresh orders to his subordinate commanders. The southern campaign would be accelerated, aimed at pushing into the Federal District and to Mexico City if possible; the immediate target was Jojutla, to be attacked in early May. Zapata received fresh encouragement from news arriving from the north, where at least two revolutionary leaders were active: on April 24 troops under Pablo González walked virtually unopposed into Monterrey, the biggest city in the north; Villa in Torreón was preparing for an advance southward against the mining town of Zacatecas, the final obstacle between his army and Mexico City. At the same time reassuring reports revealed that the Americans did not intend to march farther inland from Veracruz.

By the end of April only two federal strongpoints remained in Morelos, at Jojutla and Cuernavaca. Troops from the rest of the state had been withdrawn or eliminated, and Zapata's justifiable confidence in his hold over the area was underlined by the fact that his headquarters were arrogantly situated between these last two federal concentrations. In the first days of May he directed his attention southward, to Jojutla, eight miles from his Tlatizapán base. Revolutionaries moving up from Puebla and Guerrero united with his own forces from the center of the state, until the besiegers of Jojutla outnumbered the 1,200 federal defenders about three to one. Zapata signaled the attack: the revolutionaries rushed forward at all sides of the town—none of the defenders must be allowed to escape with their arms and ammunition. Many of these federals were without stomach to fight, and the will to resist crumbled even quicker as the revolutionaries surged onward. Outlying houses fell rapidly, and the smoke and incessant rifle fire swept closer to the main garrison. Within four hours of the start of the battle the *Zapatistas* controlled the suburbs. Street by street they advanced. With escape virtually hopeless, and tempted by promises from Zapata that prisoners would be well treated, the majority of Huerta's unwilling conscripts threw down their arms. The last defenses surrendered or were overrun; only about 90 federals managed to sneak through Zapata's lines back to Cuernavaca—where once again they spread fear and disillusionment among the garrison. [11]

Zapata's men gathered up the captured weapons and ammunition and prepared for the next move. In mid-May they began to surge north, a vast column moving endlessly over the mountain tracks to the west of the Yautepec River and then following the railroad which snaked twenty miles through the hills to the state capital. But also by mid-May depressing news arrived from Villa's camp. Splits had appeared between the commander of the Division of North and Carranza. The latter arrived at Villa's headquarters in Torreón before the advance began on Zacatecas and Mexico City; the first chief now began to reveal that no longer would he sit idle: he intended to be leader of all opposition to Huerta, and he aimed to be Huerta's successor, ruling in whatever fashion he felt; and he would allow no rival to stand in his way. His first aim was to remove the risk of Villa's success overshadowing his own position. Carranza feared his hopes of becoming president might be thwarted if Villa occupied Mexico City before he could fully establish his political authority; Carranza therefore insisted that the Division of the North should turn aside and take Saltillo. Villa objected to this diversion, especially as Pablo González's Division of the Northeast was within easy reach of the town, but Carranza remained obstinate. Villa reluctantly obeyed his orders and began to move against Saltillo on May 11; the town fell on May 20, but the success only heralded further quarrels between the general and the first chief. The disputes became increasingly bitter in the last days of the month, and they threatened to disrupt the successful conclusion of the northern campaign.

By now Zapata's forces in the south were firmly positioned in the mountains around Cuernavaca. Before first light on Tuesday, June 2, his troops began to filter down these steep mountain slopes, probing along gullies and streams swollen by the rainy season which had just begun. The revolutionaries enjoyed plentiful cover from the rocks and ravines, cloaked with thick brush, and darkness covered this first predawn assault. Outlying federal positions were attacked and the defenders hacked down. Frantically the main federal defenses tried to fight back.

"Listening carefully," wrote Rosa King in Cuernavaca, "we could tell that both the cannon inside the town and those placed outside at La Herradura, the horse-shaped hill where I had always picnicked, were in action. The light crack of rifle fire was all about us. The *Zapatistas* were attacking Cuernavaca from all sides at once—a fierce battle, without quarter." Mrs. King, crammed with other frightened civilians in her Bella Vista hotel, continued: "This was real warfare and we were in the midst of it. Before, we had been on the outskirts. For four days and nights the fighting never ceased. At night Cuernavaca was an inferno. The *Zapatistas* had bombarded and destroyed the electric light plant outside the town, the officer stationed there to protect it having been too frightened to resist; and complete darkness was added to the other horrors. Hundreds of poor people had taken refuge in the Spanish monastery, and we would have gone there too, but the bishop sadly informed us that it was already overcrowded and there was no more room." Zapata organized his forces from his headquarters in the nearby foothills: he directed detachments from one sector to another, attempting to seize upon federal weaknesses. Around him the women were attempting to nurse the growing numbers of wounded, with most of these casualties caused by artillery fire. Still Zapata maintained the pressure, pushing reinforcements along the walled lanes which led over the rough ground to the smoke-shrouded city. "The *Zapatistas* were winning on all sides," wrote Mrs. King. "By Friday the government troops were very tired. Until then we had been comparatively safe, because the Bella Vista was located in the center of the town. But now flying bullets were falling in many parts of the hotel and we dared not cross the courtyard for fear of them."[12]

But General Romero, commander of the outnumbered Cuernavaca garrison, enjoyed the advantage of the natural defenses around the city—which had been the reason for the ancient Aztecs to site their settlement in this location, and which had encouraged Cortés to build upon their foundations. The deep ravines cutting around Cuernavaca prevented massive, all-out assault, and meant that the state capital could be held by relatively few men. Zapata pressed to the very outskirts, yet found it difficult to cross the last few hundred yards; the battle dragged on. Then, on the seventh day, Zapata suffered a serious setback. Huerta had already ordered Romero to fight to the last; now he considered the occupation of Cuernavaca to be important enough to warrant the dispatch of reinforcements, even though he could ill afford this further weakening of strength elsewhere; and, on Tuesday, June 9, about 2,000 men under Colonel Hernandez managed to force a way through to the besieged city. Federals in Cuernavaca rejoiced with relief.

"They were weary and battered enough," remembered Mrs. King, "but fresh and strong-looking besides our poor garrison; and the sight of them filled us with joyous confidence. They had come on foot from Tres Marías, high in the mountains, which was as far as the trains could go. The *Zapatistas* had made them fight every inch of the way, and it had taken them a day and a night to cover a distance which in peacetime is a three-hour walk. .. . ."[13] Yet this influx of extra men brought problems: food was already short in the city and now there were 2,000 more mouths to feed. "They were ravenously hungry, as it had been impossible to stop on the way for food," commented Mrs. King, "but the women of Cuernavaca were only too glad to scurry about and prepare hot food—such as still remained—for our deliverers." Under prolonged siege, the deliverers might precipitate the downfall of the city. And on June 10, twenty-four hours after the arrival of these reinforcements, Zapata ordered direct attacks to cease. His forces pulled back into the hills and settled down for a full siege: this would be conducted by a small proportion of the revolutionary force, while the remainder pushed onward; hence Zapata's instructions on the 10th informed commanders that all forces except rear guards would "continue our advance toward the capital of the Republic."[14]

The guns fell silent. People in Cuernavaca reacted with premature relief and without even trying to ration food. Mrs. King's account continued: "The shops, closed since the first day of attack, opened again and business was resumed. How good it looked to see the main street alive with people and the merchants' stocks spread out. . . . We deluded ourselves with the thought that our men had decisively driven back the enemy, but I can see now that this was not so. The *Zapatistas* had simply retired . . . and though they had withdrawn, they kept their ring about us like wolves waiting for the prey to weaken."[15]

As Zapata's main force embarked on its almost unimpeded advance from the state of Morelos, the revolutionaries in the north suffered further dissension. Hostility between Villa and Carranza reached a climax on June 13, when Villa resigned his command. Almost immediately he regretted his impulsive outburst, but Carranza looked upon the resignation of his chief rival as a godsend, and instructed Villa's senior officers to choose a new general. Ángeles, commanding the artillery in the Division of the North and Villa's right-hand man, voiced the officers' opposition in a telegraph to Carranza on the 14th. "We do not accept your decision. . . . We know well that you were looking for the opportunity to stop General Villa . . . because of your purpose to remove from the Revolutionary scene the men who can think without your orders, who do not flatter and praise you."[16] Politically, the future of the revolution seemed daily more dark. But the military successes continued. Villa took it upon himself to resume his command, and he moved the Division of the North toward Zacatecas on June 17 without bothering to consult Carranza; battle at the town rose to full force on Tuesday, June 23. By early evening all resistance had been overcome and the last federal obstacle before Mexico City shattered. "Later reports confirmed my estimate that out of 12,000 defenders of Zacatecas no more than 200 escaped," commented Villa. "They left us their cannon, their machine guns, and almost all their rifles. . . . As I contemplated the battlefield and the streets, the magnitude of the holocaust was visible. Those who came out to meet me, men, women and children, had to leap over the corpses to greet me. Besides the enemy dead many of my soldiers lay resting, sleeping in pools of blood."[17]

Also on June 23 an American agent in Mexico City reckoned an occupation of the capital by Zapata must be considered imminent. The Liberating Army of the Center and South proceeded steadily past the northern slopes of Mount Popocatepetl and by the end of the month began to cross into the Federal District. Ahead lay the town of Milpa Alta, close to Mexico City's southern suburbs. But Zapata still moved cautiously. Federal defenses on the outskirts of the capital would be strong, and his ammunition remained limited; his advance had to be slow enough to draw in all available revolutionary forces from Morelos. Even at this moment of fast approaching climax, Zapata's army remained composed of farmers and planting time was only just finishing. In the capital Huerta tried to weaken Zapata's offensive by offering to negotiate, but the commander brushed these approaches aside. Nevertheless, although Zapata remained intent on the complete destruction of Huerta, others might be tempted to compromise, and on July 1 he therefore issued instructions to subordinate officers: no declarations must be published without these first being cleared by central headquarters, "to avoid evil interpretations, disastrous deviations, and twisted intentions whose realization would damage the cause of the People."[19] Another reason existed for Zapata's caution: events in the north emphasized the danger of the whole revolution splitting apart at the moment of triumph, and these northern events made it increasingly likely that if Zapata attacked the capital, he would do so alone, without Villa's support. Pancho Villa lay immobilized at Zacatecas, a victim of Carranza's attempt to maintain authority as chief revolutionary. The first chief had diverted precious supplies of coal, needed to power the trains carrying the Division of the North onward to Mexico City. These coal stocks went instead to Obregón, now approaching Guadalajara, and to Pablo González near Torreón. González became entangled in a clumsy attempt to heal the breach between Carranza and Villa, and his own advance halted; Obregón, although taking Guadalajara on July 6, had still to cross the width of the country before he could attack Mexico City.

For a few days in early July an uneasy silence dropped over the battlefronts. Zapata hesitated to attack Mexico City unsupported; quarrels still hampered operations farther north. The whole country seethed with rumors and uncertainty. Cuernavaca experienced the horror of siege; daily the deaths from starvation rose. "I inquired twice," wrote Mrs. King, "and was told that twenty-seven had died one day and fifteen the next; after that I took care never to ask again, as I was powerless to give relief." Soon the inhabitants were reduced to eating weeds and *guayabas*—a hard, sour fruit normally used only for jellies. Then these too were exhausted, and the people only had sugar, which they dissolved in water to drink —"the sugar which had made the *hacendados* rich and wiped out the homes of the poor with its planting."[20] The monotonous beating of rain on the tiles wore on everyone's nerves.

Nerves everywhere were stretched tight during these last days. Zapata crept closer to Milpa Alta. And Huerta finally cracked. On Thursday, July 9, he began to prepare his escape, appointing Chief Justice Francisco S. Carvajal as his Secretary of Foreign Relations, and thus placing him in an easier position to assume the presidency. Within a week, on Wednesday, July 15, Huerta submitted his resignation to the Chamber of Deputies and fled to Puerto México in the Isthmus. He boarded the German cruiser *Dresden* on the 17th and sailed immediately for exile in Europe. Also on the 17th Zapata received his first news of Huerta's resignation, and his reaction proved simple: war continued unchanged. Huerta's appointed officials remained in power, and Zapata viewed Huerta's successor with especial suspicion: just over three years earlier Carvajal had been the Díaz negotiator with Madero for the infamous Ciudad Juárez treaty, which brought about the destruction of so many hopes.

"We will carry out no transactions with any government," Zapata told his officers on the 17th, "if it does not turn over the Supreme National Powers to the Revolution, without any kind of conditions."[21] Zapata elaborated this demand for unconditional surrender when he received revolutionary agents who had been hiding in Mexico City: these men expressed fears over Zapata's plans, and said many in the capital were anxious to persuade him not to storm and sack the city. Zapata refused to soothe their fears. Twenty thousand of his men would advance on Mexico City, he declared, and the capital would be occupied within three days; although his men would receive strict orders to respect lives and property, he would give no guarantees, and he would grant no political concessions. Zapata had received too many disappointments in the past, and his experiences taught him no politician could be trusted. The old ruling order must be completely rooted out; this time the revolution, and the peasants who supported it, must not be betrayed. On Saturday, July 18, Zapata's offensive for the capital began with a powerful attack against Milpa Alta. On the same day the last battle between the Constitutionalists and the government forces in the north ended with the capture of San Luis Potosí, the town used by Madero for the title of the plan which launched Zapata on his revolutionary career.

Now began a tense period of maneuvering for peace while Zapata continued to wage war. This time Zapata's stubbornness provided his opponents with valuable advantage. Carranza also declared he refused to compromise, but of the two leaders Zapata's reputation made him the man most likely to keep his word. Carranza, previously pro-Díaz and an ex-governor of Coahuila, was himself part of the old established order. Federal politicians therefore started their task of persuading Carranza to accept settlement, and while this persuasion took place they threw all available forces to the south of the capital to block Zapata's threat. The southern rebel leader, always independent from the Constitutionalist movement in the north and always the most determined revolutionary commander, emphasized his doggedness in an Act of Ratification of the Plan of Ayala issued on July 19. This statement, drawn up by Palafox and signed by Zapata, declared that the southern revolution would "always oppose the infamous pretension of reducing everything to a simple change in the people who govern."

Two revolutionary aims remained paramount, which Zapata and his chiefs pledged to fulfill "even at the cost of their blood and their lives." First, the agrarian provisions in the Plan of Ayala must be "raised to the rank of constitutional precepts"; second, the campaign would not be concluded until "the servants of *Huertismo* and other characters of the old regime" were thrown out, and a new government created "of men devoted to the Plan of Ayala, men who immediately carry agrarian reform into practice."[22]

The Act of Ratification destroyed Zapata's last frail chance of seizing victory in this new struggle for peace. By remaining true to his original aims, he showed himself completely intractable and uncorruptible. Milpa Alta fell on July 20, but stiff federal defenses still lay ahead; Zapata's army suffered increasingly from shortages of ammunition; the authorities in Mexico City intensified negotiations with the Constitutionalists in the north.

Zapata revealed rising suspicions of the Constitutionalist leader. He had long held doubts over Carranza's trustworthiness, and the first chief's recent behavior with Villa seemed to indicate the type of deviousness which might by employed. A *Carrancista* envoy reached his camp on the outskirts of Mexico City on July 28, to be told by Zapata that "all the revolutionaries of the Republic [must] recognize the Plan of Ayala." But on August 11, while the *Zapatistas* were still battering against the federal defenses, Carranza arrived by train in Teoloyucan, only twenty miles north of Mexico City, and started to talk with the enemy. Interim president Carvajal had already fled into exile on Huerta's heels. And Carranza's loud refusal to compromise failed to hinder him reaching a highly satisfactory agreement: Constitutionalist forces under Obregón would take over the city without bloodshed; the federal garrison would stay until the last moment—preventing the *Zapatistas* moving in first—and then these government troops would withdraw southeast toward Puebla, in Zapata's direction. Obregón insisted, however, that the federals must leave behind their arms and ammunition before their last-minute evacuation.

Authorities from the War Department surrendered the federal army to Obregón at Teoloyucan on Thursday, August 13, without even a *Zapatista* observer being present. Forty-eight hours later Obregón entered Mexico City, meeting no opposition; only at the last moment did the federals on the southern suburbs cease firing at the *Zapatistas*. Next day Carranza wrote to Zapata, arrogantly granting the southern leader a "personal interview" at some neutral place in the Federal District, between the Constitutionalist and *Zapatista* front lines. Zapata sent an immediate reply. He claimed the "triumph of the cause of the people, which you say has arrived," would remain insecure "until the revolution of the Plan of Ayala" entered the capital; he insisted that Carranza and the other northern chiefs must therefore sign this southern plan. He agreed to a meeting, but at a place of his own choosing. And the town Zapata selected for this confrontation revealed his recognition that Carranza's duplicity had brought the Constitutionalists to power in Mexico City, and that Zapata's own revolution had been defeated by its allies. "I recommend that you come to this city of Yautepec," wrote Zapata, "where we will talk in full freedom." By the time Carranza made his triumphant entry into Mexico City on Tuesday, April 18, Zapata had already withdrawn south, back into the mountains of his Morelos.[23]

9

• • • • • • • • • • •

Fractured Triumph

First Madero, now Carranza. Each time the rewards of Zapata's military success were snatched away from him by politicians, even though, ironically, Zapata above all Mexican revolutionary generals insisted that military matters should always be allied to political aims. If he had sought mere battlefield glory the result might have been different. Yet Zapata remained resilient. "Revolutions will come and revolutions will go," he warned a *Carrancista,* "but mine will continue."[1]

Meanwhile the country lay in turmoil. Carranza's troops blocked the *Zapatistas* from Mexico City and ran riot in the capital; *Zapatistas* kept jealous guard on territory won, surrounding and disarming a force of 300 Constitutionalists who strayed into their area searching for fodder. The troops were sent to the headquarters at Yautepec, questioned, and then set free, but the officers remained in custody as hostages.[2] Zapata had completed his control over Morelos when his troops at last entered Cuernavaca on Thursday, August 13, the same day that the federal army surrendered to the Constitutionalists at Teoloyucan. Morelos had been won for the revolution, but Mexico had still to be saved, this time from Carranza. "I will tell you in all frankness," wrote Zapata on August 21 to Lucio Blanco, one of the senior Constitutionalist generals, "that this Carranza does not inspire much confidence in me. I see in him much ambition, and an inclination to fool the people."[3] On the same day Zapata also wrote to Pancho Villa, who had departed for the northern area of Mexico to recruit men for the impending clash with Carranza. Zapata warned him that the first chief's ambitions were "very dangerous" and likely to precipitate another war, "for in no way will we revolutionaries who support the Plan [of Ayala] permit it to be mocked in the slightest."

Carranza sent emissaries in an attempt to win over the southern leader and talks took place at Cuernavaca in the last week of August. Zapata either absented himself from the meetings or sat silent while his officers harangued the *Carrancistas*. Manuel Palafox insisted that any meeting between Zapata and Carranza should be held in Morelos, not in Mexico City as the Constitutional leader now preferred, and that the southern movement, being the older, must take precedent over the Constitutionalist policies. Finally, Carranza's emissaries were detained in Cuernavaca for the moment, not as prisoners, but as hostages to secure the safe transit of representatives of Pancho Villa through Mexico City. These messengers from Villa conferred with Zapata on August 25, and were treated "with the highest consideration," according to Charles Jenkinson, the Red Cross agent at Zapata's headquarters. Villa's men took back with them another letter from the southern chief to their leader. "The time has come for a provisional government to be established," wrote Zapata, adding that this authority should be created by the revolutionary chiefs.[4]

Tedious discussions continued in war-battered Cuernavaca, where the *Carrancista* delegates found themselves in an alien world of scruffy, dirty peasant soldiers. Carranza signaled his refusal of the agrarian policies insisted upon by Zapata and his spokesmen, and attempted to strengthen his hold in Mexico City with plans for an assembly of Constitutionalists who would back his claim for the presidency. Zapata and his officers grew increasingly disillusioned and even more stubborn. Late in August the *Zapatistas* published a declaration to the Mexican people setting forth their case; this, written for Zapata by his young secretary Antonio Díaz Soto y Gama, came as an emotional appeal for justice for the peasants. The country demanded more than "vague utterances," proclaimed the manifesto. "It wishes to crush feudalism once and for all." The peasants were aware that "with elections and without elections, with effective suffrage and without it, with Porfirian dictatorship or with the democracy of Madero, with a muzzled or free press, their portion is bitterness. They continue to suffer poverty and humiliations without ending. . . ." The men of the south would continue to fight for the cause of the people, and would refuse to yield to the "false promises" of the Constitutionalist leaders.[5]

The manifesto exactly matched the feelings of the mass of the people in Morelos. To them Carranza appeared increasingly suspect. As the historian John Womack commented: "A senator in Porfirian congresses, a corpulent, imperious old man with a ruddy face, blue-tinted spectacles, and Boulanger whiskers, sitting in his saddle as if in a chair, Carranza was politically obsolete. Rebel and revolutionary he might now be, but in another world—an established and civilized world of clean linen, breakfast trays, high politics, and ice buckets for wine. . . . Morelos country folk acted through Zapata; and as they drew back from Carranza in disgust, distrust, and disappointment, so, as one of them and as their chief, Zapata drew back too. . . . In Morelos now allegiance to a man like Carranza was impossible."[6] Villa felt the same, and he received Zapata's letters with sympathetic agreement. On September 3 the northern general held talks in Chihuahua City with Obregón, leader of the Constitutionalist advance into Mexico City on August 15. The two men produced a nine-point plan designed to eliminate the danger of further war; Villa insisted, and Obregón reluctantly agreed, that Carranza should only be named as interim president charged with arranging presidential elections which would exclude Carranza himself.[7]

But Carranza showed no inclination to move out of the National Palace. On September 5 he provided the press with his official reply to Zapata's proposals: he refused to accept the Plan of Ayala or to agree to a further demand that a revolutionary convention be assembled to name an interim president. He affected a willingness to discuss agrarian reform, and invited the Army of the South to send a delegation to discuss this subject, but he would go no further. Meanwhile he maintained strong detachments of Constitutionalist soldiers in the former federal garrisons to the south and west of the capital.[8] Occasional shooting broke out between Constitutionalists and *Zapatistas*. The latter refused to give ground, and on September 8 Zapata continued to display his political defiance by issuing a decree from his Cuernavaca headquarters that Article 8 of the Ayala Plan should be executed. This referred to the total nationalization of goods belonging to "the landlords, *científicos* or bosses" who opposed the Plan of Ayala "directly or indirectly." Rural property taken in this way would be handed to *pueblos* who needed lands, or would be used to support orphans and widows of the revolutionary dead. Already the program had started in Morelos, with *Zapatista* generals or colonels supervising proceedings in the various districts; Eufemio Zapata, for example, presided at Cuautla.[9] The decree of September 8 seemed to indicate the breakdown of any remaining hopes for alliance between the *Zapatistas* and *Carrancistas:* on September 12 the American agent John Silliman reported to the State Department that further dealings between Zapata and Carranza were out of the question.

Failure also resulted from Carranza's attempt to win over Villa. The latter continued discussions with Obregón, often heated and almost violent, during September, and Villa found the Constitutionalist general increasingly useless as an ally: his suspicions of Obregón steadily rose. At the end of the month the Division of the North prepared to move south, against Mexico City, and on the 30th Villa issued a "Manifesto to the Mexican People," repudiating Carranza and inviting all Mexicans to join him in replacing the Constitutionalist leader with a civilian government. But Obregón and other senior officers still worked to avert full-scale war, and talks with *Villista* leaders at Zacatecas at the start of October resulted in an important decision: a full convention representing all elements of the revolution should meet in the town of Aguascalientes, 330 miles northwest of Mexico City, on October 10, aimed at restoring unity and to plan for Mexico's future. *Zapatistas* would be welcomed. The proposal cut the ground from beneath Carranza's own plan to have a Constitutionalist conference in Mexico City: this still took place, attended by 79 delegates, all of whom were Carranza supporters or personally invited by the would-be president, but the conference agreed to adjourn on October 5 and to reconvene five days later at the aptly named Aguascalientes— "hot springs."[10]

The revolutionary convention at Aguascalientes marked the last chance to avoid full-scale renewed civil war. On October 3 Zapata

refused to accept an invitation, but he nevertheless sent an observer and his contact soon grew closer. On the 12th, the third day
of the conference, General Felipe Ángeles proposed that a formal
invitation should again be sent to the *Zapatistas:* three days later
this former military commander in Morelos agreed to a suggestion
that he himself should go to Cuernavaca and persuade the *Zapatistas* to attend. He reached the Morelos state capital on the
evening of the 19th; next day, at noon, Zapata met his previous ad-
versary for the first time.

Ángeles, of whom Villa once commented: "He taught me there
was such a thing as mercy," was remembered in Morelos for his
humane and restrained methods in attempting to deal with his
counterinsurgency tasks. Zapata welcomed him cordially. Past differences were easily forgotten; the two men discussed the situation amicably, and Ángeles proved helpful. Zapata said he had been placed in
a difficult position. The assembly at Aguascalientes, with the delegates known as "Conventionalists" to distinguish them from the
Constitutionalists, was clearly important because it remained outside Carranza's direct control, and because only a minority of the
members seemed in sympathy with the first chief. Moreover, on
October 14 the Conventionalists had declared themselves the sovereign authority in the country: Zapata would have to either recognize this authority or fight alone with no support from other revolutionary groups, including Villa. Yet the conference had still to
accept the Plan of Ayala, to which Zapata was pledged, and until
this happened he found it impossible to recognize the assembly as
legitimate. Zapata explained his problem to the sympathetic
Ángeles: how could he present his case to the convention and persuade it to recognize the Plan of Ayala, without his prior recognition of the convention itself? He added that the *Zapatista* high
command would have to be consulted before any decision could be
reached; accordingly a top-level *Zapatista* conference began at
Cuernavaca on October 22. Ángeles spoke most, and he displayed
all his urbanity and diplomacy: he felt sure that a compromise
could be reached between the Conventionalists and, in his careful
words, "the faction which we might call exclusively agrarian, sym-
bolized by the revolution in the south." The minutes of this meeting reveal the method adopted by Ángeles and the *Zapatistas* to

avoid the awkward question of recognition. According to the draft of these minutes the conference agreed that "it is necessary that . . . the Convention recognize the Plan of Ayala," but then the last four words were scratched out, and above them written this alteration "the principles of the Plan of Ayala." With compromise achieved, Zapata and his chiefs agreed to send a full delegation to Aguascalientes, and this 26-man team left the following day.

Zapata, still cautious and reserved, stayed behind in Cuernavaca. Leading the delegation was Paulino Martínez, the revolutionary politician whom the villagers of Anenecuilco had asked for advice back in September 1909; also included in the mission were Antonio Díaz Soto y Gama, the radical young lawyer responsible with Palafox for much of the drafting of Zapata's manifestos, and Gildardo and Rodolfo Magaña, both staff secretaries at the headquarters.[11] Much depended on the success of this delegation. Zapata's decision to send his men indicated at least limited recognition of the Convention, and benefits accrued from *Zapatista* attendance must therefore balance this partial loss of independence for the southern movement. Probably with this in mind, Zapata had planned an unexpected move aimed at bolstering his position. The delegation reached Mexico City on October 24, crammed into the same cars in which Ángeles and his men had traveled out to Cuernavaca; next day the *Zapatistas* boarded a train for Aguascalientes, where a reception party awaited them on the platform. But the train roared on without stopping, past the welcome committee, and not until the train traveled another 100 miles north did Zapata's delegation alight: at Guadalupe, headquarters of Pancho Villa. There the mission spent one day conferring with the commander of the Division of the North—"exchanging impressions." Villa seemed determined to adopt a neutral policy over the conference at Aguascalientes. He had taken his oath of allegiance to the convention on October 17, when his emotional speech to the members was rendered even more incoherent by his frequent outbursts of weeping, but soon afterward he had returned to his headquarters. Now he and his senior officers discussed the situation with Zapata's men, and the latter emerged reassured that Villa held the interests of the southern movement at heart; on October 26 the *Zapatistas* finally arrived at Aguascalientes.

The wary *Zapatistas* entered the Morelos Theater, venue of the meetings, and received a warm welcome. They seemed apprehensive despite the clapping and cheers: according to the Convention's recording secretary, Vito Alessio Robles, they looked like a troop of soldiers tiptoeing across a dangerous defile. The *Zapatistas* wore their normal clothing—skin-tight trousers, white shirts, huge sombreros—and some of the Mexico City gentlemen present tended to sneer at their peasant appearance. One politician, Martin Luis Guzmán, commented about Soto y Gama: "Anybody who did not know him would have taken him for the driver of a *pulque* wagon." But the majority of the assembly members were revolutionary soldiers, with whom the *Zapatistas* enjoyed an immediate affinity, and they soon responded to the atmosphere: the raucous shouts and interruptions, the highly charged emotion, the method of signifying applause by crashing rifle butts upon the floor. Speeches were sometimes punctuated by sudden pistol shots fired at the ceiling. Guzmán wrote: "I had only to take one look at that military assembly to be convinced that nothing would come of its deliberation. . . . It lacked the civic consciousness and the far-seeing patriotism that was needed at that moment. But . . . as a show it was a brilliant success. . . . At times the show provoked laughter; at times it left one perplexed and bewildered; at other times it produced its catharsis, for it was a tragedy in fact if not in form, with its fatal struggle between two irreconcilable forces."[12]

With the arrival of the *Zapatistas* the conference burst alive. By the time the morning session began on October 27, when the southern spokesmen were scheduled to speak, the *Zapatistas* had lost their hunted look and were full of self-assurance. Paulino Martínez walked to the rostrum amid the cacophony of rattling, thumping rifle butts and cracking pistols. He spoke well. He scorned liberal beliefs that magic words such as "effective suffrage" and "no reelection" could salve Mexico's wounds: action was required. The real needs of the people were not ballot-box slips, but "bread and justice." These could only be provided through the policies of Villa and Zapata—"Indians, both of them"—and only under the banner of the Plan of Ayala. "Land and liberty!" shouted Martínez. "Land and justice! With these the Plan of Ayala will bring economic liberty to the Mexican people!" Roars and massive cries of

"*Viva* Zapata! *Viva* Villa!" shook the building. Martínez continued above the cheering: the Army of the South did not struggle for special privileges or for riches, nor did it seek the President's chair. It fought for "a home for every family and a piece of bread for all those who have been deprived of their heritage . . . farms . . . land for all!" The Constitutional plans would never achieve these aims, he declared: the *Zapatistas* rejected Carranza as the chief of the revolution. Martínez concluded with an exhortation for the conference to embrace the only true program, the Plan of Ayala. Tumultuous applause followed Martínez as he walked back down the aisle, especially from the *Villistas*.

But then came the speech by Soto y Gama. This thirty-year-old always talked too much; previously he had felt overshadowed by Palafox at Zapata's headquarters; now, in the Morelos Theater, his opportunity to display oratory had apparently arrived. He seized the opportunity with an explosive and highly dangerous speech. He began by listing history's great leaders: Buddha, Jesus Christ, St. Francis, Karl Marx—and Zapata. Then his oratory carried him away from his prepared words. He suddenly seized the Mexican flag, so beloved by citizens throughout the nation and by those tough soldiers seated in front of him. Soto y Gama intended to point out that individual honor was more important than mythical honor to a symbol, but he failed to transmit his argument in simple enough terms for the delegates. His failure almost cost him his life.

"What's the good of this dyed rag, bedaubed with the image of a bird of prey?" cried the militant lawyer, crumpling the sacred flag in his fist. "How is it possible, gentlemen of the Revolution, that for a hundred years we have been venerating this silly mummery, this lie?" Murmurs of indignation hummed among the audience, and cries of "No! No!" came from the back of the hall. Soto y Gama recklessly continued. "We are making a great revolution today to destroy the lies of history. And we are going to expose the lie of history that is in this flag. . . ." Shouts erupted on all sides, drowning the lawyer's words; it seemed a fusillade of shots would at any moment riddle the arrogant young *Zapatista* on the stage. An eyewitness described the scene. "The members jumped to their feet, faces livid with indignation, trembling and shaking their fists at the speaker, who stood calmly in the tribune above them, awaiting the passing of the storm." The eyewitness, León Canova, continued: "The beautiful flag, which was affixed to the left side of the tribune, was snatched away and borne to the center of the stage while on the floor pandemonium was rampant. Delegates screamed at one another, with left hands pounding their chests, and right hands on their pistols. . . . The chairman was pounding the bell for order, but no sound of the bell could be heard. . . . From the crowded boxes and galleries of the theatre, humanity was tumbling over itself in a mad effort to escape imminent danger." Soto y Gama stood unmoved until the uproar died down, then he said calmly: "If you've finished, I'll go on." He refused to apologize, but maintained he meant no disrespect for the flag: instead, he had meant to show the importance of the Plan of Ayala. "For *that* banner . . . we men of the south have come to do battle!"

The *Carrancista* Eduardo Hay hurried to the rostrum to reap benefits from Soto y Gama's mistake. He picked up the flag and kissed the cloth gently, as if soothing its injured pride, a theatrical gesture which brought loud applause. Then he declared: "You, Señor Soto y Gama, if you want—you may come here to preach socialism. We have socialists here, but not those who simply talk. . . . Our socialists are those who can act without preaching about it. We know that our people will not be ready to listen to socialistic doctrines until they get bread and peace. Without these, socialism would turn into anarchism"—a reference to Soto y Gama's reputation as an ardent anarchist. Clearly, the convention suffered greater division than ever before: as Guzmán commented: "Two profound aspects of the same nationality were locked here in a death struggle." The *Carrancistas* ranged themselves against the *Zapatistas*, and the moderates among the audience were dismayed by Soto y Gama's display: here, they believed, was direct evidence of the erratic extremism which characterized these peasants from the south. But with the *Zapatistas* were allied the *Villistas*. One by one the officers from Villa's headquarters strode forward to defend Soto y Gama and the southern movement. "I am in accord," shouted one *Villista*, Roque González Garza, "with absolutely everything that Señor Soto y Gama has said. . . . I announce in the name of Villa that the principles of the Plan of Ayala are those of the Division of the North." Ángeles spoke up. "If there are any doubts about the matter, I should like to declare personally that I adhere to the principles of the Plan of Ayala. . . ."

Quarrels continued for the next four days: each faction claimed that it, and not the other, held the interests of the people closest to heart. The *Zapatistas* and *Villistas* denounced Carranza and declared he must go; Villa felt so strongly about this point that he had already said he would retire if Carranza agreed to depart in return. Back in Mexico City, Carranza seized upon this statement by the commander of the Division of the North, and on October 29 Obregón opened a sealed envelope just handed to him at the convention. Inside was a letter from Carranza. He agreed to retire— if this were matched by the simultaneous retirement of both Villa and Zapata; but he warned that if the convention failed to find "patriotic means" of solving the present problems, then he would rally all Constitutionalist forces to fight against "the enemies of the liberty of the Mexican people." The most massive uproar so far greeted this reading of Carranza's message. Fighting broke out in the theater as the *Zapatistas* showed their outrage that their leader should be linked with Carranza as a threat to the freedom of the people. Quarreling continued the next day, October 30, until the assembly finally managed to agree they should move into secret session. With the public removed from the balconies, the delegates voted overwhelmingly in favor of the retirement of Villa and Carranza: the latter still had a minority of supporters at the convention and less than two dozen now expressed their wish to keep him in power. The question of Zapata's retirement was left unanswered. Ángeles telegraphed Villa for his support, and the general agreed to go with characteristic emotion: "I propose not only that the convention retire Carranza from his post in exchange for retiring me from mine, but that the convention have us both shot."[13]

But the Convention's decision and Villa's apparent acquiescence failed to ease the confusion. Jumbled talks carried on into November. Carranza refused to quit his office, maintaining that the conditions he demanded for his retirement had not been complied with; Villa, in turn, intended to stay in command until Carranza had formally retired, and the roundabout continued to whirl closer to war. Carranza left the capital for Tlaxcala on November 1, and by the time the final session of the convention took place on November 13 most of the Constitutionalists had complied with his order to follow him into rebellion. These *Carrancistas* included Obregón, until now hesitant; on November 19 this able general formally declared war on Pancho Villa and organized his forces in Mexico City. He prepared to evacuate the capital and take the field; his troops moved out on November 20, commandeering trains, cars and horses.

Villa had written to Zapata on November 10 that "the time for hostilities has come," and the northern general now received the appointment as commander-in-chief of the Conventionalist forces. The nominal political head of these anti-Constitutionalists was Eulalio Gutiérrez, chosen by the Convention on November 2 as presidential candidate in place of Carranza. Nicknamed by the *Zapatistas* as *el presidente accidental*, Gutiérrez enjoyed acceptable qualifications to be political leader: a former fisherman, stevedore, shopkeeper, and small-time lawyer, who had displayed bravery in the revolutionary fighting as a dynamiter of "inventive capacities." But he totally lacked political experience. Turmoil continued in the north as both sides began maneuvering for conflict. The Conventionalists surged forward to occupy Mexico City as a base. Carranza obtained his base through the courtesy of the United States government. With Huerta gone, the last flimsy pretext had departed for the Americans holding on to Veracruz, and early on November 23 evacuation from this valuable port began. Carranza moved eastward, preparing to move in.

While this shuffling for position took place, Zapata packed up his headquarters in Cuernavaca. He rode northward with his peasant army, in close correspondence with Villa and with the members of his delegation who had remained with the Conventionalists. Late in the evening of November 24, soon after the last Constitutionalists evacuated the capital, the first detachments of the *Zapatista* army entered Mexico City. At last they had arrived. But the entry, which should have been one of total triumph, was marred: instead of marking the victorious end to war, it merely opened the next round in bloody revolution.

10

• • • • • • • • • • •

Reluctant Rebel

No riotous celebrations accompanied the arrival of Zapata's sandaled army into Mexico City. These peasants from the south seemed overawed as they filtered into the capital; an eyewitness described them as "little brown fellows, with heavy cartridge belts buckled around their gaunt bellies and over their shoulders, and antiquated arms in their holsters." They stared amazed at the palatial buildings, and almost shuffled along the magnificent avenues. The bravest went into restaurants and ordered meals; most followed their normal rural custom and knocked on strange doors asking for food. One evening a fire engine clanged down the street, and some *Zapatistas* opened fire, fearing the machine to be a new form of artillery; they killed a dozen firemen.[1]

Zapata stepped off the train late on November 26, forty-eight hours after the arrival of his first troops. Like them he seemed subdued, and he savored no triumph. The collapse of hopes for peace and the prospect of war filled him with greater disillusionment than ever before. Having been disappointed so many times, now his natural suspicion ruled his emotions. He refused to go to the National Palace, and took a room at the small, dingy San Lázaro hotel, situated close to the suburban railway station of the same name, from which trains left for Morelos. Reporters interviewed him the next day, November 27, but were unable to persuade him to say more than a few muttered sentences. He remained in his room for much of the day, declining an invitation to attend ceremonies at the palace. Visitors found him unsmiling and preoccupied with his thoughts. Outside in the streets some of his troops were beginning to recover their buoyancy, especially when they discovered items in this alien world with which they were familiar, such as horses: one foreign lady, Mrs. Leone Moats, saw "a most disconsolate-looking bride and groom sitting in their carriage minus the horse, which had been led away by *Zapatistas*. They presented a thoroughly pathetic spectacle, poor things, marooned there in the middle of the main thoroughfare."[2] Pancho Villa stayed outside the city at nearby Tacubya, and talks between representatives of the two military leaders took place during the 27th aimed at bringing about the first historic meeting between them. But this would not take place in the capital: Zapata left on November 28, barely forty-eight hours after his arrival, reaching Cuernavaca the same day. His troops moved out of Mexico City soon afterward, before the approach of *Villista* detachments under General Ángeles. Agents of Villa had to travel through the mountains to confer with Zapata in his own territory; they tried unsuccessfully to persuade him to return to Mexico City. Zapata would only agree to a conference at Xochimilco, twelve miles south of the capital.[3]

On December 4 the two chiefs journeyed to this small market town, for an event supposed to herald a magnificent and overpowering revolutionary alliance. Zapata took with him his principal staff officers including brother Eufemio; other members of his family also tagged along—his cousin Amador Salazar, his sister María de Jesús, even his small son Nicolás. Pancho Villa rode south with a small escort of his elite troops known as the *Dorados*, the Golden Ones, because of the gold insignia they wore on their khaki uniforms and stetsons. Just on noon Villa and his men reached the town, which had been gaily decorated with streamers and flowers. "So many were the bouquets and wreaths," remembered Villa, "that our men could not carry them and our horses were walking on them while we rejoiced in our hearts." Zapata and his entourage waited for them at the municipal school. Montaño delivered a short but hearty speech of welcome, then introduced the two men; after a few polite greetings, formal and slightly stilted, Zapata drew Villa inside and up the stairs to a crowded first-floor room.

Present among the fascinated audience in the room were two American agents, George Carothers and León Canova, who had driven down from Mexico City early that morning: finding the town still deserted they had turned back again—only to meet Villa's group jogging down the road. Canova later wrote an extremely detailed dispatch for the Secretary of State in Washington which provided an illuminating description of the scene now taking place in the hot, stuffy schoolroom. Villa and Zapata contrasted sharply, noted Canova. Villa was "tall, robust, weighing about 180 pounds, with a complexion almost as florid as a German, wearing an English [pith] helmet, a heavy brown sweater, khaki trousers, leggings and heavy riding shoes." Zapata seemed from a different country. His skin was colored very dark, and in comparison with Villa his face was thin with high cheekbones; shorter than Villa, he probably weighed around 130 pounds. He sat uneasily in his chair, "his immense sombrero sometimes shading his eyes so that they could not be seen"—his eyes, said Canova, were dark, penetrating, and enigmatic. "He wore a short black coat, a large light blue silk neckerchief, pronounced lavender shirt and used alternatively a white handkerchief with a green border and another with all the colors of the flowers. He had on a pair of black, tight-fitting Mexican trousers with silver buttons down the outside seam of each leg." Villa seemed to wear no jewelry, but "Zapata wore two small old-fashioned gold band flat rings on his left hand." Canova's meticulous account also covered Zapata's sister, although he mistook her for Zapata's wife. "Everything she had on her person could probably have been purchased for about $5 American money. Her fingers were covered with the flat band old-fashioned rings, that looked more like brass than gold, of which she had more than a dozen." Next to her lay Zapata's son, curled up asleep through the whole conference and "clothed in a pair of loose-fitting white cotton trousers and shirt of the same material, home-made and badly made."

Canova enjoyed ample time to make these observations: for thirty minutes the two leaders sat "in an embarrassed silence, occasionally broken by some insignificant remark, like two country sweethearts." Zapata seemed to be studying Villa closely, but clearly these men of action found the going difficult. Then the desultory conversation touched on the subject of Carranza, and with this topic the conference came alive. "Carranza," remarked Villa, "is a man who is very—well, very insolent." Zapata suddenly sat straighter, nodding vigorously, and he exclaimed: "I've always said so! I always told them Carranza is a son of a bitch!" The two men poured out their mutual hatred of the Constitutionalist leader. Villa also attacked Carranza's followers: "Those are men who have always slept on soft pillows. How could they ever be friends of the people, who have spent their whole lives in nothing but suffering. . . ." "On the contrary," interrupted Zapata, "they have always been the scourge of the people." They found themselves agreeing on every point as they continued to slam the *Carrancistas*, the Mexico City politicians, the cowardice of supposed allies during the anti-Huerta fight, the lack of progress for the people. . . . Now, united, all would be different. Villa and Zapata became increasingly voluble, and, unfortunately for future harmony, Villa waxed overenthusiastic. "I have here close by the capital 40,000 Mausers and some 77 cannons and some . . ." "Very good! Very good!" exclaimed Zapata. Villa continued: ". . . 16 million cartridges and plenty of equipment. When I saw that that man was a bandit, I began to buy ammunition." The garrulous conversation went on with mutual self-congratulations and back-slapping. "I'm a man who doesn't like to fawn on anybody," confided the emotional Villa, "but you surely know that I've been thinking about you for a long time." Zapata rushed to reply. "And we too. Those who have gone up north, of the many who have gone . . . they have told me that things looked hopeful for me up there. He is, I said to myself, the only one I can count on. And so, let the war go on! I'm not going to make deals with anybody. I'll continue to fight, even though they kill me and all those who follow me. . . ."

Zapata turned in his chair and called for cognac to celebrate the friendship. Villa, a strict teetotaler, pleaded for a glass of water instead, but Zapata thought he was joking. He poured out two large tumblers full of brandy and passed one to Villa to toast "our fraternal union." Villa could hardly refuse. He lifted his glass and gulped. Canova watched the result with amazement. "Villa nearly strangled. His face contorted and tears sprang to his eyes, while he huskily called for water." Still spluttering, he offered Zapata the rest in his glass. "No", replied his host, "you go ahead and drink it." Outside a military band began to beat out a rowdy tune, drowning all conversation; Zapata rose to take Villa to a quieter, private room, and the two men went through the doorway arm in arm.

This second conference lasted ninety minutes, and seemed as successful as the first. Discussion covered practical military matters, and the two leaders decided upon a common strategy. The Army of the South was to drive on Puebla while Villa's Division of the North moved on Veracruz via Apizaco. Zapata mentioned his lack of arms and ammunition; Villa, still overenthusiastic about his own military supplies, promised to send sufficient to cover the southern needs, especially artillery. All appeared well. The formal discussion ended with a dinner and plentiful speeches, and Canova sent his dispatch to Washington: he saw evidence of a "good understanding . . . which holds great promise for the early establishment of peace in Mexico." Zapata and Villa agreed that their armies should pass in review in a joint occupation of Mexico City on the following Sunday, December 6.[4]

Rarely before had the city seen such a military spectacle as this formal occupation on the 6th. Parades began in the morning and lasted until five in the afternoon. "The people of the city welcomed us all with the greatest enthusiasm and affection," wrote Villa. "How the young ladies showered us with their flowers! They made a little basket of Zapata's sombrero until the bouquets bent the brim with their weight and overflowed." Zapata rode a superb white stallion and wore a silver-braided *charro* suit which glittered with silver buttons; this time Villa seemed determined to equal his partner's finery, dressing himself in an elaborate suit of dark blue and gold. "Hardly recognizable as the Villa I had seen on the border," commented Allen Tupper Wilkes, writing for *Harper's Weekly*. Wilkes described the "soldiers afoot in khaki and felt or straw sombreros, mounted soldiers in the most original of *charro* suits, wearing hats that were large to the point of being caricatures. Wonderful hats, some gold or silver trimmed. . . ." The two generals had themselves photographed in the National Palace, Villa sitting grinning in the presidential chair beneath the carved eagle of Mexico, Zapata siting on his left, staring at the camera in a self-conscious pose and clutching his twenty-gallon sombrero on his knee. Their men celebrated together in the city, and this time the bars remained open—the revolutionaries crowded into "pulque joints" with fanciful names such as "The Dream of Love," "The Men Without Fear," "The Emotions" and "The Early Mornings of April." The day ended with a banquet thrown by Eulalio Gutiérrez, the provisional president; next morning, December 7, the two military commanders called upon Gutiérrez at the National Palace to inform him of their campaign plans. The visit seemed no more than courtesy dictated: Villa and Zapata rarely mentioned the nominal political leader in their discussions, and clearly they intended to pay him minimum attention.[5]

Zapata left Mexico City on Wednesday, December 9. When they said their farewells he and Villa remained full of confidence: the campaign would now begin, with Veracruz the target. They departed to lead their respective armies, which would give a combined total of 60,000 men. They never met again. The bubble of optimism burst with shattering suddeness. Zapata's disillusionment had been lifted by his meeting with Villa, but hopes proved false again. Even on his way south from Mexico City, Zapata heard reports of ex-federal agents infiltrating the ranks of the revolutionaries, spreading distrust; once more the fine ideals of the revolution were being polluted. Even Zapata's trust in Villa received a shaking. Villa's promised artillery for the Army of the South arrived late, and only after repeated requests, and even then the *Zapatistas* had to haul the cannon through the mountains because Villa found himself unable to spare transport trains. Zapata was obliged to wait outside Puebla City while these guns arrived, and on December 13, during this delay, he heard reports of fighting between *Villistas* and his officers in Mexico City. Puebla City fell two days later, with the garrison abandoning their defenses and fleeing back to Veracruz, but to Zapata the victory seemed hollow. Hopes of firm union with the Army of the North, which had seemed so certain in the flower-scented schoolroom at Xochimilco, appeared worthless. "Our enemies are working very actively to divide the North and South," wrote Zapata to Villa the day after he entered Puebla City, "for which reason I see myself compelled to recommend that you take the greatest care possible on this particular." The formal language in the letter differed drastically from the jocular words spoken at Xochimilco; likewise, Zapata's next actions departed completely from the agreed plans. He abandoned the campaign. Not only did he decline to advance further, toward Veracruz, but he withdrew the bulk of his army from Puebla City despite its strategic importance.

Back went Zapata to Morelos. The year 1914, which had seen such triumphs and such disappointments, ended dismally. Zapata and his army seemed finished with revolution, for many reasons. To hundreds of *Zapatistas*, the goal had been reached: they had been to Mexico City, and had found it unpalatable; their world and their country was not Mexico, but Morelos, which they now ruled with Zapata their leader. They wanted nothing more than to return to their fields. Harvest time had come again. To Zapata, the accumulating reports of dissension between north and south, of dwindling cooperation, of quarrels, all amounted to a colossal burden of disillusionment which bowed him down. Zapata's behavior in December 1914 showed him to be utterly weary of war. He wanted to retire. He held Morelos; there he would introduce his own peaceful reforms. So, in the last days of the year, he rode from the stench of cordite and settled to live with his family in the tranquillity of Tlaltizapán, where green laurels cast cool shadows and where water rippled from the fountains and through the streams in the fields.

War raged around Zapata while he attempted, with success, to introduce social improvements in his state. Detachments of his army continued to fight, but he displayed only minimum interest in directing operations. Events in Mexico City justified all his suspicions: Villa squabbled with Gutiérrez, and by Christmas the provisional president had begun to negotiate secretly with Obregón, the *Carrancista* general at Veracruz. Villa hesitated to launch a firm offensive, and the Constitutionalist forces under Obregón regrouped to drive inland from Veracruz early in the new year, 1915. On January 4 they pushed out the remaining *Zapatistas* from Puebla City, while a second army thrust to about sixty miles of Mexico City.

Gutiérrez hurried from the Mexican capital on January 16 to escape both Villa and the approaching Constitutionalists, and after wandering from one point to another in north Mexico, he settled in the obscure desert town of Doctor Arroyo. He still claimed to be provisional president, but on the day of his flight from Mexico City the Conventionalists named the twenty-nine-year-old *Villista* Roque González Garza as their political leader. Confusion increased still further as Obregón approached the capital. On January 26 the revolutionary government under González Garza fled south to Zapata's own state capital, Cuernavaca. Two days later the Constitutionalists entered Mexico City. In the chaotic political and military situation both sides behaved with a rising frenzy of cruelty, and as always the innocent civilians suffered most. Mexico City experienced mounting misery, both from Obregón's harsh methods of attempting to quiet opposition and from the rebel blockade of food and water to the metropolis. By the end of February the situation had become critical. Bread and meat were exhausted: alley cats were sold for up to $10 American each. "It was a time of filth and pestilence," wrote Mrs. Moats. "The city was full of lice, and there was a terrific epidemic of typhus fever. . . . The poor people were absolutely starving. In her entire history Mexico has perhaps never experienced such widespread privation."[6]

The situation in Morelos seemed idyllic in contrast. Zapata still concerned himself more with agriculture than with armies, and he extended his influence into González Garza's revolutionary government, known as the Convention: Zapata's secretary Palafox became Secretary of Agriculture and intended to use all the experience being gained by Zapata in the Morelos agrarian reforms. When asked by a reporter if he intended to "study" the agrarian question, Palafox replied: "No, *señor*, I'll not dedicate myself to that. The agrarian question I've got amply studied. I'll dedicate myself to carrying [reform] into the field of practice." Palafox, with Zapata's full backing, organized commissions to study all areas of Morelos and define land rights for the individual villages: these teams worked quickly and efficiently, and eventually surveyed the boundaries of almost all the *pueblos* in the state, incorporating into them most of the local agricultural land, timber patches, and irrigation works. Zapata informed the Convention president: "The matter relating to the agrarian question is resolved in a definitive manner, for the different *pueblos* of the state, in accord with the titles which protect their properties, have entered into the possession of said lands."[7]

Never before had Zapata been so beloved by the people. Mrs. King spoke to some peasants and described their reaction to her questions. "I asked them about Zapata, and then, for the first time, I felt an eagerness, a kind of expectation stirring behind their guarded words. Little by little they brought out the tales of Zapata's prowess in battle, of his terrible just anger, and his goodness to the weak. . . . I told them, in my turn, what I had heard in Mexico City, that there was no leader in Mexico so popular as Zapata, since all men knew that he fought not for his own gain, but only 'that there might be the same laws for the poor man as for the rich'; and that when he was in the capital the people would have made him president, but he would not let them, saying he was not the man for the place. 'Como no,' they nodded gravely."[8]

Yet hostile propaganda still hid from many the truth about Zapata. Edith O'Shaughnessy, the American diplomat's wife, wrote in her diary: "Zapata has been the terror of every president—Díaz, de la Barra, Madero, and Huerta—for nearly five years. His crimes and depredations are committed under the banner of 'Land for the People,' and there has been a certain consistency about his proceedings, always 'agin the government'; but that he has, after these years of bloodshed, rapine, and loot, rendered conditions more tolerable for any except the rapers and looters, is most debatable."[9]

Whether he sought it or not, war inevitably swirled closer to Zapata. Detachments of his army still fought, especially south of Mexico City, where they were responsible for blowing up the water-pumping station at Xochimilco. This reduced the pressure of water in the capital to such an extent that supplies were available for the citizens only between five and six o'clock each evening: the water pressure was insufficient to flush drainage or work the sewers and the stench became overpowering. Moreover, a return to militancy was forced upon Zapata by a threat to his area—posed by the Convention President at Cuernavaca. Once again Zapata found himself in conflict with his own revolutionary leader, and this dispute obliged him to turn unwillingly from his peaceful agrarian reform.

His concern for Morelos, and his powerful activities within the state, led to a situation bordering on semi-independence for this rich section of central Mexico. As part of this independence, the *Morelenses* sought to obtain their own currency, rejecting the bills printed by the Convention in favor of crude but valuable coinage made from silver mines in Guerrero. On February 2 the Convention president decreed that the revolution paper money be accepted in Morelos. A quarrel soon broke out between González Garza and Zapata, with the latter objecting not so much to the decree but rather to the limited amount of Conventionalist currency sent to his area. In the first week of February Zapata left Tlaltizapán to visit Guerrero, but the argument continued.

González Garza had other reasons to feel discontented with the *Zapatistas:* once the Convention moved to Cuernavaca, where it held its first session in the Toluca Theater on January 30, the President found himself surrounded by Zapata's influence. The Convention itself became dominated by *Zapatistas:* these revolutionaries clamored for more money for their state, and quarreling spread into the assembly meetings. The *Zapatistas* refused to concede to the Conventionalists the right to levy federal taxes in Morelos and insisted upon control over their own affairs, including the running of the railroads; they complained that they were unable to take a greater part in the fighting, through lack of money and war material. In this connection Zapata wrote to Villa on February 20, asking for troops and ammunition to aid the campaign in the south; the letter failed to arrive at Villa's headquarters until mid-March, when the northern general's reply stressed the necessity of seizing equipment and ammunition from the enemy.[10] Villa remained above Mexico City, seeking to consolidate this area and to keep his supply lines open to the north.

González Garza attempted to resign on February 19, but the Convention persuaded him to remain in office. He looked upon Zapata and his chiefs as obstructive and unduly quarrelsome, and the criticisms had some justification. But Zapata's attitude stemmed primarily from his unwillingness to continue the wider fight and his preoccupation, as always, with Morelos. Only rarely during the entire revolution did his sense of obligation shift from his state to the country in its entirety; in these first months of 1915 his feelings of responsibility was focused down even further, from the state as a whole to individual Morelos villages. To him, the village system was of paramount importance: the state was composed of scores of village units, and these basic communities, each with its council and chief, must be given utmost respect and protection. If they flourished, then so would the state. They represented the people, literally at ground level. Thus Zapata told Lorenzo Vázquez, now the state's governor, that he must "maintain order and tranquillity in all the *pueblos*."

Zapata rebuked military officers who interfered in village affairs, and he limited his own involvement to enforcing decisions which villagers had already reached on their own. He remained far from the dictator in his own state, and even further from being a warlord. His opponents claimed that the state of Morelos lacked law and order, because Zapata refused to organize a state police: in fact, he insisted that law enforcement should remain the province of individual village councils, and this being so, a state police system was unnecessary.

Yet despite the exaggeration and lack of understanding displayed by his critics both then and later, Zapata was undoubtedly guilty of some mistakes. Preoccupied with progress in Morelos, he proved unable or unwilling to apply sufficient control over some of his subordinate officers, and discipline sagged in the sections of the army which continued to engage in military affairs. Two drunken generals quarreled on February 17, leading to senseless hostilities between the forces under their command; reports increased of petty pillage; on one occasion a mob of *Zapatistas* broke open the door of the Toluca Theater at the Convention in Cuernavaca, seeking to intimidate the delegates at the assembly.[11]

Obregón's Constitutionalist army entrained from Mexico City on March 10 and 11. Further occupation of the capital would be useless, and possibly disastrous in view of the rebel blockade; the *Carrancista* commander now made for Pachua to the northeast of the capital for a showdown with Villa. A cautious advance guard of *Zapatistas* crept into the capital as the enemy left. Zapata remained deep in Morelos, still largely unconcerned with the war, and his men in Mexico City displayed a lack of discipline hitherto unheard-of among the soldiers from the south: houses were looted and damaged and some civilians molested. The rebels turned the

Country Club into a barracks and used the ballroom as a stable; horses were also housed in the ground floors of the luxurious mansions on the Paseo de la Reforma, while peasant soldiers and their women dossed down in the rooms above; precious Chinese tiles were ripped from the floor of another ballroom, so that the barefooted country women could dance without slipping. But in general these liberties were no more than those practiced by any army of occupation: once again they received gross exaggeration by Zapata's enemies.

The Convention reconvened in Mexico City on March 21, with González Garza optimistic that he would now be rid of the *Zapatista* influence. He rapidly suffered disappointment. The *Zapatista* majority, led by Soto y Gama and Palafox, proved vocal and belligerent. But the disputes meant little to Zapata himself: once the Convention had departed from Cuernavaca and Morelos, it ceased to interest him. He stayed at Tlaltizapán while the quarrels continued and while, in the north, the armies of Villa and Obregón clashed in battle. On April 16 Zapata received a visit from Judge Duval West, on a fact-finding tour for President Woodrow Wilson, and West's subsequent report to Washington revealed a perceptive assessment of the southern leader and his motives. West found Zapata friendly, but considered him naïve and concerned only with the situation within the state boundaries of Morelos. The peasants considered him "as a saviour and as the father," but West predicted that "his influence will eventually be narrowed to the people in the country he represents." His political philosophy was simple to the extreme, so much so that it seems hardly surprising the sophisticated West believed it naïve. "He believes it is right that the property of the rich should be taken and given to the poor." Zapata saw no need for a rigid government or standing army: instead, all men should carry arms as they worked their village fields, and if the enemy should come, then the men would turn upon them and drive them away. West left with the clear impression that life to the Morelos leader meant the soil, the clean air, the mountains of Morelos. Zapata had admitted to him that he found it impossible to live in the city: his home remained among his people. It was to secure the soil and the free air for his people

that he had led the revolution; in Morelos, this had been achieved.
Let the rest of Mexico secure its freedom and happiness in the
same way.[12]

Even acutely depressing reports from the north failed to shake
Zapata from his lethargy for war. On April 6 Villa lost heavily
against Obregón at Celaya. He advanced again at Celaya on the
13th, vowing to teach his "perfumed opponent" a lesson. Both
sides gathered all available forces, 25,000 *Villista* troops and 15,000
Carrancistas. But the latter occupied deep-dug trenches surrounded by barbed wire and covered by machine guns; time and
again the *Villistas* rushed forward, and for two days the battle continued. Then Obregón counterattacked on the 15th, and routed his
enemy, who fled north leaving up to 4,000 dead. "Bodies were
strewn on both sides of the track as far as the eye could reach," reported an American, J. R. Ambrosins. Villa would never fully recover from the defeat.[13]

Significantly, a political row rather than this military disaster
stirred Zapata from his preoccupation with Morelos reform. On
April 30, largely as a result of charges brought by González Garza,
the Convention in Mexico City voted for the dismissal of Zapata's
protégé, Manuel Palafox. News of this ejection of Palafox from the
post of Agriculture Minister reached Zapata on May 2 while he was
staying at Yautepec; he immediately telegraphed González Garza:
"I will not permit you to continue molesting General Palafox. . . .
I am coming personally to arrange the matter. In the meantime,
you will take no action." Two days later, now at Jojutla, Zapata
wired again: he was "leaving today for the capital with all my
forces." The courageous Convention president rode out with only
one aide, to confront Zapata, and the two men met at Los Reyes;
González refused to be intimidated even when Zapata pulled out
his pistol. The president insisted that he, not Zapata, must give the
orders. Zapata continued to argue as they traveled on together to
Mexico City. But the southern leader stayed only a short while in
the capital: within hours he commandeered a flat railroad wagon,
rode his horse into it, and departed back to Morelos. He never saw
Mexico City again. Zapata and González Garza apparently reached
some secret compromise: although nothing was officially an-

nounced, Palafox continued to hold his office and so too, for the moment, did the Convention leader.[14]

Both militarily and politically the Conventionalist situation deteriorated into increasing confusion. Politically, the meetings of the Convention in Mexico City were hindered by continued quarreling and by growing anxiety as the Constitutionalist forces advanced toward the capital. Militarily, Villa flung what was left of the Division of the North against Obregón's forces at León on June 3. Obregón narrowly avoided death: a shell ripped off his right arm at the elbow, and the *Carrancista* general sought to speed his death by shooting himself—he raised his pistol and pulled the trigger. But one of his aides had cleaned the weapon the previous day and had forgotten to load it, hence saving Obregón for the great role he had still to play in Mexican affairs. Meanwhile his generals destroyed the remains of the Division of the North and the *Carrancista* grip on Mexico City rapidly tightened. On June 9 González Garza was replaced by Francisco Lagos Cházaro, a former governor of Veracruz, but the presidential post was now virtually meaningless. Carranza, still based at Veracruz, organized his forces for the final push on the capital. He formed an army corps of the east under the command of Pablo González, and this began to move forward.

Zapata stayed in Morelos, for the moment, although on June 18 he ordered "all generals, chiefs and officers . . . who are passing their time in Mexico City in theatres, *cantinas* and houses of ill-fame, to report at the front for duty." [15] Some obeyed and acted as bravely as ever. Southern troops under General Rafael Eguía Lis made a stand before the Gran Canal, fifteen miles from the capital; the *Zapatistas* suffered from a chronic shortage of artillery and ammunition, but they had managed to obtain five old guns, and fire from these halted González's advance. The *Carrancistas* were unable to rush the wide drainage ditch, and next day, June 24, the *Zapatistas* counterattacked in a torrential thunderstorm to drive the enemy back. But despite their bravery these revolutionaries were fighting a hopeless battle: poorly armed, badly supplied, they had to withdraw, and González resumed his advance on Mexico City. All remaining vestiges of law and order vanished in the capital; the Convention held its last meeting on July 7, González entered on the 11th only to pull out again six days later when he received false reports of a *Constitutionalist* counteroffensive. The rebels nervously reentered, but threw themselves back in their saddles with every stray gunshot or rumor of *Carrancista* troops, and they fired wildly at everything that moved.

"There were days on end when one could not leave the house," wrote Mrs. Moats. "It required only a rumor to cause the evacuation of Mexico City." "You may go out fifty times and nothing happens," commented the British author Charlotte Cameron, "yet the fifty-first time your life may be forfeit."[16] At last Zapata entered the campaign. He rode north in the final days of July and led 6,000 men into action against 1,700 *Carrancistas* northeast of Mexico City. But the intervention came too late and with inadequate supplies; his operation failed to coordinate with similar defenses undertaken by surviving *Villistas*. All the rebels were too weak in weapons and ammunition to hold out against sustained attack, and they especially lacked artillery. Zapata withdrew. González reoccupied the shambles of a city on August 2; the capital had changed hands for the last time. Don Venustiano Carranza took up residence in the National Palace as the stub of the Convention administration fled to Toluca. Villa struggled to find arms and men in northern Mexico, while the *Zapatistas* pulled back into Morelos and Zapata himself returned to Tlatizapán. He resumed the offensive in September but was still crippled through equipment shortages. Some successes resulted from lightning raids into the Federal District and Mexico state, and in late September Zapata even managed to capture the power plant at Necaxa which supplied electricity to Mexico City, but he found it impossible to consolidate his gains, and Necaxa had to be abandoned. The *Carrancistas* enjoyed far greater firepower through their modern weapons, and pushed steadily forward in both north and south. Villa lost one key town after another; to the south the *Carrancistas* began probing through the mountains and into the Valley of Morelos. On October 10 the Convention in Toluca finally fled in all directions. *Zapatista* delegates escaped to Cuernavaca and established a rump administration under the guidance of Palafox, but this amounted to no more than a pretense. The national revolution had collapsed.

It received the death blow on October 19. On this day the American government abandoned all remaining hope of finding an alternative to Carranza as the ruler of Mexico. Efforts had been made during the previous months to find a more attractive figure, but these constantly resulted in failure. Zapata might have found favor if he had been more ambitious and less concerned with Morelos; reports such as that sent by Judge West ruled him out. William Jennings Bryan, the American Secretary of State, believed earlier in the year that Villa was "perhaps the safest man to tie to," but now Villa's power had been destroyed. A conference on the Mexican problem opened in Washington on August 5, attended by representatives from Argentina, Brazil, Chile, Bolivia, Uruguay, and Guatemala, and these delegates accepted a proposal by Robert Lansing, Bryan's successor at the State Department, that all the "secondary chiefs" in Mexico should be asked to choose a government which would exclude factional leaders. Carranza rendered this impractical idea obsolete by defeating his enemies. He refused an American suggestion that he might receive recognition if he would "guarantee religious freedom, give amnesty for political offences, institute the land reforms which had been promised, give protection to foreigners and recognize their just claims." The Washington conference therefore faced harsh reality, and on October 11 the delegates announced that the *Carrancistas* constituted "the only party possessing the essentials for recognition as the *de facto* government of Mexico." America extended this *de facto* recognition on October 19. Even though *de jure* recognition would not be given until March 3, 1917, President Wilson took the immediate step of prohibiting all arms shipments to Mexico—except to Carranza. The United States policy was rapidly adopted by Britain, France, Italy, Russia, Japan, Germany, Spain, and the majority of the Latin American countries.[17]

America and most of the rest of the world were still intensely preoccupied by events in Europe. These months saw the creation of a new monster of war, when trenches scarred the fields of France and Belgium, when slaughter on an unprecedented scale erupted in Artois, Champagne, and Ypres. The Germans would suffer 612,000 casualties by the end of the year, the French 1,292,000, and the British 279,000. America had so far shunned military involvement, but intervention might soon be unavoidable. Wilson's recognition of Carranza was, in effect, a shelving of the Mexican topic so that his desk could be cleared for more important problems. But his decision, echoed so soon by the other Great Powers, seemed a sentence of execution to Zapata's revolution in Morelos.

Yet the fight would continue. Zapata was forced onto the defensive. His supplies of arms and ammunition, shortages of which had always hindered his efforts, were now rendered even more tenuous. Carranza enjoyed a steady inflow of modern equipment and his confidence had been boosted by the political recognition from abroad, realizing his claim to sovereign legitimacy. But despite all disadvantages, Zapata remained defiant. Never before had the odds been so great; his success in facing these multiple difficulties underlined his unique talents—and emphasized the tragedy of the subsequent events.

11

●●●●●●●●●●●●

The People Reply

Zapata must begin yet again. First he had fought with Madero, and then against him; then against Huerta; then in alliance with Carranza, and now against him. It seemed Zapata had a restless need for revolution. Some abandoned the struggle, answering an amnesty offer issued by the *Carrancistas* in August; others continued to fight, but with lack of enthusiasm and questioning the wisdom of further war. By contrast, Zapata's desire for conflict fully returned. In spring 1915 he had been content to watch war rage around him because Morelos could survive as the conflict continued; the state was an island in a sea of struggle. But now circumstances were altered. Morelos stood endangered, together with all the agrarian reforms which Zapata had introduced in the state. The threat must be removed. Carranza seemed a reincarnation of the dictators of the past, under whom Morelos had suffered so grievously; the new leader had totally rejected the Plan of Ayala. More than ever before Zapata considered the security and sanctity of Morelos to be of paramount importance, and he still sought no more. The same war went on, similar to the struggle waged by Zapata against Madero and Huerta and even the same as others had fought long before him. Mrs. King rightly believed she had "caught the rhythm" of the revolution when she wrote: "It was the long continuous movements of resistance, like a rolling wave that had swelled against Cortés and his conquistadores, and the greedy Aztec war lords before them; that had engulfed the armies of Spain and the armies of France as it now engulfed the *hacendados*. It was the struggle of these people for a birthright, to develop their own way, in spite of strangers who came greedily to skim the cream, and, ignorantly, to make the people over. And so silent and vast and unceasing was the struggle that it seemed to me as though the sleeping earth itself had stirred to cast off the artificial things that lay heavy on it. . .."[1]

But harsh practicalities had to be faced. One of Zapata's most immediate problems in autumn 1915 was to convince others that threats to Morelos continued to exist. Zapata remained in control in Morelos and the peasants lived in peace, even though *Carrancista* forces approached the frontier. Zapata had to organize for war, yet while internal peace continued in the state, support would be difficult to obtain, and without sufficient appeal his revolution stood no chance of success. This dilemma confronted Zapata while subordinate generals struggled outside the border to block the advancing *Carrancistas*. Especially active was de la O, who fought hard and well during December to drive back enemy forces pushing northward from Guerrero; by the end of the year de la O's units had battered the *Carrancistas* south to Acapulco, making a mockery of plans announced by Mexico City authorities on November 28 for a victorious campaign against the *Zapatistas* "right into their hideouts in . . . Morelos."

Yet Zapata knew the government pressure would soon be rapidly increased, and if insufficient people in Morelos reacted to the danger, the state would topple before adequate preparations could be completed. And on February 1, 1916, the government announced that 20,000 troops would be dispatched to join the 10,000 already assigned to the south. Six days later Zapata issued a desperate appeal to the people: "The fratricidal struggle staining the . . . Fatherland with blood" resulted from "the endless ambition of one man of sick passions and no conscience." Zapata hurriedly attempted to organize an army and to accumulate precious ammunition: a primitive munitions factory worked night and day at Atlihuayán hacienda, refilling shells and bullets and plugging them with pieces of copper cable stolen from Mexico City tramcars and power works.[2]

Then, in the latter half of February, the revolutionaries suffered a further setback, with a serious collapse in their command structure. Zapata's forces were still organized on a semiregular army basis. The total number of troops amounted to 20,000, with Zapata as commander-in-chief and with a number of experienced generals beneath him. De la O retained some independence, but worked closely in conjunction with Zapata. Among the most valuable *Zapatista* commanders were Francisco Pacheco and Amador Salazar, the first based on Huitzilac and the second at Yautepec. Both were able commanders: Pacheco, originally a local guerrilla chief in his own right, joined forces with Zapata early in 1913 and later became the Conventionalist Secretary of War; Salazar, a cowboy and hacienda worker from Yautepec—and Zapata's cousin on his mother's side—had started fighting early in the struggle for Madero, even before Zapata, and had joined with him in 1911. He commanded the Mexico City garrison during the Conventionalist occupation in 1915. Now, in different ways, Zapata lost them both.

Already, during late 1915, doubts had arisen over Pacheco's trustworthiness after it had been noticed that the majority of defectors from the *Zapatista* cause came mainly from his division, stationed on the edge of Mexico State and the Federal District. An unreliable commander in this area could cause disaster: his division would face the main weight of an invasion from the north. During January and early February 1916, Pacheco's troops lost a number of important strategic points; other *Zapatista* commanders, notably de la O, began to argue that he should be dismissed. Zapata, remembering Pacheco's past excellent record, seemed deaf to the danger and on February 20 even entrusted him with the secret task of attempting to persuade the *Carrancista* commander, General Pablo González, to switch to the rebel side. De la O discovered this attempt, although not Zapata's part in it, and his suspicions of Pacheco inevitably soared: relations between the two generals were already unsettled because of a feud between their native villages of Santa María and Huitzilac. Zapata attempted to reassure de la O, informing him on March 4 that the plan to contact González originated from headquarters "to discover the aims of the Carrancista General Pablo González and other chiefs who support him."[3] Suddenly, on March 13, Pacheco inexplicably retreated from Huitzilac. He withdrew south to Cuentepec, allowing the *Carrancistas* to advance as far as La Cruz before de la O managed to block their path. Zapata still refused to take action against Pacheco, even though the general's withdrawal had enabled the enemy to occupy positions only seven miles from the state capital, Cuernavaca. An imminent assault was inevitable: on March 18 González arrived in the *Carrancista* forward line to supervise the final plans. De la O raged about Pacheco's treachery, only to be told by Zapata on March 23 that he must refrain from taking matters into his own hands and shooting Pacheco before he could be tried. Zapata's request went unheeded: Pacheco continued to move south, only to be caught by one of de la O's patrols and shot. Zapata refrained from admonishing de la O, and in fact Pacheco's guilt was clear.

Zapata had lost one of his ablest generals; on April 16 he lost another when Amador Salazar was hit in the neck by a stray enemy bullet near Yautepec. The bullet killed him instantly, but he stayed upright in the saddle, his sombrero covering his face, and not until the huge hat slipped did his companions realize the general was dead.

The campaign could barely have begun in worse fashion for the *Zapatistas.* Confronting them was an army of 30,000, one third more than their own strength. The enemy commander had received instructions to defeat the rebels at all cost. Events elsewhere in the country dictated that *Carrancista* authority must be enforced in full, and as soon as possible. Far to the north Villa had made another bid for glory in the early hours of March 9, this time crossing the Mexican border to raid the American garrison at Columbus, New Mexico; he returned to Mexico with the Americans in pursuit. President Wilson asked Carranza to approve this punitive American expedition into his territory; Carranza replied that he would give permission, provided the right were reciprocal and subject to certain conditions. The State Department treated this as acceptance, and the American force crossed the frontier into Sonora on March 15. The farther south it traveled, the more the American action aroused Carranza's hostility. Fighting between his troops and the "invaders" might soon follow; Zapata must be defeated before this broke out—and a union between villa and Zapata prevented.[4] Urgent orders were dispatched to González, who established his headquarters at Tres Marías in the hills above Cuernavaca on April 27.

Zapata enjoyed only one advantage. A personal comparison between him and González left Zapata much the superior. González had the reputation of being totally incompetent, and his successes so far in his career had mainly come about only after the opposing forces had voluntarily retired, usually through shortages of ammunition. Carranza admitted to the Spanish journalist V. Blasco Ibañez that: "General González commanded the largest forces in the revolution and he came out of it with the unique honor of having lost every battle in which he was engaged."[5] Hamilton Fyfe described the *Carrancista* attack on Monterrey in spring 1914, which González directed in his usual fashion. "An enormous amount of ammunition must have been used. Yet only a few hundred men in all were hit. That . . . is typical of Mexican battles. If either side could induce its soldiers to use the bayonet or was enterprising enough to train a few regiments of Lancers, and if further, they could break themselves of the habit of sitting down after victories instead of following them up, the civil war could soon be decided."[6] This snobbish description remained true of González's methods—but not those of Zapata. Pablo González, a bushy-browed ex-pedlar who wore smoked glasses in imitation of Carranza, was in fact stupid and entirely unoriginal. Yet not even this disparity in skills could enable Zapata to defend Cuernavaca. González, floppy Stetson on his head, issued his orders from his headquarters in the dismal huts at Tres Marías, and by April 29 his troops held positions surrounding Cuernavaca. The city offered excellent defenses against infantry attack—but not against artillery, which could make use of the nearby hills to fire down into the houses.

Federal guns roared from these hills slopes to cause mounting damage in the state capital. Salvo after salvo exploded in the streets; Zapata abandoned the city late on May 1, but the bombardment continued. Soon after dawn on May 2 González supervised the final *Carrancista* artillery attack, and shortly after his troops entered the defenseless city. Similar rebel withdrawals took place throughout Morelos as the *Zapatistas* found themselves completely unable to offer opposition against vastly superior federal firepower. One town after another fell to the enemy as the *Carrancistas* concentrated their artillery and machine guns on the

flimsy defenses. Even more powerful weapons were used against
the peasants: for the first time the government forces enjoyed the
use of a biplane, which clattered over to bomb the *Zapatista* lines.
Its military value was exceeded by the terror it caused—few peasants had seen an aircraft before. "One day I went to the fields to
bring squash to eat," wrote a *Zapatista* soldier. "I went with another man and we saw something in the sky. What did we know
about airplanes then! We hid between the stalks and were afraid.
What thing was up there? The plane spotted some rebel lines
marching near Yautepec and dropped two big bombs. How we
were frightened! A few days later the government troops entered
Azteca and things were very bad. The *Carrancistas* finally drove us
out. . . ."[7]

On May 6 González reported proudly to Obregón, now Carranza's War Secretary, that the campaign had virtually been won in
Morelos. His boast seemed justified. Everywhere the rebels were
fleeing, disorganized, frightened, apparently a rabble. Zapata and
his best troops clung to their Tlaltizapán headquarters, to Jojutla,
and to a few villages, but throughout the remainder of the state the
Carrancistas seemed in firm, brutal possession. During May and
early June they daily surged further forward. By mid-June the enemy threatened Tlaltizapán, and this pleasant market town, which
had been so peaceful when Zapata established his headquarters
there the previous year, now took on a desperate, dying air. Zapata
tried to organize a last defense, but his position remained hopeless.
Federal artillery pounded the rebel positions and gradually Zapata's lines began to break; increasing numbers of his peasant soldiers turned and fled. "That's where I finally had it," admitted one
Zapatista. "The battle was something awful! The shooting was tremendous! It was a completely bloody battle, three days and three
nights. But I took it for only one day and then I left. I quit the army
and left for Jojutla, without a *centavo* in my pocket. I said to myself, 'It's time now I got back to my wife, to my little children. I'm
getting out!' . . . I saw that the situation was hopeless and that I
would be killed and they would perish."[8]

Zapata retreated with the remnants of his army, first to Jojutla,
then to Huautla in the farthest corner of Morelos. The villages he
rode through lay gutted, fields neglected; the wet season had come

again, and the rain spat and hissed in the glowing embers of burned homes. González and his troops stamped their authority on the state with increasing brutality. Mrs. King crept fearfully back to Cuernavaca from the safety of Mexico City, and her reaction to the sights she saw verged on hysteria. "Black, battered, bullet-pierced walls where had been comfortable, happy homes, bridges destroyed, approaches to the town cut off, everywhere signs of the dreadful conflict that had taken place." Her Bella Vista hotel was in ruins. She lamented: "My head had known it would be like this, but my heart was not prepared. We drove down the silent streets past abandoned, deserted houses: not a soul in sight. A dog, nosing in a heap of rubbish, slunk away at our approach, and the clatter of wheels awoke strong echoes in the emptiness. . . . I was sobbing, 'But there is no one here! Where are the people? Where are the people?' " Mrs. King wandered to the outskirts of Cuernavaca and stood weeping, almost delirious in her grief. She gazed miserably over the cobbled streets, over the ravine, and across the valley. "I looked across the wasted valley to the unchanging beauty of its slopes and the encircling ranks of its protecting mountain ranges. They were strong, steadfast, eternal—but so far away. Rebelliously I called to them, 'Are you dead, too?' Then voices came across the valley: voices of Toltecs and Chichimecans from their homes of centuries ago at the feet of the white volcanoes; voices of Tlahuicans from their ancient citadel, Cuauhmáhuac, where they had battled to hold their freedom and their country: voices saying, 'The very ruins all about you are telling you we live. Freeborn men, like their mountains, will always survive.' And the motionless foothills seemed to surge with the shadows of the men I knew lay hiding there, with their rifles and their leader, finding cover and nourishing herbs among the stony ledges."[9] And so Mrs. Rosa King, casting her eyes up to the hills in her anguish, discovered the undying essence of Zapata's revolution.

"We still kept fighting," wrote a *Zapatista* during the retreat to the south. "I would leave my wife in a nearby village and would go to join the battle. . . . There were heavy losses, men and horses too. Fleeing all the time! Yes sir, to the south. . . . The people were tired. They didn't want to fight any more." One dismal day Zapata rode up to the group to which this exhausted peasant be-

longed. "If you don't want to fight any more," he shouted, "then
we'll all go to the devil! What do you mean, you don't want to
fight?" No one answered. Zapata wheeled his horse around, as
weary as his men, and muttered: "Then there's nothing I can
do."[10]

Within days Zapata proved himself wrong. His technique of
quiet persuasion worked once again. Some of his subordinate commanders used more dramatic methods of rousing their men, and
they also seemed effective. One colonel gathered together a crowd
of tired revolutionaries and shouted: "Who wants to go with me?
Let's go and break up their base! Our situation is desperate. We're
at the state boundary. Where else can we go? Then let's go back!"
He pointed his rifle high, fired—and led the men on a defiant raid
northward as far as the hills above Tlayacapán, scattering federals
who attempted to oppose him. "He killed so many in Yautepec,"
commented a *Zapatista*, "they piled up like stones."[11]

Incredibly, by early July the revolutionaries began to rally
around Zapata to resume the offensive. Three reasons accounted
for this revival. One lay in the continuing appeal which Zapata held
for so many peasants, often amounting to worship. Under Zapata
the people believed in themselves. "It seemed . . . that a single
family had reunited there," wrote an observer of a refugee crowd at
Tehuiztla, southwest of Jojutla. "Everybody talks to everybody
else with complete confidence. People lent each other help, and
men and women who had never seen each other talks as intimately
as old friends." This eyewitness noted how the men hid their families in the mountains, in "inaccessible, unheard-of places," and
then climbed down from the hills "to dispute with the enemy the
land he was trampling over."[12] And the methods of repression employed by Pablo González overshadowed even those adopted by
Huerta and Robles Domínquez in earlier counterrevolutionary
campaigns—and they constituted the second reason for Zapata's
ability to gather his forces. The people returned to him in their
misery, more bitter and more determined because now they had
even less to lose. The eyewitness at Tehuiztla commented that this
village "presented the look of a fair, but a fair of pain and rage. People's faces were furious. They would barely mumble out a few
words, but eveyone had a violent remark for the Constitutionalists

on the tip of his tongue." The introduction of agrarian reform in Morelos during spring 1915 had revealed to the peasants the rewards of revolution, which were once again being taken from them by the federals.

Thirdly, Zapata's success stemmed from the form of war which he now adopted. As always, he chose the right tactical methods to fit the current situation. Faced by 30,000 well-armed federals, plentifully supplied with heavy-caliber artillery, Zapata abandoned all attempts to meet the enemy in full battle, and he reverted to guerrilla operations. Rather than deploying his forces in numbers equivalent to divisional strength, the *Zapatistas* were rapidly reorganized into units of 100 to 200 men, which could stab far and wide into federally held territory. These small detachments based themselves in districts where they enjoyed detailed knowledge of the local terrain; their low numbers provided them with increased mobility and security, enabled them to find provisions more easily, and reduced the number of discernible targets. The guerrillas were instructed to inflict maximum damage and confusion, using the minimum of ammunition.

The more González attempted to reap the results of his military success, the more he sowed the seeds of his defeat. His barbaric methods were introduced early in the campaign. On May 5, three days after taking Cuernavaca, González ordered every person in Morelos to hand over his arms under threat of "severest penalties" for disobedience; on May 8 one of his generals, Rafael Cepeda, shot 225 prisoners. The previous system of exiling *Morelenses* was reintroduced: by mid-May nearly 1,300 people had been sent north. In mid-June the federal troops ran riot in the laurel-lined streets of Tlatizapán, Zapata's former base, and 286 people were executed, including 112 women and 42 children.[13]

González proclaimed that his "supreme duty and decided goal" was to "re-establish order and work in the whole State," and he then proceeded to strip the state of all available booty. Vast quantities of loot flowed north: timber, crops, cattle, sugar, machinery, locomotives, paper, coal, copper, dynamite, tons of household belongings—even including Mrs. King's bathtubs from the ruins of her Bella Vista hotel. The federal troops, *los Constitucionalistas*, were better known as *los consusuñaslistas*—"the ones with their fingers ready."[14] Mrs. King, who noted that the federal commander sought to crush "his elusive foe in any way he could encompass it," complained to González over the deplorable situation in wrecked Cuernavaca. "This is no time to talk of reconstruction," he snapped. "The work of destruction is not yet completed. Will you not comprehend, señora—I am about to destroy what still remains of Cuernavaca!"[15] "According to his enemies," wrote Blasco Ibañez, "in his youth Don Pablo González was a peon in a factory at $20 a month. To-day he is considered one of the richest men in Mexico, both in real estate and personal property. How did he work the miracle? By becoming a General."[16]

Zapata and his guerrillas fought back with ever-rising fury as the violations accumulated. The Constitutionalists found it impossible to match their enemy's speed, nor to prevent them suddenly appearing in a totally unexpected areas to outflank or dart behind the main federal strongholds. These raids grew in scope and audacity during July and August. The guerrillas either struck like mountain lightning, disappearing back into the rains and mists of the hills before the federals could recover, or they came on against federal machine guns regardless of casualties. "The truth is they are devils," cried one *Carrancista* after a sudden, violent action. "Who can guess how many are dead? I didn't know what a volley really was. It's frightful! Are they dogs? If one fell, the others went right over him. We couldn't even take aim without trembling with fear."[17] Zapata organized the multiple operations from his Huautla headquarters: his chiefs took their men into every corner of Morelos—in the southwest around Tetecala and Puente de Ixtla, in the south around Jojutla, in the southeast around Jonacatepec, around Cuautla, in the area from Cuautla over to Yautepec, and down to Tlaltizapán, where Eufemio Zapata operated. De la O controlled his forces with customary skill and energy in the northwest and west, reaching into the Federal District, Mexico state, and right down to Guerrero. In early July about 1,000 guerrillas, an unusually large number, struck deep into the Federal District as far as Milpa Alta, almost on the outskirts of Mexico City; they withdrew back into the mountains after capturing valuable military supplies. Other victories soon followed: *Zapatistas* engaged the enemy for seven hours at Tlayacapa on July 16; 200 *Zapatistas* attacked

Tlaltizapán next day. . . . So the humiliations continued for González. On July 9 the federal commander issued a Manifesto to the Natives of Morelos, in which he warned he would "proceed with especial severity against all the state's *pueblos*" if the people continued to provide support for Zapata: the whole population would incur "the most terrible responsibilities" and would suffer "summary punishment without right of appeal of any kind."[18]

Zapata replied a month later with a manifesto urging the people to render even greater support; the declaration also condemned local chiefs who were avoiding the fight, describing them as "the cowards or egoists . . . who are content to live in towns or camps, grabbing from the *pueblos* or enjoying wealth they have obtained while others fight the revolution." As always, Zapata insisted upon strong discipline from his troops; he warned in the manifesto that he would weed out "chiefs, officers and soldiers who instead of fighting the enemy use their weapons to harm the citizens of the *pueblos,* and to steal from them their scanty means of subsistence."[19]

González's manifesto went virtually unheard; Zapata's received full response. Daily, fresh reports of ambushes reached the *Carrancista* headquarters in Cuernavaca: whole battalions of troops were pinned down by handfuls of *Zapatistas* hidden in excellent positions in the rocks above vulnerable mountain trails; attempts to pursue the guerrillas were almost invariably disastrous. Federal casualties averaged about 100 men killed each week, three times as many as the number in the *Zapatistas*, and scores of the *Carrancistas* deserted to the revolutionary cause. As in previous campaigns, the government authorities relied increasingly upon arbitrary conscription to fill the ranks, scouring the cities and countryside for manpower. "I know a Mexican General," wrote Blasco Ibañez, "who enjoys a great reputation among his admirers for his skill in raising troops. 'He takes to the mountains,' they told me, 'with one attendant and a few rifles. He turns up at the end of the month with 500 men. Give him two months and he will have 5,000, and so on till he gets his army.' "[20]

The only method of reply which González could think to use against the guerrillas was further repression. On September 30, 180 more inhabitants of Tlaltizapán were executed, of both sexes.

But next day Zapata revealed that his military campaign was being subtly altered, in a way even more damaging to the federal prestige. "There is not a single line of communications which it can be said is controlled by *Carrancismo*," declared Zapata in a public announcement. Immediately, he set out to prove his words. His aim was to stress to foreign interests, and especially to the United States government, that Carranza remained incapable of ruling Morelos. Three days after his manifesto, significantly titled "An Exposition to the Mexican People and to the Diplomatic Corps," his troops struck at Xochimilco pumping station which supplied Mexico City with water: the battle, reported the American *chargé d'affaires*, was "one of the heaviest . . . in months."[21] An even bolder raid took place a week later, when guerrillas attacked San Ángel, a southwest suburb of Mexico City. During early November railroad stock formed Zapata's principal target, and his dynamite men became highly adept at destroying this expensive equipment: on November 7 citizens in Mexico City were disturbed by a mighty roar just outside the capital—a train had been blown up, killing about 400 military and civilian passengers; similar attacks took place elsewhere on the fringes of Morelos, usually with appalling casualties.

By now Zapata's force had regained control over most of the Morelos countryside. The main fighting shifted to the frontiers— in Puebla, Tlaxcala, Hidalgo, Mexico state, the Federal District, Guerrero, and Oaxaca. Zapata seemed tireless; his base remained at Huautla, but he constantly rode from one section of the state to another, always appearing where least expected and where most needed. He finished any *Zapatistas* who misbehaved with civilians, and issued further orders on October 9 and 23 dealing with this point; he praised subordinate commanders who gave enthusiastic support to this policy; one, Fortino Ayaquica, received a special commendation on October 26 for ordering his officers to shoot on the spot any person caught in banditry or abusing local rights. González continued to be equally rigid, but at the other extreme: on November 11 he issued instructions that "anyone who directly or indirectly supports Zapata, or any other group opposing Constitutionalism, will be executed by firing squad with no further requirements than identification." Anyone caught on roads without a pass issued by the Cuernavaca headquarters would also be shot immediately, as would anyone discovered near railroads "without adequate reasons" or anyone not resettled in specified towns.[22]

Fighting dwindled in mid-November. The time for annual harvest had come again, and for a short while the guerrillas returned to their fields wherever possible. During these weeks the *Zapatistas* left the continuing destruction of the enemy to the diseases which swept the federal garrisons, especially malaria, typhoid, and dysentery. The latter was caused from eating fruits such as the mango: one *Zapatista* described how his local commander seized advantage from this incapacitation of the enemy. "He finished off practically all the *Carrancistas* of the north because they ate mangoes and got sick, and while they were stretched out Marino went in and just had to take aim and *zas, zas,* he finished them. That's why they named him General Mango." This peasant continued: "At that time, the peasants brought their mangoes to Yautepec. There was nothing to eat so the people ate mangoes. A detachment of *Carrancistas* was there, and when the peasants entered the city carrying their net sacks the soldiers took away their fruit and ate it. In a few days, *zas,* the entire army was shivering with chills, they were all dying of malaria. All of them! And what doctor was there then? What medicine? The streets were full of corpses and the women who followed their men in the army searched among the bodies to find their dead."[23] About 7,000 sick federal soldiers lay in the military hospitals or huddled in railway boxcars or screen huts because the wards were full. Occasional batches of morphine and quinine reaching Cuernavaca were resold on the black market to profiteers from Mexico City.[24] The horrors increased as the dry season grew more intense. The streets of the towns stank from the corpses and excreta; flies clustered thick; typhoid rapidly spread. Federal troops, already demoralized with victory apparently snatched away from them, slumped at their posts.

And at this moment Zapata struck. The harvest had been collected and the peasants took up their arms again. During the last days of November orders were issued from Zapata's headquarters, now back at Tlaltizapán, and on December 1 the offensive began. Simultaneous surprise attacks were launched against federal garrisons at Cuernavaca, Yautepec, Jojutla, Jonacatepec, Axochiapan, Paso del Muerto, Matamoros, Chietla, Atlixco in Puebla, and against a host of lesser targets. González had left the state for a brief leave in Mexico City; he was summoned urgently to the War Department, where the telephone lines from Morelos were jammed with frantic appeals for help. Time and again the wires crackled with last despairing messages from isolated garrisons as the *Zapatistas* swarmed over them. Jojutla and Trienta haciendas fell the first day, causing 500 federal casualties; other targets were taken the next day, December 2, and others were under tight siege. Guerrillas severed all rail communication eastward between Cuernavaca and Iguala in Guerrero. This time Zapata maintained the pressure. Brittle propaganda stories issued by González, still in Mexico City, were answered in the field by further *Zapatista* successes. The rebel took Jonacatepec on January 7, 1917; on the 8th they battered into Yautepec; on the 10th they took Cuautla. Cuernavaca fell during the next seven days.

"The nightmare of *Carrancismo*, running over with horror and blood, is at its end," announced Zapata from his Tlaltizapán headquarters on January 20.[25] He organized his forces for the final days of the campaign, concentrating them at the key mountain passes around the border of Morelos. Only a few federal troops remained active within the state; González managed to reach federal outposts at Tres Marías in early February, to assess the situation, but after three weeks in the mountains he hurried north again—taking with him the last federal garrisons. Morelos had been swept clean. González kept up a pretence during this spring of 1917, seeking more men and equipment for a proposed counteroffensive and feeding the federal newspapers with outrageous stories of *Zapatista* defeats. Then, on July 7, González admitted defeat: he received a two-month leave of absence to visit America "on a personal basis."[26]

12

•••••••••••

In Death, Victory

Victory over Pablo González heralded the beginning of Zapata's defeat. Morelos now stood free and defiant. But freedom was an illusion and defiance an empty cry on the wind. Zapata, the skilled military leader, knew better than most that military victories were insufficient, and that without political success the military triumph remained a hollow shell.

Zapata ruled Morelos; but Carranza ruled Mexico. Morelos could never survive indefinitely alone, and this was especially true in these months of 1917. The state lay crippled and exhausted, both through the ravages of war in general and through the policy of destruction instituted by González. "Never did anyone believe," wrote Juan Espinosa Barreda, a secretary at the Morelos headquarters, "that there would be ruffians who surpassed Huerta . . . *pueblos* completely burned down, timber levelled, cattle stolen, crops that were cultivated with labor's sweat harvested by the enemy." The peasants had been uprooted from their villages and their homes destroyed behind them. The village structure, upon which Zapata relied so much in 1915, was shattered. The plantations, upon which the life of the state had originally been based and which Zapata always saw as a vital section of the community, were in ruins and deserted. Weeds covered the fields; mills were gutted and the machinery looted or rusted. The peasants had neither their villages nor their previous places of employment, and the people starved: they clustered in miserable groups, bewildered and hopeless, and without the village system to help breathe life back into the land, the task of reconstruction was impossible for the state alone to handle. Morelos was bankrupt, and with no income to be derived from plantation production, finance would continue to be nonexistent. Zapata might rule, but his kingdom was a wilderness.

By comparison, Carranza's situation stayed strong despite the loss of Morelos. The flow of oil and mineral products to the Western Front in Europe, where the war reached a new intensity with each terrible month, brought in vital wealth. With this firm economic base, Carranza could afford to be generous, and as early as December 1914 he started to acknowledge the movement for agrarian reform. This recognition was contained in the Constitution of Mexico promulgated by Carranza on February 5, 1917. Article 27 of the Constitution undermined the revolutionary call for revolt by stressing the rights of the *pueblos* to hold land in common.

At last the federal government appeared to agree that the farmers of Morelos were entitled to what they wanted. "Ownership of the lands and waters within the boundaries of the national territory," declared Article 27, "is vested originally in the Nation, which has had, and has, the right to transmit the title thereof to private persons, thereby constituting private property. Private property shall not be expropriated except for reasons of public use and subject to payment of indemnity. The Nation shall at all times have the right to impose on private property such limitations as the public interest may demand, and the right to regulate the utilization of natural resources in order to conserve them and to ensure a more equitable distribution of public wealth."[2] This section of the Constitution coincided with the statement in Zapata's Plan of Ayala concerning nationalization, especially Article 9, "the laws of disamortization and nationalization will be applied as they fit." Differences between Carranza's Constitution and Zapata's plan rested upon the respective trustworthiness of the two men themselves. In 1915 and 1916 Zapata would have had no difficulty in persuading the people that Carranza must not be believed. But now his task was infinitely more difficult. The people were exhausted; moreover, the Constitution contained a clause which introduced a very important check on the President's power, thereby helping to remove fears that the new leader would merely be another dictator:

the principle of no reelection was established, specifying that at the end of four years the President would have to yield up his place. This, for many Mexicans, was the basic reason why the whole revolution against Díaz had been initiated so many painful years before.

Carranza wasted no time before holding elections under the new Constitution. These took place on March 11 in every state except Morelos. As a result, Carranza at last officially became president of Mexico, with the inauguration ceremony on May 1. Much still depended on Carranza himself, but however much Zapata might suspect and dislike him, he would experience mounting difficulty in persuading the bulk of the peasants to share his view. Carranza spoke from a position of economic, political, and military strength. Militarily, Mexico City was secure. Zapata's army hovered on the edge of Morelos, but lack of arms and ammunition prevented a large-scale advance. Moreover, the military situation in the north of Mexico now enabled Carranza to concentrate additional strength around his capital. The American punitive expedition which crossed the frontier in pursuit of Villa in March 1916 had remained in Mexico under the command of General John J. Pershing, but efforts to catch Villa were in vain, and the 10,000 American troops gradually returned toward the border. By early January 1917, agreements had been reached between the Mexican and United States governments concerning withdrawal, and this started on January 30. So ended this potential source of conflict between American and federal forces over the violation of Mexican sovereignty. Villa remained in being, but rarely managed to muster more than 1,000 men; he might threaten northern cities and even occasionally occupy towns, but his scope was extremely limited.

Carranza's consolidation of power reduced Zapata's ability to promote military and political aims for which the peasants could fight. In 1917 there seemed much less reason for war. Zapata's very success worked against him; in a sense, driving González from Morelos aggravated Zapata's problem—with the enemy gone, it became more difficult to hold the people together in a common revolutionary cause. Zapata struggled to prevent the disintegration of the revolution during these dreary, exhausted months of 1917 when the state suffered a severe feeling of anticlimax. His success proved limited. Signs of drastic splits rapidly grew, and especially serious were those in the upper hierarchy of Zapata's organization. Quarrels broke out between Palafox and Soto y Gama on the one hand and veteran field commanders on the other. One of the latter, Lorenzo Vázquez, a *Zapatista* since 1911, found himself outvoted by the two intellectual officers at the headquarters; he grumbled to Otilio Montaño, the schoolmaster who had been responsible for much of the drafting of the Plan of Ayala. Montaño showed himself to be sympathetic, and the two men discussed whether they should quit the movement. Matters reached a climax at the beginning of May 1917, when a revolt broke out at Buena Vista, only four miles up the road from Zapata's native village of Anenecuilco. Zapata ordered an attack on the mutineers on May 5, and he arrived on the scene himself with 10,000 men and with de la O providing support. The loyal *Zapatistas* stormed the Buena Vista hacienda and suppressed the main mutiny within a few hours, although isolated pockets held out in the hills for a number of days.[3]

Reprisals were sharp and potentially disastrous. The headquarters at Tlaltizapán announced on May 7 that the veteran Lorenzo Vázquez had been hanged for treason; Montaño, implicated by captured mutineers, was placed on trial at Tlaltizapán on May 15. Zapata left the town on the day his old comrade stood trial, wishing to be away from this painful episode, and he did not return until Montaño had been executed just before noon the following day.[4] Within a month Zapata suffered another loss, even more personal. His brother Eufemio had turned increasingly to drink in an effort to lift the depression he felt during these difficult days. In mid-June, probably drunk, he lost his temper with the father of one of his subordinate officers, Sidronio Camacho, and beat the wretched old man. Camacho sought Eufemio out in revenge and gunned him down in the street; he died the same evening, June 18, while Camacho fled north with his men and surrendered to the federals.

Other officers also deserted during these anxious summer months of 1917. Zapata's revolution weakened, and by mid-August he knew he could no longer stand alone. He began to make contact with other rebel groups in Mexico including the *Villistas*, in an attempt to forge a common revolution, but he failed to make progress. Zapata persisted, trying to lift the struggle from being merely the lost cause of one state: on September 1 he published a Manifesto to the Nation, which he asked Villa to sign. This declared that Carranza was a bogus revolutionary, and that the fight must continue for the basic aims "whose most concrete expression is the Plan of Ayala."[5] Villa failed to respond.

The federals replied with renewed military opposition in November. *Carrancista* columns pushed into Morelos from the east, still under the command of Pablo González. He urged his generals on, and the officer who proved most energetic was Sidronio Camacho, the ex-*Zapatista* who had shot down Eufemio Zapata the previous June. The federal battalions took Cuautla on November 19, and marched onward as the *Zapatistas* withdrew through lack of ammunition; Zacualpán, on the Puebla border, fell on the 24th, and the federals also occupied Jonacatepec. But then stalemate arrived, familiar to veterans of both sides: the guerrillas took to the hills and proved impossible to prize out, while the federals, with greater firepower, could not be dislodged from the major towns. The federal campaign suffered the usual demoralization as the guerrillas remained undefeated, and Zapata attempted to make use of the deadlock. In February 1918 he sent a number of proposals to Carranza. As a "preliminary base for any action towards peace," Zapata insisted on a ceasefire with the troops in their present positions, combined with a federal promise of civil guarantees to the villages and towns. In return, the *Zapatistas* would avoid attacking federal lines of communication and would protect tradesmen and officials crossing the lines. The *Zapatistas* would then negotiate to restore regular rule in the south. Zapata therefore continued to hope for semi-independence for Morelos, with his forces remaining in existence.[6]

Carranza refused even to reply. Zapata returned to his search for allies and now, in early 1918, this effort began to spread over into the international field. The Great War bled slowly to death in Europe; soon the Great Powers might resume their interest in Mexico, and especially the United States. In February 1918 an American arrived at Zapata's Tlaltizapán headquarters—William E. Gates. This archeological expert considered himself a spokesman of the American administration and a skilled assessor of the

Mexican scene. He hated Carranza and believed the Mexican President owed his position to the income derived from supplying materials for the war in Europe. Gates therefore delivered a strong warning to Zapata: the southern revolutionaries must unite as soon as possible with other factions, or it would be too late: Carranza would almost certainly fall with the ending of the Great War, declared Gates, and he warned that America would not tolerate renewed internal conflict in Mexico. "See that Mexico does not make intervention necessary for her own salvation." Gates added: "Mexico must not go on in self-destruction." "I don't want to hear it," interrupted Zapata. He believed the threat: either Carranza would unite all factions behind him to face the common enemy, America, or America would seize the nation's sovereignty. The only way to avert both disastrous steps was to forge alliance with the other dissident organizations. Zapata even moderated his aims in the hope of achieving greater success in the search for allies.

On April 25 a Manifesto to the Mexican People emerged from his headquarters, signed by Zapata: the statement made no mention of the original Plan of Ayala, and was clearly intended to appeal to all types of revolutionaries. As a result, the language was lacking in power and incisiveness. Revolutionaries should fight "to redeem the indigenous race, giving it back its lands and by that its liberty; to have the laborer in the fields, the present slave of the haciendas, converted into a man free and in control of his destiny through small property; to improve the economic, intellectual, and moral condition of the worker in the cities, protecting him against the oppression of the capitalist; to abolish dictatorship and win ample and effective political liberties for the Mexican people. . . ."[8]

Zapata relied heavily on Gildardo Magaña during the campaign for allies. Magaña, in his mid-forties, had joined the *Zapatistas* soon after the destruction of the Tacubayan Conspiracy in March 1911, to which he had belonged; paunchy, smooth-faced, yet persuasive, he proved an agile negotiator. He sought to contact possible moderates among the federals, including General Cesáreo Castro, commander in Puebla, and he delved into the complicated, intricate arena of political opposition to the president from within Carranza's own party. Magaña was highly adept: an intelligent, perceptive debator, with an acute political sense, he could discern

undercurrents and subtle political tendencies. Zapata, more ideal-
istic, plain, and straightforward, was totally unsuited for this work
and he allowed Magaña full authority to speak on his behalf, constantly urging him on to seek more openings. But even Magaña's
energy and talents failed to bring success.

And as Zapata received constant reports of these political setbacks, he also had to witness the suffering of his people. The harvest of 1918 turned out to be disastrous, largely owing to the ne-
glect which the land had suffered the previous year. The
countryside reminded Gates of the Belgian landscape ravaged by
war; he wrote later that it seemed like "Rheims and Ypres and St.
Quentin in the small."[9] No longer did the comfortable slap-slap
sound from the villages as the women shaped tortillas; children
stood pot-bellied and large-eyed in the deserted doorways; their fathers quarreled over the meager produce from the fields and jeal-
ously guarded the seeding of the next crop. The constant buffeting
affected Zapata's character: his reserved nature became un-
healthily withdrawn and he spent long hours brooding. "His normally taciturn character," wrote one of his young officers at headquarters, "became dark, crabby, irritable, somewhat raw-nerved,
to such an extent that even men in his bodyguard feared when he
called to them."[10] Another long-serving *Zapatista* broke down:
Manuel Palafox, once so quick-witted, now deteriorated to a nervous wreck.

While the miseries accumulated in Morelos, Carranza enjoyed
power and prestige in Mexico City. His promise of land for the
landless remained unfulfilled. And yet his behavior also revealed a
feeling of insecurity and fear. "When Don Venustiano receives a
visitor," wrote Blasco Ibañez, "the first thing he does . . . is to
back his chair against the nearest window. By this simple maneuver he places himself in semi-darkness so that his body becomes a
silhouette from which the face stands out like a faint white spot. In
this posture he cannot be observed closely, while he, on the other
hand, can scrutinize at pleasure the face of his visitor."[11] Moreover, under the Constitution which he had been obliged to introduce in early 1917, Carranza's term as president was limited, and
already an opposition movement had begun to grow. Alvaro Obregón, the one-armed general who had resigned from the post of

Secretary for War on the day of Carranza's formal inauguration, now showed signs of abandoning his retirement as a chick-pea farmer in Sonora. Obregón might provide the focus of a movement to which Magaña could attach the *Zapatista* movement. Blasco Ibañez provided this description of the potential opposition leader. "He is still young—not quite 40. He has a strong and exuberant constitution. You can see at once that the man is brimming over with vitality. . . . Obregón, with his short, thick neck, broad shoulders and small, sharp eyes . . . reminds you of a wild boar."[12]

Zapata wrote to Obregón in mid-August 1918, with the letter drafted by Magaña, urging him to declare opposition to Carranza. No evidence exists that Obregón replied to this appeal from his former enemy, but Magaña continued to hope that contact might be made, and distributed a *Zapatista* leaflet titled "A Toast to Alvaro Obregón." Meanwhile Carranza stayed in power despite the ending of the Great War on November 11. Ten days after the armistice Zapata wrote to Felipe Ángeles, former military commander in Morelos and afterward Villa's right-hand man in the north. Ángeles was in exile in Texas; Zapata knew he had been educated in France and had recently been in the country, and his letter on November 21 revealed how Zapata clutched at every straw. Would Ángeles use his "intimate friendship" with Field Marshal Foch, the French commander, to win "powerful moral influence" for the revolution?[13]

Daily, the suffering of the *Morelenses* increased. During the winter months of 1918–19 a Spanish influenza epidemic swept south from Mexico City, where the death rate had soared to 42 per 1,000, compared with 17.5 per 1,000 in the European capitals.[14] The peasants in Morelos, already weakened, fell in scores as the influenza hit them. Bodies piled up faster than they could be thrown into hastily dug graves. The population of Cuautla dropped to 170 people in December; only 5,000 remained in Cuernavaca; scores of villages seemed deserted. In Mexico City, the *Carrancista* newspaper *Excélsior* gloated in a headline on November 26: "Spanish Flu Continues Its Pacification Work in Morelos." The ranks of Zapata's army were decimated and his staff reduced by half.[15]

During these days of peak *Zapatista* weakness, the federals resumed their offensive. The start of the dry season enabled the roads to be used for artillery transport; reinforcements were rushed to the state boundaries and González ordered the move forward in mid-December. Over 11,000 federal troops marched into the towns of Yautepec, Jojutla, Cuernavaca, and Tetecala and into the outlying villages, where they found the peasants mostly fled, or dead. Officers reported hamlets literally abandoned to "the peace of the grave." Once more Zapata's guerrillas took to the hills; their chief issued another defiant manifesto on New Year's Day, 1919, calling upon the people to take up arms and throw out Carranza, because only then "will we again be the masters of our destiny."[16] A fresh federal push in January drove Zapata from his Tlaltizapán base and he established new headquarters near Jojutla, only to have to retreat again in late February, first toward Jonacatepec and then along the border toward Tochimilco. On March 17 Zapata signed a belligerent letter to "Citizen Carranza," in which he declared he appealed not "to the President of the Republic, whom I do not recognize, nor to the politicians, whom I distrust [but] to the Mexican, the man of feeling and reason, who I believe must be moved sometimes (if only for an instant) by the anguish of mothers, the suffering of orphans, the worries and anxieties of the Fatherland." Although probably drafted by his secretary, the letter perfectly expressed Zapata's feelings, not only in these first months of 1919, but throughout the last decade of revolutionary struggle. And within a tragically short time this protest would assume even greater significance.

"As a citizen," declared Zapata to Carranza, "as a human being with the right to think and speak out; as a peasant knowing the necessities of the humble people to whom I belong; as a revolutionary . . . who has had an opportunity to know the national soul . . . with its miseries and hopes . . . I address myself to you. Since you first had the idea of rebelling . . . since you first conceived the project of making yourself Chief and Director of the misnamed 'Constitutionalist' cause, you . . . have tried to convert the revolution into a movement for your own gain and that of your little group of friends . . . who helped you get to the top and are now helping you to enjoy the spoils of war: riches, honors, business, banquets, luxurious feasts, Bacchanalian pleasures, orgies of satiation, of am-

bition, of power and of blood. It has never crossed your mind that
the Revolution was for the benefit of the masses, for the great le-
gion of the oppressed which you aroused with your preach-
ings. . . . Haciendas have been given or rented to favorite generals: the old landlords have been replaced in not a few cases by
modern landlords dressed in *charro* costumes, military hats, and
with pistols at their belts; the people have been rocked in their
hopes . . . nor have lands been distributed to the workers, the
poor peasant and those truly in need. . . ."[17]

Zapata therefore continued to identify himself with the peasants, and while he retained this union he remained virtually inde-
structable. He constantly insisted that his troops must show respect and orderliness, in complete contrast to the federals and
their commanders. "When asking for food you will do so with good
words," Zapata told his men in March, "and whatever you want,
ask for it in a good manner, and always showing your gratitude. . . . The better we behave, the sooner will we triumph and
have all the *pueblos* on our side."[18] No peasant sought to betray
Zapata; he obtained sanctuary wherever he wished. His guerrilla
organization had been perfected to such an extent that the hard
core could withstand all blows the enemy might deliver in a military campaign: Zapata's veterans displayed flexibility and resilience, against which the federals could not compete. Zapata retained the hope that Carranza's position might be eroded. This
hope received a powerful raise in January, when Gates published
an article in the *North American Review:* Gates attacked Carranza
and praised Zapata, declaring: "The Mexican Revolution (really
started by Zapata in 1909, before Madero) will never end until the
mountain peasants of Morelos come into their own. . . ." In turn,
Carranza received encouragement from an editorial in *The New
York Times* on March 18: "Order, the resumption of sugar planting, the sugar industry and agricultural work generally, the revival
of communications, education, and peaceful life depend in Morelos
upon the utter downfall, the permanent absence, or the extinction
of ZAPATA. . . ."

Now, in early 1919, Zapata's tragedy reached its climax. The
military stalemate could have continued indefinitely. Presidential
elections would take place in June 1920, and although Carranza

was unable to stand under the Constitution, his party seemed sufficiently strong to ensure his replacement by someone equally hostile to the southern leader: among possible candidates was General
González. Without the downfall of Carranza or his party, which Zapata could never achieve through military means alone, the revolution would never triumph. Zapata could introduce no new policy or
method which would enable the revolution to progress. He had
tried all means during the last years; each had brought him further
from success. He had instituted agrarian reform in Morelos during
early 1915, but only by attempting to ignore the war around him;
the war had overtaken him and he had thrown himself into the conflict again to remove the threat to the state; he won Morelos, but in
doing so ruined his agrarian revolution and the state now starved.
No matter how successful Zapata might have been, he could go no
further. His search for allies failed, and one reason for this disappointment originated from Zapata's own personality and reputation: possible allies only knew him as a man who refused to abandon his principles, an idealist, above all a military leader. Such a
person would ill fit a situation of political compromise and nego-
tiation. However skilled Magaña might have been, he remained
overshadowed by Zapata, and the very character of his leader hindered his efforts. Yet Carranza could never win total power in Morelos while Zapata survived: the guerrillas would continue to exist
as long as Zapata retained his appeal with the people of his state. As
The New York Times had declared, Zapata must be extinguished.

A half-breed Yaqui colonel in the federal army, Jesús Guajardo,
quarreled with his federal commander in mid-March. González
found Guajardo drinking at a local cantina after he had been ordered into the hills around Huautla to hunt *Zapatistas*. Guajardo
was arrested as a coward, even though this daredevil was well
known among the garrison for his boasts of wishing to meet Zapata
"man-to-man" to win the honor of taking the rebel leader. Spies
from Cuautla reported this upset to Zapata; on March 21 the agents
slipped back into the federal base with a note from Zapata to Guajardo, suggesting he should defect. During these days Zapata was
under pressure from his subordinates to exercise greater care, and
to retire into Puebla; Zapata had already refused to accept this advice, and now appeared to be going to the other extreme by allow-

ing his characteristic caution to slip. He seemed excited with the idea of winning over Guajardo, who was considered to be the best cavalry officer in the south.

Zapata's letter failed to reach Guajardo. General González ripped it open and read the words instead, and even this torpid general saw the opportunity offered. He immediately received authorization from Carranza for his plan, and on the evening of March 30 he summoned Guajardo to the officers' mess. He kept the young colonel waiting while he sipped his black coffee and talked casually with other officers. Then Guajardo was told to enter: to be accused by the irate González of being a traitor. Shocked and frightened, Guajardo took the letter waved before his face, and he read Zapata's invitation. González ranted at him unmercifully, driving him to tears. And then the general offered Guajardo one opportunity to save himself from the firing squad: he must pretend to accept the invitation, and lead Zapata into a trap. Guajardo hurriedly scribbled a reply to the rebel leader.

Zapata responded to this answer with another letter, sent on Monday, April 1. His aides at the headquarters still considered him to be untypically reckless, but Zapata seemed extremely enthusiastic over his scheme. "He was going with great vigour," wrote a young aide afterward, "with new spirit, like someone who knows he is going to complete a good job."[19] Zapata asked Guajardo to mutiny against his fellow officers the following Friday, April 4: first Guajardo must arrest a group of amnestied *Zapatistas* in Jonacatepec—these men, led by Victoriano Barcenas, had provided the federals with valuable help. Guajardo replied almost immediately. He agreed to the plan, but asked for more time, claiming he needed to obtain a shipment of 20,000 rounds of ammunition due to arrive in Cuautla on Sunday, April 6. Zapata showed impatience, yet nevertheless continued to declare his belief in the other's sincerity. Officers at the rebel camp pleaded with him to take more care, but he refused to listen.

The plan went into action on Monday, April 7. Zapata ordered rebel attacks to be made to divert federal attention during the day. Next morning Guajardo mutinied in Cuautla and marched out with his men. He reached Joncatepec on the 9th, occupied the town in

Zapata's name, and proclaimed his faith in the rebels. He arrested the band of ex-*Zapatistas* led by Victoriano Bárcenas; and then, contrary to Zapata's instructions, he calmly had these former rebels shot.

Also on this Wednesday, April 9, Zapata waited a few miles south of Jonacatepec at Pastor Station, a small, desolate railway halt. His group of guerrillas stood beneath sparse trees by the railroad, tense and increasingly nervous. The morning dragged by. Then they saw a rider hurrying toward them down the track from Jonacatepec: the messenger brought news of the events in the town. Zapata's spies reported rumors of a possible federal plot, but the guerrilla chief again pushed aside his normal caution. He sent word back to Guajardo: he must ride out to meet Zapata, bringing only 30 men with him—the same number as Zapatas bodyguard. Zapata even intended to welcome Guajardo himself, rather than staying in the background for better safety: six months before, such recklessness would have been completely rejected.

Throughout his career Zapata constantly urged caution. By nature suspicious, he had always felt his way forward rather than rushing headlong like so many other guerrilla commanders. Unlike many of these rebel leaders, he had survived so far. Now he acted completely out of character, against the advice of his aides, against the reports of his spies, although now, early this Wednesday afternoon, he admitted his suspicions had been aroused. They made no difference. His behavior can be explained in one of three ways: either he believed the prize to be worth the risk, or he still chafed against those in his headquarters who had recently advised him to retire and he intended to show he could still be active. Both of these reasons were hardly important enough to warrant the abrupt reversal of all Zapata's natural inclinations. A third possibility exists: that Zapata judged—correctly as it happened—that the revolution stood better chance of ultimate success with his death. His murder might break the stalemate by rousing the people, and by causing a wave of anti-Carranza feeling even among those who would never normally associate themselves with the *Zapatistas*. In this connection three interesting words are contained in Zapata's letter to "Citizen Carranza" which he had written on March 17: he said that he addressed himself to the ordinary Mexican peasant for "the last time," almost as if he knew he would be throwing himself into a situation such as the one he now entered.

At 4:30 in the afternoon a thick column of dust could be seen approaching from the north. Zapata's thirty men took up positions. The dust cloud billowed closer, and men could be seen, line after line of federal cavalry with Guajardo at their head. The colonel had brought 600 troops with him, plus a mounted machine gun, despite Zapata's instructions to limit the number of soldiers to thirty. Yet Zapata still welcomed Guajardo. He even embraced him. He suggested that they ride south two miles to Tepalcingo; Guajardo agreed, although both then and later he acted in a strained fashion. He refused repeated invitations to eat with Zapata and his officers during the evening and kept to his room instead, complaining of a bellyache. Later that night he requested permission to return immediately to Chinameca hacienda, ten miles east, claiming he wanted to protect his stores of ammunition stacked in the plantation buildings. Zapata still voiced no objections; instead he agreed to meet Guajardo at Chinameca early the next morning to discuss the next step—even though Zapata would travel deeper into federally held territory for this discussion at the hacienda. Guajardo left, and soon afterward Zapata rode out to spend the night in nearby hills.

Shortly after first light next morning, Thursday, April 10, Zapata rode toward Chinameca. The only added protection to which he would agree was a bodyguard of about 150 men, still far fewer than the force under Guajardo's direct command, to say nothing of other federals that might easily be in the area. At 8:30 A.M., with the sun already rising high, Zapata and his small force rode out of the hills and down to Chinameca, scene of Zapata's split-second escape from Huerta's men in 1911.

Zapata showed no sign of hesitation. He rode directly up to the hacienda, met Guajardo in one of the plantation outbuildings, and began discussions. Within minutes a report reached the two men that federal troops were believed to be in the vicinity. Zapata ordered Guajardo to guard the hacienda while he left with his men to investigate. No federals were found, and Zapata returned at 1:30 P.M. He dismounted outside the hacienda. Only Guajardo's troops were inside the walls, with the *Zapatistas* posted as sentries in the surrounding area. Zapata checked their positions, then accepted an invitation from Guajardo to enter the hacienda and eat with him. The time was 2:10 P.M. Zapata mounted a beautiful sorrel given to him by Guajardo the day before, named "The Golden Ace," and he heeled the horse forward through the main gate. He took only ten men with him.

Inside Zapata met Guajardo's troops lined up in neatly drilled ranks, as if a guard of honor. The bugler stepped forward and blew the call to present arms—three long notes. These sounded as Zapata rode slowly across the square, swung himself from the saddle, and put his foot on the first step leading up to the house. The third note ended. And at that moment the soldiers moved their weapons from the present-arms position, raised them to eye level, and fired. Two volleys struck Zapata at point-blank range. The black cloth on the back of his jacket jerked as if plucked by invisible fingers; he crashed forward, his face hitting the wooden veranda, killed instantly. Insufficient time had even been allowed for him to draw his pistol or to turn and face his executioners.

Zapata's body lay slumped across the hacienda steps as ear-shattering firing exploded from all sides. One *Zapatista* inside the building with Guajarda was killed by his host; two others, in Zapata's escort, died in the first moment, two more were cut down at the gate, and four others were wounded. The rest fled southward down the Cuautla River.

Even while this firing continued, Guajardo screamed at his troops to drag Zapata's body inside the hacienda: he needed the corpse as proof of his success. At 4:30 P.M. the federals hurried northward from Chinameca. Guajardo took back his prize sorrel, and Zapata's body was thrown across a mule, arms dangling on one side, legs lolling on the other. At 7:30, as darkness began to blur the outlines of the rising mountains, the federals reached the first small town—Villa de Ayala. Guajardo ordered a soldier to telephone the good news to Cuautla; he stood only a few paces from the point where Torres Burgos and Zapata had begun their revolution on March 11, 1911. The macabre procession continued into the night, winding less than a mile from Zapata's village of Anenecuilco. Just after 9 P.M. the federals rode into Cuautla, reining their horses on Galena Street by the central *plaza*. González almost ran to meet them; Guajardo ordered the ropes to be cut and Zapata's body slithered onto the pavement. González turned it over with his boot, clicked his flashlight, and turned it upon the face. The federal commander sighed with relief: the face, bloody on the bridge of the nose and above the right eye where it had smashed against the hacienda veranda, was Zapata's. The body was carried to the local police station, identified conclusively, and photographed for posterity with large white words scrawled across the snapshot—"*Emiliano Zapata. Mora.*" Emiliano Zapata. Dead.[20]

González ordered cameras to record Zapata's burial at the Cuautla cemetry two days later, Saturday, April 12. But many peasants refused to believe the shocking news; even a generation later some *Morelenses* still say Zapata lives. They swear they see him, on the back of a nervous horse up high in the mountains. Others accepted his death, but with even greater anguish. One typical villager summed up the emotion felt by thousands: "Ah! I was on the way back from Guerrero when the news of Zapata's death came. It hurt me as much as if my own father died! I was a *Zapatista* down to the marrow of my bones. . . . I had a lot of faith in Zapata's promises, a lot of faith. I did indeed! I was one of the real *Zapatistas!* I felt very bad. . . . I believed the news. Yes, I believed it right away. . . . They tricked him, that's what they did. They tried many tricks on him before, but he never fell for them. I guess his time must have come. . . ."[21]

His time had come. The time when the revolution would prosper better without him, when a wave of revulsion would wash against Carranza, when the peasants were united by Zapata's death. After internal wrangling, the diplomatic peace-maker Gildardo Magaña emerged as Zapata's successor six months later. Before this, on June 1, 1919, Obregón announced his candidacy in the forthcoming presidential elections, disgusted by Carranza's attempt to force his own nominee, Ignacio Bonilla, upon the people. Pablo González, passed over by his leader, announced himself as a challenger. And now Magaña completed the move started by Zapata and allied the southern cause with Obregón; support for the former general rapidly rose. Carranza hit back in all directions. In the north, his troops captured Ángeles early in November 1919,

and the general was executed on the 26th; Villa survived until riddled by assassins' bullets at Canutilla on July 20, 1923.

On April 20, 1920, Obregón announced from the *Zapatista*
stronghold of Chilpancingo that he was abandoning his presidential
campaign; instead, weapons would have to be taken up to "safe-
guard the virtues which the government is seeking by arms to destroy."[22] With Obregón fought the *Zapatistas*, his major source of
strength. Carranza fled from Mexico City on May 7, on board a
train of colossal length, crammed with loot from the capital, and
with thirty other trainloads of supporters following behind. He
lumbered toward Veracruz, came under increasing attack, and finally left his train and his booty to continue on horseback for northern Puebla. On May 20 he was killed by guerrillas at the squalid
village of San Antonio Tlaxcalantongo. Obregón had already entered Mexico City, on May 9, and with him rode the *Zapatistas*.
From now on they formed an essential part of the government, especially in the Department of Agriculture, and the administration
instituted populist agrarian reform as an essential part of national
policy. Obregón's government marked the seventy-third since
Mexico secured her independence less than a century before, and
these included the thirty-year rule of Porfirio Díaz. But at last
peace came to Morelos and to the *Zapatistas:* a peace which had
been hindered by Zapata himself, who sought only nonmilitary reform for the people yet whose continued presence would have
stood as a symbol of war.

"Though society defames us," wrote Zapata, "history will justify
our actions, when the new generations come to enjoy the fruits of
our battles, fought with our bodies and the tears of our women.
And this same society which attacks us today for our crimes will
cover us with blessings."[23]

Sources

Full details of all the books noted below are contained in the bibliography.

Chapter 1
SCATTERED SEEDS

1. Lewis 89
2. King 294
3. Lewis 87
4. Sotelo Inclán 138–43
5. Womack 7–8
6. Lewis 3
7. Womack 46
8. Palacios 20
9. King 33–34
10. Lewis 74
11. Womack 53
12. Ibid. 53, 39
13. Ibid. 63
14. Barba González 36–45
15. Womack 37
16. Ibid. 52
17. Lewis 462
18. Sotelo Inclán 179
19. Ibid. 182
20. King 3–4
21. Ibid. 39, 37
22. Calvert 105
23. O'Shaughnessy, *Diplomatic Days*, 74
24. King 59; Sotelo Inclán 217
25. Sotelo Inclán 217
26. King 59
27. Ibid. 60

Chapter 2
SEASON OF REVOLT

1. Lewis 76
2. Sotelo Inclán 218
3. Womack 60
4. Atkin 49
5. Ross 122
6. Atkin 50–51; Bell 61
7. King 61
8. Womack 70
9. Cumberland 125–26
10. Womack 72
11. Ibid. 76
12. Atkin 55

Chapter 3
REVOLUTION

1. Cumberland 121, 122
2. Magaña, I, 98–99
3. King 61
4. Magaña, I, 99
5. Ibid. 100; Womack 78
6. Womack 78
7. Almazán 19
8. Dunn 52, 53
9. Magaña, I, 101
10. Womack 84
11. Magaña, I, 111
12. Dunn 64

13. Ibid. 64, 65
14. *Archivo de Zapata* (Box 12)
15. Womack 87
16. Cumberland 150
17. *Times*, May 19, 1911
18. U.S. National Archives,
    812.00/1981
19. Womack 90

Chapter 4
BARREN HARVEST

1. King 62
2. Ibid. 66
3. Ibid. 63
4. Womack 95
5. King 68
6. Cockroft 187
7. King 70
8. Womack 93
9. Ibid. 79
10. Dunn 112
11. Moats 70; Atkin 78–79;
    Cumberland, 157
12. Magaña, I, 158–61; Cumberland
    173
13. King 68–69
14. Dunn 121–22
15. Womack 100
16. Atkin 85
17. Magaña, I, 164–65
18. *El País*, June 22, 1911

Chapter 5
RETURN TO REVOLT

1. Womack 107
2. Magaña, I, 205–06
3. Ibid. 247
4. Womack 105
5. Ibid. 107; Calvert 93
6. King 82
7. Womack 108–09
8. Sherman, 150; Meyer 220; Calvert
   108–09
9. *Archivo de Zapata* (Box 12)

10. Calvert 94
11. Taracena, *Madero*, 451
12. *Archivo de Zapata* (Box 14)
13. Taracena, *Madero*, 453
14. *Archivo de Zapata* (Box 13);
    Womack 114
15. Magaña, I, 219–24
16. Womack 118
17. Cumberland 180
18. Ibid. 180; Womack 119
19. Magaña, I, 311
20. Cumberland 180
21. Womack 119
22. Magaña, I, 245–57
23. Ibid. 257–58
24. Ibid. 258–59
25. Womack 121
26. Magaña, I, 326
27. Almazán 22
28. Atkin 110
29. King 88
30. *Archivo de Zapata* (Box 30);
    Womack 122
31. King 83–86
32. Womack 121–22
33. Ibid. 122-23, 394
34. King 86

Chapter 6
BETRAYAL

1. King 77
2. Womack 123
3. Magaña, II, 38–39
4. Atkin 88
5. O'Shaughnessy, *Intimate Pages*,
   137
6. Magaña, II, 65–66
7. Ibid. 66–68; Womack 125
8. Magaña, II, 67–78
9. Womack 126
10. Ibid. 400–04
11. Magaña, II, 80–83
12. Ibid. 95; Womack 127
13. Cumberland 1S7–89; Atkin 92, 93
14. Womack 131
15. Ibid.

16. *Diario del Hogar*, January 25, 1912;
    Womack 135
17. Magaña, II, 108–09
18. King 88
19. Womack 137
20. *El País*, August 31, 1912
21. Womack 139
22. King 92, 93
23. Ibid. 94
24. Lewis 91
25. King 89
26. Lewis 91
27. King 89
28. Womack 139–40
29. Bell 155
30. Cumberland 195, 196
31. Womack 142; Magaña, II, 133
32. Bell 167–69
33. Womack 142
34. Atkin 97
35. Ibid. 96
36. Harris 46; O'Shaughnessy,
    Diplomat's Wife, 159
37. Womack 148
38. King 97–98
39. Womack 145, 146
40. King 99
41. Womack 148–50
42. Ibid. 151
43. Guzmán, *Memoirs of Pancho Villa*,
    76-90
44. King 105
45. Díaz Soto y Gama 119

Chapter 7
TEN TRAGIC DAYS

1. Atkin 106
2. Cumberland 233–34
3. King 108
4. Ibid. 110–12
5. U.S. National Archives,
   812.00/6225
6. Bell 303
7. Magaña, III, 92
8. Ibid. 92–93

9. Fyfe 14–15
10. Atkin 132–35
11. U.S. National Archives,
    812.00/6849
12. Ibid.
13. Magaña, III, 160–61
14. Womack 166, 167
15. Magaña, III, 138–39
16. Lewis 100
17. King 121–22
18. Womack 172
19. Magaña, III, 267–68
20. Womack 173
21. Lewis 92
22. Womack 173
23. Lewis 91
24. Fyfe 56
25. Ibid. 14
26. King 141
27. Womack 174
28. Ibid. 175
29. *Archivo de Zapata* (Box 12)
30. Atkin 147–50
31. Calvert 131
32. Magaña, III, 252–57; *Archivo de
    Zapata* (Box 27)
33. Atkin 151–52
34. Baker 286
35. Fyfe 4
36. Magaña, III, 294–95
37. Fyfe 122; Reed 57

Chapter 8
TO MEXICO CITY

1. Guzmán, *Memoirs of Pancho Villa*,
   160–63
2. U.S. National Archives,
   812.00/11356
3. Guzmán, *Memoirs of Pancho Villa*,
   163–70; Atkin 182–83
4. King 121–22, 127
5. Stephenson 265–66
6. Reed 273–74
7. Atkin 190
8. Baker 321–22
9. Magaña, IV, 183, 187–97

10. U.S. Foreign Relations, 1914, 485–86
11. Magaña 215–29
12. King 170–71
13. Ibid. 174
14. Womack 187
15. King 175–76
16. Guzmán, *Memoirs of Pancho Villa*, 220
17. Ibid. 228–29
18. U.S. National Archives, 812.00/12323
19. *Archivo de Zapata* (Box 27)
20. King 183–84
21. *Archivo de Zapata* (Box 27)
22. Ibid.
23. Dromundo

Chapter 9
FRACTURED TRIUMPH

1. Womack 197–98
2. Magaña, IV, 241–42
3. *Archivo de Zapata* (Box 27)
4. U.S. National Archives, 812.00/12986; *Archivo de Zapata* (Box 27)
5. U.S. Foreign Relations, 1914, 592
6. Womack 210–11
7. Atkin 217
8. Quirk 67–68
9. Womack 211–12
10. Atkin 221
11. Magaña, V, 230–31
12. Guzmán, *The Eagle and the Serpent*, 264, 267
13. Quirk 108-17; Atkin 224–25; Guzmán, *The Eagle and the Serpent*, 272–73

Chapter 10
RELUCTANT REBEL

1. Strode 246
2. Moats 182

3. *Archivo de Zapata* (Box 27)
4. U.S. National Archives, 812.00/14061, 14048
5. Guzmán, *Memoirs of Pancho Villa*, 378–79; Quirk 140
6. Moats 171
7. Womack 234–35
8. King 294
9. O'Shaughnessy, *Diplomat's Wife*, 218
10. Quirk 200–01
11. Quirk 207; Taracena, *Mi vida ...*, 336
12. U.S. National Archives, 812.00/14832
13. Atkin 251–52
14. Quirk 239–40
15. Ibid. 258
16. Moats 181; Atkin 259
17. Quirk 280; U.S. Foreign Relations, 1915, 734–66

Chapter 11
THE PEOPLE REPLY

1. King 295
2. *Archivo de Zapata* (Box 27)
3. *Archivo de Zapata* (Box 31)
4. Calvert 182
5. Blasco Ibañez 75
6. Fyfe 46–47
7. Lewis 101
8. Ibid. 102
9. King 298–99
10. Lewis 101
11. Ibid. 102
12. Womack 258
13. Ibid. 254
14. Ibid. 264
15. King 298
16. Blasco Ibañez 77–78
17. Lewis 108
18. *Archivo de Zapata* (Box 28)
19. Ibid.
20. Blasco Ibañez 185–86
21. U.S. National Archives, 812.00/19449

22. *El Universal,* November 14, 1916
23. Lewis 102
24. Womack 271
25. *Archivo de Zapata* (Box 30)
26. Womack 283

Chapter 12
IN DEATH, VICTORY

1. *Archivo de Zapata* (Box 28)
2. Calvert 176
3. Lewis 107
4. Womack 286
5. *Archivo de Zapata* (Box 29)
6. Ibid. (Box 30)
7. W. E. Gates, *World's Work* magazine, April 1919
8. *Archivo de Zapata* (Box 29)
9. W. E. Gates, *World's Work* magazine, April 1919
10. Womack 288
11. Blasco Ibañez 3–4
12. Ibid. 54
13. Womack 311
14. Atkin 303
15. Calvert 192
16. *Archivo de Zapata* (Box 30)
17. Ibid.
18. Ibid.
19. Reyes Avilés 45–46
20. Parkes 309; Gruening 310-11; Palacios 276-87
21. Lewis 108
22. Atkin 314
23. Kirk 109

Bibliography

Almazán, Juan Andrew, *En defensa legítima* (Mexico 1958)

Archivo de Zapata, National University, Mexico City

Atkin, Ronald, *Revolution! Mexico 1910–20* (London 1969)

Baker, Ray Stannard, *Woodrow Wilson, Life and Letters* (London 1932)

Barba González, Silvano, *La lucha por la tierra. Emiliano Zapata* (Mexico 1960)

Bell, Edward I., *The Political Shame of Mexico* (New York 1914)

Blakemore, Harold, and Smith, Clifford T., *Latin America: Geographical Perspectives* (London 1971)

Blasco Ibañez, V., *Mexico in Revolution* (London 1920)

Callcott, Wilfred Hardy, *Liberalism in Mexico, 1857–1929* (Hamden, Conn. 1965)

Calvert, Peter, *Mexico, Nation of the Modern World* (London 1973)

——, *Revolution* (London 1970)

Casasola, Miguel y Gustavo, *Historia Gráfica de la Revolución*, 4 vols. (Mexico 1960)

Cockroft, James D., *Intellectual Precursors of the Mexican Revolution, 1900–1913* (Austin, Texas 1968)

Cumberland, Charles Curtis, *Mexican Revolution: Genesis under Madero* (Austin, Texas 1952)

Díaz Soto y Gama, Antonio, *La revolución agraria del Sur y Emiliano Zapata, su Caudillo* (Mexico 1960)

Dillon, Dr. E. J., *Mexico on the Verge* (London 1922)

——, *President Obregón—A World Reformer* (London 1922)

Dromundo, Baltasar, *Vida de Emiliano Zapata* (Mexico 1961)

Dunn, H. H., *The Crimson Jester* (London 1934)

Fyfe, H. Hamilton, *The Real Mexico* (London 1914)

Gruening, Ernest, *Mexico and Its Heritage* (New York 1928)

Guzmán, Martín Luis, *Memoirs of Pancho Villa*, trans. Virginia H. Taylor (Austin, Texas 1965)

————, *The Eagle and the Serpent* (New York 1965)

Harris, Larry, *Pancho Villa and the Columbus Raid* (El Paso 1949)

Johnson, William Weber, *Heroic Mexico* (New York 1968)

King, Rosa E., *Tempest over Mexico* (London 1936)

Kirk, Betty, *Covering the Mexican Front* (University of Oklahoma 1942)

Lewis, Oscar, *Pedro Martínez: A Mexican Peasant and His Family* (London 1964)

Magaña, Gildardo, and Perez Guerrero, Carlos, *Emiliano Zapata y el agrarismo en México*, 5 vols. (Mexico 1951-52)

Meyer, Michael C., *Huerta, a Political Portrait* (Lincoln, Nebraska 1972)

Moats, Leone B., *Thunder in Their Veins* (London 1933)

O'Hea, Patrick, *Reminiscences of the Mexican Revolution* (Mexico City 1966)

O'Shaughnessy, Edith, *A Diplomat's Wife in Mexico* (New York 1916)

————, *Intimate Pages of Mexican History* (New York 1920)

Palacios, Porfirio, *Emiliano Zapata* (Mexico 1960)

Parkes, Henry Banford, *A History of Mexico* (London 1962)

Pinchon, Edgcumb, *Viva Villa! A Recovery of the Real Pancho Villa* (London 1933)

————, *Zapata the Unconquerable* (New York 1941)

Quirk, Robert E., *The Mexican Revolution 1914–1915* (Bloomington, Ind., 1960)

Reed, John, *Insurgent Mexico* (New York 1969)

Reyes Avilés, Carlos, *A History of Mexico* (London 1962)

Ross, Stanley R., *Francisco I. Madero, Apostle of Mexican Democracy* (New York 1955)

Sherman, William L., and Greenleaf, Richard E., *Victoriano Huerta, a Reappraisal* (Mexico 1960)

Simpson, Eyler N., *The Ejido: Mexico's Way Out* (University of North Carolina 1937)

Sotelo Inclán, Jesús, *Raíz y razón de Zapata. Anenecuilco. Investigación histórica* (Mexico 1943)

Stephenson, George M., *John Lind of Minnesota* (Minneapolis 1935)

Strode, Hudson, *Timeless Mexico* (New York 1944)

Tannenbaum, Frank, *Peace by Revolution* (Columbia University 1933)

————, *Mexico, the Struggle for Peace and Bread* (New York 1950)

Taracena, Alfonso, *Madero* (Mexico 1937)

————, *Mi vida en el vértigo de la Revolución Mexicana* (Mexico 1936)

U.S. Foreign Relations Papers, 1911–20 (Library of Congress, Washington)

U.S. National Archives, Mexican Affairs, Group 59 (Library of Congress, Washington)

White, Jon Manchip, *Cortés* (London 1970)

Womack, John, Jr., *Zapata and the Mexican Revolution* (New York 1970)

Index

251

Chietla, 61
Chihuahua, 121, 131–132, 151, 165–166
Chihuahua City, 137, 165
Chilpancingo, 169–170
Chinameca hacienda, 106; Zapata's death at, 240–241
científicos, 140
Ciudad Juarez, *see* Juarez, Cuidad
Coahomulco, 128
Coahuila, rebellion in, 151
communal lands, *see* land disputes
Constitutionalists, 151, 172, 188, 202–203, 206; *see also Carrancistas*
Convention, revolutionary, 202–206, 207, 210; first meeting at Aguascalientes, 188, 190–195
Conventionalists described, 189
counterinsurgency methods, moderate, 138–141; repressive, 126–130
Creelman, James, 24, 26, 34
Cuahuixtla hacienda, 19, 25
Cuauhtémoc, 17
Cuautla, 17, 20, 27–28; Madero-Zapata meeting in, 99–100; *Zapatista* attack on, 63–70; Zapata burial in, 242
Cuernavaca, 17, 25, 96; *Carrancistas* in, 216–217, 231, 235; the Convention in, 203–206; reform legislature in, 138–140; *Zapatista* conference in, 189; *Zapatista* occupation of, 80–82; *Zapatista* sieges of, 153–154, 171, 177–179, 181

Dávila Madrid, Manuel, 83
de Jesús, María, 197, 198
de la Barra, Francisco León, 71–72, 90, 96, 101, 102, 104, 105; moves against Zapata, 101–105; negotiations with Huerta, 97–99; Plan of San Luis Potosí opposed by, 93; pro-planter bias of, 82; reaction to Zapata's petition, 109
de la O, Genovevo, 28, 29, 81, 97, 122, 125, 126, 127, 139, 149–150, 156, 171, 214, 215, 216, 222, 230
de la Torte y Mier, Ignacio, 31
de Mendoza, Antonio Hurtado, 33
Diario del Hogar, 123, 125
Díaz-Madero negotiations, 66–67,68
Díaz, Encarnación, 170
Díaz, Félix, 143, 144, 145, 147, 148; revolt and imprisonment of, 141
Díaz, Porfirio, 21, 24, 25, 26, 27, 34–35, 37–38, 40, 43–44, 46, 48; reaction to Morelos revolution, 58–59; resignation of, 71–72; suppresses *Maderistas*, 40–41; suppresses Tacubayan conspiracy, 57

Díaz Soto y Gama, Antonio, *see* Soto y Gama, Antonio Díaz
Division of the North, 176–177, 179–180, 181, 188; *Carrancista* destruction of, 209
Division of the Northeast, 177
Division of the Northwest, 172
Domínguez, Alfredo Robles, 83, 84
Dunn, H. H., 65, 85, 88
"dynamite boys," 65, 69–70

El Imparcial, 89, 90, 161
El Independiente, 174
El País, 90–91, 95, 127, 128, 130–131, 133
Eguía Lis, Gen. Rafael, 209
Escandón, Pablo, 25–29, 31–32, 33–34, 35–36, 37, 39, 44, 50, 54–55, 64, 83, 133
Espejo, Josefa, *see* Zapata, Josefa (Espejo),
Espinosa Barreda, Juan 227
Estrada, Roque, 38
Excelsior, 234

federal army, strength of, 124; rebel leniency in surrender of, 170, 176; weaknesses of, 50–51
Figueroa, Ambrosio, 62, 63, 68, 96; denounced in Plan of Ayala, 118; moves against Zapata, 101–105; named governor of Morelos, 111; private truce by, 66; relationship with planters, 71–72, 83; resignations of, 125
Figueroa, Francisco, 62
Figueroistas, 72, 79, 86, 89
Flores, Eduardo, 41
Flores Magón, Jesús, 139
Fyfe, H. Hamilton, 151, 158, 159, 164, 167, 217

García Granados, Alberto, 94
Gates, William E., 231–232, 233, 236
Gómez Palacio, 170, 171
González, Gen. Pablo, 166, 181, 209–210, 218, 219, 237; described, 217; heads drive into Morelos, 231; moves against Tampico, 173; ousted from Morelos, 226; repressive measures of, 219, 220–222, 223, 224–225; role of, in death of Zapata, 237–238, 242
González Garza, Roque, 205, 207; meeting with Zapata, 208; named Convention president, 203; ousted as president, 209; speech of, at Convention, 193–194
González Salas, Gen. José, 112; suicide of, 131
Guadalupe, 190
Guajardo, Col. Jesús, role of, in death of Zapata, 237–242

Guerrero City, 43
guerrilla warfare, basic stages of, 44–45; tactics used by Zapata, 123–124, 221, 222, 223
Gutiérrez, Eulalio, named provisional president, 195; ousted as provisional president, 202–203
Gutiérrez, Octaviano, 28
Guzmán, Martin Luis, 191, 193

hacienda system, 19, 22–24, 29
Hay, Eduardo, 100, 193
Hidalgo, Father Miguel, 38
Hospital hacienda, 19, 32–33, 36–37
Huautla, 218, 222; Federal "attack" on, 160–161
Heurta, Gen Victoriano, 132, 136–137; alcoholism of, 107–108, 133, 159, 167; American actions against, 163–164, 173–174; Chihuahua campaign of, 133, 137; Congress dissolved by, 163; negotiations with de la Barra, 97–98; repressive policies of, 106, 107, 152, 155–156; resignation of, 181; role in Madero plot, 145–148; moves against Zapata, 95–97, 103–105, 110–111
Huitzilac, 215
Hutchins Hotel, 38

influenza epidemic, 1918–19, 234
Izúcar de Matamoros, *see* Matamoros (Izúcar de)

Jenkinson, Charles, 186
Jiménez Castro, Brig. Gen. Adolfo, 162
Jojutla hacienda, 29, 63, 218, 226; federal mutiny in, 169; federal occupations of, 134, 235; *Zapatista* occupations of, 54–56, 132–134, 176
Jolalpan, 62
Jonacatepec, 17, 59; federal occupations of, 134, 231; *Zapatista* occupation of, 152–153
Juan del Río, 109
Juárez, Ciudad, 137; Orozco attack on, 48; rebel occupations of, 66–67, 165; *see also* Treaty of Ciudad Juárez

King, Mrs. Rosa, notes on Mexican revolution by, 20, 25, 33–34, 36, 37, 38, 41, 54, 79–80, 82, 83, 87–88, 96, 107–108, 109, 111, 126, 128–130, 137–139, 142, 146, 147, 154, 159, 171, 177–179, 181, 204, 213–214, 219, 221–222

Lagos Cházaro, Francisco, named Convention president, 209

land disputes between villages and haciendas, 22–24, 29–30, 31–34, 36–37
land question, interim governor Villamar on, 140; Madero's equivocation on, 86; in Plan of San Luis Potosí, 42–43, 70, 82; in Plan of Ayala, 119
Lansing, Robert, 211
León, Village defeated at, 209
Leyva, Gen. Francisco, 26, 27, 58–59, 69, 79
Leyva, Patricio, 26, 27, 28, 48, 58, 81; assumes governorship of Morelos, 141
Leyvistas, 26–29, 30, 35, 37, 59
Liberating Army of the Center and South, 162, 180
Liberating Army of the South, command system in, 122
Limantour, Señor, 71
Lind, John, 172, 173
London Daily Mail, 146, 147–148, 165
London Times, 71
Los Hornos, 128
Lugo, Col. García, 147

Maderista Revolution, beginning of, 52–53
Maderistas, 35, 40–41, 43–44
Madero, Alfonso, 38
Madero, Francisco I., 34–35, 38, 39–40, 43–44; army plot against, 141, 143–148; assassination plot against, 93–94; attempts compromise in Morelos, 97–100; attempts to negotiate with Zapata, 139; betrays Zapata, 114–117; declares martial law in Morelos, 125; denounced in Plan of Ayala, 118; elected president, 111; inaugurated, 113–114; on land question, 82, 86; meeting with Zapata at Cuautla, 99–100; murdered, 149; response to Plan of Ayala, 123; and Treaty of Ciudad Juárez, 71–72; sends ultimatum to Zapata, 90;
Madero, Gustavo, 38, 143, 144; arrested by Huerta, 148
Madero, Julio, 38
Madero, Raúl, 38, 100, 101, 103
Magaña, Gildardo, 190, 232–233, 234, 237; becomes Zapata's successor, 242
Magaña, Octavio, 57
Magaña, Rudolfo, 57, 190
Manifesto to the Mexican People, 232
Manifesto to the Nation, 231
María Lozano, José, 112
Martínez, Abrahám, 88, 94, 125–126
Martínez, Paulino, 30, 190; speech at the Convention of, 191–192
Matamoros (Izúcar de), 61
Maya, Ignacio, 170

Mayo, Rear Adm. Henry T., 173
Mazatlán, siege of, 172
Mendoza, Francisco, 122, 124, 132, 171
Merino, José, 23, 29
Merino, Col. Rafael, 50, 55
Mexico City, 131–132, 183–184, 209–210
Mexico Nuevo, 25, 26
Mila Alpa, 180, 181, 182, 183
military discipline among revolutionists, 52, 55, 61, 65–66, 81, 82, 157, 158, 224
Miranda, Alfonso, 81
Miranda, Joaquín, execution of, 175
Moats, Mrs. Leone, 197, 203, 210
Moctezuma Hotel, 25–26
Mondragón, Gen. Manuel, 143, 144
Montaño, Otilio, E., 120, 122, 150, 156, 165, 230
Montes, Andrés, 23
Morales, Federico, 72, 106
Morales, Jesús, 122, 124, 175
Morelos, 17; condition in 1917, 227–228; condition under Zapata, 202–206; land ownership in, 29; martial law in, 97, 125; legislature of, 138–140, 150, 152; repressive policies in, 23, 27–28, 106, 107, 124, 126–131, 152, 156, 159–160, 219–225
Morelos Theater, 191–195
Moreno, Lucio, 47–48, 53, 57

Naranjo, Francisco, moderate policies in Morelos of, 125–127, 135–140
nationalization program, 188
Navarro, Jesús, 122
Neri, Felipe, 125, 132
New York Times, 236, 237
Nexpa, 128
North American Review, 236

Obregón, Álvaro, 151, 166, 172, 174, 181, 183, 184, 187, 188, 206, 209, 218, 233, 234; war with Villa, 195, 208; defeats Villa at Celaya, 208; occupies Mexico City, 202–203; overthrows Carranza, 242–243
Ocotepec, 128
Olea, Gen. Antonio, 161
Olea, Hipolito, 28
Orozco, Pascual, 43, 48, 66, 126, 131, 133, 135, 141, 151, 156, 161; cruelties of, 136; offered leadership by Zapata, 118
O'Shaughnessy, Edith, 35, 113, 204

Pacheco, Francisco, 215–216
Palafox, Manuel, 153, 165, 168, 183, 203, 207–210, 230, 233
Parras, 82
Pearson's Magazine, 24

peasants, lands retaken by, 70; life of, 18–20, 22–24, 34; and Plan of Ayala, 120; Zapata supported by, 19–20, 123
Pérez, Eugenio, 23
Pershing, Gen. John J., 229
Pimentel, García, 29
Pino Suárez, Gen. José, 149
Plan of Ayala, 118–120, 122, 136, 187–194 *passim*, 231, 232; amendment of, 156; press publication of, 123; rejected by Carranza, 213; and Carranza constitution, 228; Zapata's ratification of, 182–183
Plan of San Luis Potosí, 39–40, 52, 54, 55, 57, 70, 93, 118–119, 120; land question in, 42–43, 82
plantations, growth of, 22–24
planters, political activities of, 24–29, 71–72, 82, 83–84, 87, 89–90, 94
presidential elections of 1910, 34–35, 40; of 1911, 111
Puebla City, 40, 93–94

Quintana Roo, 23
Quintero, Carmen, 23

Rasgado, Gen. Alberto T., 161
Reed, John, 136, 172
Rellano, battles for, 131, 133
revolution, the, political base for, 42, 46, 112
revolutionary army, 44, 49–50, 53–61, 122, 156–157; *see also* guerrilla warfare
revolutionary Convention, *see* Convention, revolutionary
Reyes, Gen. Bernardo, 111, 121, 141, 143, 144
Robles, Gen. Juvencio, 134–137, 151, 152, 161; repressive policies of, 126–130, 155–156, 159–160
Robles, Vito Alessio, 191
Robles Domínguez, Gabriel, 88, 90, 101, 114–117
Romero, Gen. 178
Ruiz de Velasco, Tomás, 83, 84, 89, 90

Salazar, Amador, 125, 132, 197, 215; death of, 216
Salazar, José, 20
Salgado, Jesús, 169, 170, 171
Salinas, Miguel, 100
San Andrés, 43
San Ángel, 224
San Antonio Tlaxcalantongo, 243
San Luis Potosí, 182
San Luis Potosí, Plan of, *see* Plan of San Luis Potosí
San Pedro de las Colonias, 172
San Rafael, 128

Santa Clara hacienda, 29
Santa María, 127
Sarabia, Juan, 106
Serdán, Aquiles, 40
serfdom, 19, 22–23
Sonora, 151
Soto y Gama, Antonio Díaz, 186–187, 190, 191, 207, 230; speech at Convention of, 192–193
"strategic hamlet" concept, 128
sugar production, Morelos, 22–24

Tacubayan conspiracy, 57
Tampico, 173–174
Tehuiztla, 220
Tenextepango, 19
Teoloyucan, 183
Tepepa, Gabriel, 47–49, 53–56, 59, 60, 72
Tepoztlán, 132, 134
Tetecala, 235
Ticumán, 128
Tierra Blanca, 165–166
Tixtla, 169, 170, 171
Tlaltizapán, 132, 202, 207, 210, 218, 221, 222, 225, 230
Tlaquiltenango, 55, 132,
Tlayacapa, 222
Toluca Theater, 205–206, 210
Torreón, 133, 159, 162, 169–170
Torres Burgos, Pablo, 27, 28, 29, 41, 43, 45, 47, 48, 50–55
Treaty of Ciudad Juárez, 71–72
Tres Marías, 216, 217, 226
Triente hacienda, 226
Trinidad Ruiz, José, 122, 125

Uructa, Jesús, 145
U.S.S. Dolphin, 173

Vázquez, Emilio, 94, 121
Vázquez, Dr. Francisco, 121
Vázquez, Lorenzo, 132, 206, 230
Vázquez Gómez, Francisco, 165, 172
Vazquistas, revolt of, 121
Veracruz, 141, 174, 195, 202
Villa, Francisco "Pancho," 17, 28, 66–67, 136, 141, 151, 159, 165–166, 174, 189, 194, 195, 205, 209, 211, 229, 231; actions of, against Torreón, 159, 162, 169–170; advantages of, 172; attack on Columbus, New Mexico, by, 216; assassinated in Canutilla, 243; conflict with Carranza of, 176–177, 179–180, 181; "Manifesto to the Mexican People" of, 188; quarrel with Gutiérrez, 202; and Zapata, 59–60, 185–186, 187, 197–201

Villa de Ayala, 19, 20, 21, 22, 27, 30, 41, 49, 52–53, 114–116, 241
village lands, *see* land disputes
Villamar, Aniceto, 140
Villar, Gen. Lauro, 144, 145
Villistas, 193, 197
Vivanco, José, 37, 41
von Hintze, Adm. Paul, 113

West, Judge Duval, 207, 211
Wilkes, Allen Tupper, 200–201
Wilson, Henry Lane, 43–44, 107, 131–132, 147, 148, 149, 152
Wilson, President Woodrow, 164, 173–174, 207
Womack, John, Jr., 157, 187
women in rebel armies, 60–61
World War I, effect of, on Mexican revolution, 211–212, 228, 231–232

Xochimilco, 197–200, 224

Yáñez, Refugio, 27, 37
Yautepec, 17, 215, 220, 225, 235

Zacatecas, 176, 180
Zalcuapán, 231
Zapata, Cleofus, 20
Zapata, Cristino, 21
Zapata, Emiliano, 18–19, 21, 26; American help sought by, 165, 172; area controlled by, 17; and conflict with Carranza, 182–183, 184, 185–186, 187–188, 210, 214; consolidation of ascendancy in South by, 55–60, 79–81; death of, reasons for, 239–241; descriptions of, 18–20, 59–60, 233; disillusionment with Madero, 89–90, 116–117, 139; drafted into army, 30–31; family history of, 19–21; financial support of, 57, 81; leadership of revolution assumed by, 156; as *Leyvista*, 27; as a *Maderista* leader, 41–42, 48; Manifesto to the Mexican People of, 232; Manifesto to the Nation of, 16, 231; marriage of, 92, 95; meeting with González Garza, 208–209; meeting with Villa, 197–201; meetings with Madero, 85–87, 99–100; peasant support of, 19–22, 123; petition to de la Barra, 108–109; Plan of Ayala issued by, 118–120; Plan of Ayala reaffirmed by, 182–183; reaction to American landings, 174–175; relatives seized as hostages, 127, 160; strategy and tactics of, 45–46, 49–50, 54, 63–70, 105–106, 110–111, 121–124, 134–135, 150, 153, 164–165, 168; union with Obregón sought by, 234; views on agrarian